MEMORIES

BY THE SAME AUTHOR

Women
Singular Encounters
Of a Certain Age
More of a Certain Age
A Woman a Week
Speaking for the Oldie
Asking Questions
In Conversation with Naim Attallah
Insights
Dialogues
The Old Ladies of Nazareth
The Boy in England
In Touch with His Roots
Fulfilment and Betrayal 1975–1995
No Longer With Us
No Longer With Us II

MEMORIES

The charms and follies of a lifetime's publishing

Naim Attallah

QUARTET BOOKS

First published in 2020 by Quartet Books Limited
A member of the Namara Group
27 Goodge Street, London, W1T 2LD

Copyright © Naim Attallah 2020

The moral right of the author has been asserted by him in accordance with the Copyright, Designs and Patents Act, 1988

All rights reserved.
No part of this publication may be reproduced, stored in a retrieval system, or transmitted in any form or by any means, without the prior permission in writing of the publisher, nor be otherwise circulated in any form of binding or cover other than that in which it is published and without a similar condition including this condition being imposed on the subsequent purchaser

Reasonable efforts have been made to find the copyright holders of third party copyright material. An appropriate acknowledgement can be inserted by the publisher in any subsequent printing or edition

A catalogue record for this book
is available from the British Library

ISBN 9780704374799

Typeset by Avon DataSet
Printed and bound in Great Britain by TJ International Ltd, Padstow, Cornwall

For Joseph Ghazal
A most faithful and generous friend

FOREWORD

'Old age ain't no place for sissies'
BETTE DAVIS

She had a point. I've almost reached my ninth decade and it is tough going. There's not much I can do to alleviate the aches and pains. I can try and avoid the uneven pavements, use the lift, whereas once I bounded up the stairs (though I still can totter upstairs to my office every working day). My memory is not as sharp as it was either. What I do have though is what in the publishing trade we call 'a backlist'. Fifteen books of various shapes and sizes; memoirs and interviews, published over the past forty years. I've also written a blog for the past ten years where I was free to cover all number of topics and it was the reaction to that blog that made me wish to create a small book which somehow solidified the jottings and thoughts in a more permanent form.

What follows is a potpourri of vignettes selected from those books and blogs which convey the varied and many moments in my life which both amuse and console in my old age. Hopefully they may also amuse and interest my readers.

NAIM ATTALLAH

MEMORIES

A TRIBUTE TO THE HASHEMITE PRINCESS WHO HAD NO EQUAL

The death, aged 91, of Princess Dina Abdul-Hamid in August 2019, was noted by some media sources but we have yet to see the comprehensive coverage which usually follows the passing of a personage of world-ranking importance. She was an exceptional person with remarkable gifts.

Dina Abdul-Hamid told a very personal story in *Duet for Freedom*, which Quartet published in 1988, with an introduction by John Le Carré. As a member of the Hashemite dynasty, Princess Dina had been briefly married to King Hussein of Jordan, but her book gave an epic account of events following the capture of her second husband, Salah Ta'amari, a spokesman for the PLO, during the 1982 Israeli invasion of Lebanon. By an extraordinary chance, her attempts to contact Salah and free him from the hidden labyrinth of the notorious prison camp of Ansar, opened up the chance of negotiating with the Israelis for the release of thousands of Palestinians and Lebanese in exchange for six captured Israeli soldiers. *Duet for Freedom* was a true love story with many wider implications. Princess Dina was honorary godmother to my son Ramsay – honorary because of our religious differences, she being of Islamic descent while we belong to the Greek Catholic church.

In his Introduction, John Le Carré ended with the hope that 'if there is ever to be a peaceful solution to the Palestinian-Israeli conflict, it will be found not in acts of violent suppression and expulsion, nor in acts of violent retaliation, but in the deliberations of two people who have done so many awful things to one another that they have finally scared themselves sufficiently to give up heroics and talk like men. If that ever happens, they might do worse than have Salah along, with Dina at his side.'

That was written nearly forty years ago and yet its message is still as potent now as it was then. Princess Dina worked ceaselessly for peace and reconciliation. She deserves a proper recognition of her place in history.

A TRUE PALESTINIAN PATRIOT

Quartet lost a good friend in August 2018, when Said K Aburish died after a long illness. He was a distinguished journalist, a brilliant writer and had that rare quality: the courage of his convictions. We were very fortunate to be able to add his name to our list of authors, in 1993, when we published *The Forgotten Faithful*.

Said was born in the biblical village of Bettany, near Jerusalem in Palestine, in 1935. One of his grandfathers was a judge of the Islamic Court and a lecturer at the Arab College. The other was Village Headman. His father was correspondent for the London *Daily Mail*, the *New York Times*, *Newsweek* and *Time*. Said attended schools in Jerusalem and Beirut, and then at universities in the United States. He returned to Beirut in late 1950s as a reporter for Radio Free Europe and the London *Daily Mail*. After a varied career, which included positions as a consultant to two Arab governments, he returned to fulltime writing in 1982. At this time, he took up residency in London and contributed articles to the *Washington Post*, the *Independent* and *Libération*, amongst others.

The Forgotten Faithful was about the Christians in The Holy Land, particularly those in Jerusalem and its surroundings who were cruelly treated by both the Israeli government and Muslim fundamentalists. The book was very well received and drew world-wide attention to this outrage.

In the early sixties, when my budding banking career took me to Intra Bank, which had its head office in Beirut, I became acquainted with Said's father, who for almost forty years had held court at the bar of Hotel Saint Georges in his capacity as correspondent *par excellence* of so many international newspapers. When he was not at the hotel's bar he held *majlis* at his office, attended by many of his admirers. We clicked on the spot and became great friends – just a few years before I met Said, who was truly his father's son.

Said inherited his charisma as well as his charm, but above all his father's great journalistic flair. Said wrote many books, some of which were hard hitting and controversial but always worthy of note. He will be remembered for his patriotic zeal as a Palestinian who loved his land and his people and never denied his origins. He died were he was born and he would not have wished to be buried anywhere else.

He will be sorely missed.

REMEMBERING WILFRED

In August 1981, I received a phone call from Wilfred Burchett, with whom I had become friends after our first meeting at the Plaza Hotel in New York in the late 1970s. He was in America advising the Nixon administration in its conduct of clandestine talks with the Vietcong with a view to ending the Vietnam conflict. At that time the Americans were sustaining heavy losses and their toll of dead and injured was steadily rising to levels that were politically indefensible. Their problem was to find a way of extricating themselves from the conflict without loss of face. Wilfred was a *bête noir* for the administrations in both America and his native Australia for having covered the Vietnam war from the 'other side', sending out his dispatches from behind the lines in the jungle. His knowledge of and contacts with the Vietcong, however, took on a value that Nixon and his advisers were unable to ignore in the changing political climate of the United States and the rising radical tide of its peace movement.

Wilfred was now retired and living behind the Iron Curtain in Sofia with his Bulgarian wife. His proposal was that I should visit him with my wife Maria and our son Ramsay, if he could manage to secure an invitation for us from the Bulgarian authorities. I was delighted to hear from him in the first place and in the second overwhelmed by this unexpected gesture. My response was immediate and positive: we would love to come. Wilfred was a giant among the journalists of his generation, and a warm-hearted, larger than life character. He may have held many controversial political views, but at heart he was a courageous humanitarian, a champion of the poor and the oppressed, and had my unconditional admiration.

Wilfred's initial clash with American interests had come head-on in 1945 when, as a young war correspondent entering Japan with the US invasion forces, he defied the exclusion zone declared by General MacArthur to cover the cities of Hiroshima and Nagasaki after their destruction by atomic bombs. He was the first Western journalist to enter Hiroshima after the attack and sat on a surviving lump of concrete with his Hermes typewriter in the radioactive wilderness, having seen the evidence of obliterated humanity and the plight of those who were dying from their injuries and a mysterious sickness previously unknown to medicine. The technical terms to describe their illness were not yet in place, but Wilfred was in no doubt about the enormity of the implications. He began his report, published as a world exclusive in Lord Beaverbrook's *Daily Express* in London, with the words: 'I write this as a warning to the world.'

The scenes he went on to describe in graphic detail seemed almost beyond the scope of the human imagination. The official American line on atomic warfare, then and for long afterwards, was that death and destruction were caused by the bomb blast, radiation being a harmless side-effect. From the American point of view, Burchett's talk of 'bomb sickness' needed to be refuted and dismissed as Japanese propaganda. The official press report on Nagasaki, which denied the effects of radiation, was prepared by William Laurence, a science writer on the *New York* Times, who also happened to be in the pay of the US War Department. Laurence and the *New York Times* were awarded a Pulitzer prize for journalism in recognition of their efforts (now seen as dishonourable), but Burchett's forebodings never went away. At a press conference he openly challenged General MacArthur when he made attempts to pour scorn on Burchett's Hiroshima account.

With the polarization of positions and loyalties that inevitably came with the Cold War, Wilfred's sympathies were certainly not in America's favour. His highly controversial dispatches from the Korean war after it began in 1951 were obtained under Chinese press accreditation. He enraged the Americans by revealing that a captured general, William F. Dean, was fit and alive in the north as a prisoner of war when they were trying to use his supposed slaughter to bring pressure to bear on negotiations. The Americans branded Burchett pro-Communist and there were attempts in Australia to have him declared a traitor. Though no formal charges were ever laid against him, the Australian government declined to renew his passport at the start of hostilities in Vietnam, forcing him to remain in exile from his homeland for many years.

At one point his reports from Vietnam from among the Vietcong forces provoked the Nixon administration to such an extent that they put a bounty on his head; but in 1980, one of the most distinguished of American war correspondents, Harrison E. Salisbury, the 1955 Pulitzer prize-winner for international reporting, described him in these terms:

Wilfred Burchett is a man who defies classification. There is hardly a war or revolution in the past forty years at which he as a journalist has not been present. There is hardly a left-wing movement with which he as a radical (or 'progressive', as he likes to call himself) has not sympathized. In his ceaseless travel he has met most of the diplomats and national leaders of his time and most of his fellow correspondents. There is probably no other man living who was on intimate terms with both Ho Chi Minh and Henry Kissinger. He was reviled by the right in his native Australia, but became a hero for his country's growing peace and anti-nuclear movements. Australian war journalist Pat Burgess wrote: 'No correspondent was better loved by his colleagues or more bitterly detested.' This in itself testified to the power of what he had to say. Burchett himself made clear his standpoint: 'My duties as a citizen of the world go beyond my responsibilities only to my own country. In other words, I reject the "my country – right or wrong".' During a press conference he stated, 'I've certainly not been a traitor to the Allies. I've opposed policies in Vietnam. I oppose Australians being killed on Vietnamese soil. If I were a Vietnamese invading Australian soil, I'd be supporting Australia.'

In Britain another distinguished war correspondent, James Cameron, gave his recollections of him in 1977:

I have had the good luck to know Wilfred Burchett off and on ever since we toiled together in the Fleet Street vineyard of the Chateau Beaverbrook. We abandoned this patronage at almost exactly the same time, though for marginally different reasons. To his [Beaverbrook's] dying day, which took a long time to come, the lord believed that our defections had been politically coordinated; he was, as so often, quite wrong. In fact at the time I had never even met Wilfred. Indeed I did not know his name was Wilfred.

As an Australian he worked for the *Express* during the war in the Pacific; I was in Asia and Europe. He signed his file simply: Burchett. They had to find an acceptable by-line for this gifted but remote correspondent, so someone or other arbitrarily called him

'Peter'. Fleet Street was always pretty cavalier about identities. Nevertheless, for some time after I established a kinship with this wayward old mate, I had a job unscrambling the Peter from the real man. And it is a real man.

Where Burchett's invitation to me and my family was concerned, he was as good as his word. Hardly a week had passed after his phone call before all our travel arrangements were concluded. The official invitation arrived, accompanied by three air tickets on Bulgarian Airlines. We flew to Sofia, where we stayed for one night before taking an onward flight next day to the Black Sea resort of Varna. There we found ourselves occupying a suite in what was then the resort's most luxurious hotel. It had a stunning outlook on to the Black Sea and, as it happened, a grandstand view of the Russian fleet on exercise. We watched their manoeuvres with guarded curiosity and restrained ourselves from taking any pictures in case we found ourselves in breach of some security regulations and landed ourselves in trouble.

Despite the obvious severity of the regime and the signs of Russian influence that were everywhere evident, Wilfred managed to make us feel totally at home with his display of friendly hospitality. The shortage of consumer goods was obvious, and although food was reasonably available, it lacked variety – though not, of course, if you were a government official of some standing. In that case, miraculously, the unobtainable would suddenly appear.

We experienced this phenomenon one lunchtime when we were telephoned by a high-ranking notable from the Ministry of Tourism, who announced that he was waiting for us in the hotel lobby and would like to entertain us to lunch. Normally at that hour we would have been going to take our lunch in the very same restaurant, sampling its minimalistic menu and having any request for something extra acknowledged with a smile and a nod but never fulfilled. Suddenly, as the official snapped his fingers, there was a dramatic transformation of the scene. Trays of food showed up as if from nowhere, their contents equalling anything you would find in the West, with no hint of any shortages in the sizes of the portions being offered.

There was also the unusual spectacle of the waiters, who seemed positively panic stricken, running back and forth to satisfy every little whim and gesture of our host. The normally languid service became fast and furious to a point of manic precision. It was an abuse of authority that may have been morally deplorable, but at least it provided us with an excellent meal which was more than welcome in the circumstances. In Varna leading party and trade-union officials taking their annual vacations by the Black Sea were allocated what were, by their standards, luxurious apartments for their stay. By and large they were the elite, enjoying the perks due to them as a reward for their loyalty to the regime. They were carefully selected individuals and there was no mistaking who they were in our hotel. In the afternoons they took tea and cakes and listened to 'palm court' classical music being performed live by a little ensemble of young musicians. We also spent part of the afternoon having tea and cake since it seemed the thing to do. There was an oddness, however, about the way a generously large pot of tea would arrive but then turn out to contain precisely enough tea to fill three cups. The measurement was so accurate that there was no allowance for any margin of error. The cake portions were cut to a similar exactitude, avoiding any risk of excess and ensuring the size was in compliance with a strict dietary regime. The average American tourist, accustomed to large intakes of food to keep up energy levels when on their travels, would have been disappointed with the culinary rewards of Varna in the Soviet era.

Even so, our stay there was made highly enjoyable by the fact that we spent most evenings with Wilfred and his wife, who entertained us faultlessly. To have the opportunity to get to know the man at close quarters, and hear his own accounts of his exploits together with his insights and conclusions, was a very special privilege. He combined a rare modesty with a zest for living despite the many tragedies he had encountered. The optimism he retained clearly illustrated his belief that in the end the dignity of man would always triumph. His own body had been riddled with bullets and he had had many brushes with death, surviving against the odds. The scars he carried were a testimony to his relentless efforts in the battlefields of South-East Asia to bring the truth to the outside world. He may have been misguided on many issues. His political perspective meant he was slower than others on the left to recognize the real nature of Stalinist control and oppression within the Soviet bloc and the post-war purges and show trials. He wrote in support of the Pol Pot revolution in Kampuchea during its early years, but later altered his opinion after its savagery became all too apparent. His errors of judgement provided his enemies with ammunition to use against him, but while he was fallible in some respects, he was startlingly clear-sighted in others. In Hiroshima he felt that not only was he seeing 'the end of World War II' but also 'the fate of cities all over the world in the first hours of a World War III'. All Wilfred's actions and opinions were informed by humanitarian instincts: the Australian spirit of fair play writ large. This is why I loved the man most dearly. He had never been member of a communist or any other party, he would say if asked, but thought of himself as an international socialist.

The night before our departure from Varna was one we would remember for a long time to come. It was as if all the pent-up forces of history burst in a violent storm around the Black Sea, with a ferocity that seemed to make the hotel rock. The rolling of the thunder, the lightning forking over the sea, the clouds lit up as if by fire – it was awe-inspiring: nature's devastating forces on display in front of our very eyes. It was a dramatic farewell to Varna. Once back in the capital, Sofia, we were provided with a black Mercedes and a chauffeur to go with it. There was so little traffic we were able to explore the city thoroughly, always in the company of Wilfred and his wife. We dined at the few functioning restaurants and drank dark Bulgarian wine, some of which was really rather nice. The evenings we spent in sorting out the problems of the world.

The qualities in Wilfred that impressed me most were compassion for his fellow human beings and extreme loyalty to his friends. John Pilger, an illustrious war correspondent for the later television age, recalled in one of the pieces in his book *Heroes* (Vintage) how in the spring of 1980, shortly before he was due to leave for an assignment in Kampuchea, he received a phone call from Paris. It was Wilfred on the line.

> A familiar, husky voice came quickly to the point. 'Can you postpone,' he said. 'I've heard about a Khmer Rouge list and you're on it. I am worried about you.' That Wilfred was worried about the welfare of another human being was not surprising; the quintessence of the man lay in what he did not say. He neglected to mention not only that he was on the same 'list', but that a few weeks earlier, at the age of seventy and seriously ill, he had survived a bloody ambush laid for him by Khmer Rouge assassins, who wounded a travelling companion. (Wilfred's intelligence was as reliable as ever; I narrowly escaped a similar ambush at the same place he was attacked.) I have known other reporters; I have not known another who, through half a century of risk-taking, demonstrated as much concern for others and such valour on their behalf. He took risks to smuggle Jews out of Germany, to drag American wounded to safety during the Pacific war, and to seek out prisoners of war in Japan, in 1945, to tell them help was coming; the list is long. He sustained a variety of bombardments, from Burma to Korea to Indo-China, yet he retained a compassion coupled with an innocence bordering at times on naivety which, it would seem, led him into other troubles. Such qualities were shared by none of the vociferous few who were his enemies.

As a publisher I had the privilege of publishing three of Wilfred Burchett's books under the Quartet imprint. They were: *Catapult to Freedom* in 1978; *Memoirs of a Rebel Journalist* in 1980; and *Burchett Reporting the Other Side of the World, 1939–1983*, edited by Ben Kiernan, with a preface by John Pilger in 1986. Two years after our visit to Bulgaria, Wilfred Burchett died in Sofia in September 1983 from a cancer that he himself was convinced could be attributed to his visit to Hiroshima in 1945. His epitaph should reflect his own words hen, in Paris in 1974, he said: 'Truth always turns out to be much richer than you thought.'

LATIN SPLENDOUR

I'm glad to read in a Sunday newspaper that Latin passion is due to come to the Proms on Wednesday. Marin Alsop, the American conductor who shattered more than 100 years of inequality when she became the first woman to lead proceedings at the 'Last Night of the Proms' in 2014, returns triumphantly to the Royal Albert Hall with the Sao Palo Symphony Orchestra. She fully intends to bust another stereotype that Europeans are considered superior to everyone else when it comes to creating and performing classical music.

'Last time we came to the Proms people were surprised by the world class musicians of this orchestra,' she smiles. 'I think they'll be even more amazed this year.' Alsop has been music director of the orchestra since 2012 and like a benign and proud mother she refers to them in glowing terms describing the unique qualities her musicians will bring on Wednesday night to one of the most important musical festivals in the world.

'They're very devoted to the work, yet still maintain their identity in terms of bringing that Latin sense of passion and emotionality to the table.' With a programme showcasing some of Brazil's finest composers, their summer's tour in Europe – the orchestra will also play at the

Lucerne and Edinburgh International Festivals – is 'an enormous opportunity for us to connect with the broader world.'

Growing up in New York City, Alsop, 59, did not see any women on orchestral podiums. However, she remembers being taken by her musical parents to a young people's concert conducted by Leonard Bernstein and becoming 'obsessed'. She was nine years old. 'It was a religious calling. I never even questioned it.'

In those days female maestri were as rare as hen's teeth, but Alsop says 'I did think about the gender issues. Bernstein was my idol and my hero and then he became my teacher and I had parents who were incredible role models particularly my mother, who believed that you can do anything you want to in life.'

Her remarkable career does seem to be forged on such principles. When New York's Juilliard School rejected her for their post graduate conducting programme she founded her own orchestra, Concordia, and honed her craft with them. When the musicians of the Baltimore Symphony rebelled at her historic appointment as their Music Director, she simply put her head down and got on with the job. Ten years on, Baltimore is considered as one of the most impressive symphony orchestras in the world and it has renewed Alsop's contract not once but twice. She will be there until at least 2021.

When asked if she ever felt a victim of prejudice, she carefully replied: 'I don't think in terms like that. Everyone's probably a victim of prejudice to one degree or another and there are certainly many people who are more mistreated for the wrong reasons than I am. So I feel mostly privileged.'

She's excited about showing off the Sao Paula orchestra this week: 'Brazil has a very rich musical heritage and their composers have a wonderful way of blending the popular idiom into their classical works. Some classical conductors would be horrified at the prospect about bring anything "popular" to the classical concert hall. Well, I think when we let down those barriers there can be an incredible hybrid that can connect people to our art form in a much deeper and more relevant way. I like the idea of not so many barriers and boundaries between things.'

What a far-sighted conductor she has proved to be. The fact that she was tutored by Leonard Bernstein speaks volumes for a lady who has become remarkable in her own way. Bernstein happens to be my hero also. Having met him on one occasion at the book launch of Quartet's *Hashish*, published in September 1984, we seemed to have clicked congenially and the memory of that encounter remains with me to this day.

PUBLISHING A CLASSIC

Hashish was a sumptuous and strikingly beautiful book production with stunning photographs by Suomi La Valle and a text by John Julius Norwich. Hashish had long been in use in the Middle East before it was discovered by the European literati of the nineteenth century. It had become part of the alternative culture of the 1980s, being praised and vilified in equal measure, the controversy over the relative benefits and harm done by its pharmacology continuing to the present day. Aside from the arguments, hashish was and is a means of livelihood for many people in Nepal and Lebanon. Suomi La Valle had gained the trust of the peasants who cultivated the plant, *Cannabis sativa*, and taken a series of astonishing photographs. John Julius Norwich, who had lived for three years in Lebanon, wrote about it with deep scholarly knowledge and level-headed lucidity. As he said:

> My own purpose will be to try to put this extraordinary plant in its historical and literary perspective: to assess the effects – political, cultural and even etymological – that it has had over the two and half thousand years or so that have elapsed since its peculiar properties were first discovered; and finally perhaps to remove at

least some of the mystique that – among those who have no direct experience of it – has surrounded it for so long.

The *Standard* reported how John Julius Norwich had tried hashish when he was with the British Embassy in Beirut in the early 1960s, smoking the stuff through a hubble-bubble at the home of a Lebanese high-court judge. 'I puffed diligently away,' he recalled, 'but the incident made little lasting impression.' My own experience was similar, though in a different environment. I enjoyed it at a certain stage of my life, but was never dependent. It was a passing phase, like some others one enjoys in the heyday of youth. There are those – mostly politicians – who have problems admitting they ever indulged. Others of us have the courage and honesty to admit it, acknowledging it as a step on the way to becoming more sophisticated and complete human beings. The party for Hashish was attended by a less predictable mixture of guests than usual. Its risqué aspect attracted a wider circle than the normal crowd of book-launch attenders. Suomi La Valle's wife, being the owner of an exclusive fashion boutique called Spaghetti in Beauchamp Place, Knightsbridge, invited elements from the fashion industry who were not unfamiliar with 'the weed' and its uses. They joined the motley company of beautiful people who were intent on not being excluded from an event tinged with notoriety because of its subject matter. Leonard Bernstein, new to the London party circuit, was there too. So was the more familiar figure of BBC Television's weatherman, Michael Fish, seen deep in conversation with the model Marie Helvin; which only went to show that modelling and weather forecasting might have more in common than is generally supposed. *Hashish* sold quite well, though it never achieved the figures we hoped for. We were definitely dealing with a book ahead of its time and lost out as a result. After the original print run of thirty-five thousand copies was either sold or remaindered, the book was never reprinted, and like various other Quartet titles it has become a collector's item. Whenever copies in good condition surface today, they are sold at a high premium. *Hashish* has become a cult book throughout the world.

SELINA BLOW

In the autumn of 1991, Selina Blow (ex-Quartet) was living in New York and making a name for herself in the world of fashion. The New Yorkers loved the architectural and horticultural inspiration that she brought to her designs, giving them a dotty English look that was perfectly in tune with her personality. An illustration for an article in *Avenue* magazine showed her one spring Saturday afternoon, walking two Austrian pugs along the upper reaches of Park Avenue, dressed in an iridescent purple velvet jacket (modelled on one worn by her aunt in 1905), a man's simple white dress shirt, nondesigner blue jeans, and a pair of gold leather Robert Clergerie ankle boots. Around her neck was a big silver cross, à la Madonna, decorated with large faux stones. On her finger she displayed a crystal ring surrounded with water sapphires and a variety of moonstones. A large brass belt completed her colourful ensemble. Its buckle featured a brass replica of Blow's company logo: an exotic two headed peacock, plumes spread to the wind.

In the interview Selina's passage through Quartet was covered by the following account:

> After high school, she pursued furniture restoration and interior design before settling in at Quartet Books, the publishing house run by the flamboyant Palestinian Attallah. Her job as a press officer brought her into London's fashionable circles, where she became known as one of Attallah's gaggle of well-connected young women. 'We had to go to all his parties and dress up in these plastic dresses,' Blow recalls. 'I was actually enormously

fond of him. But through the eyes of others,' she adds, 'this must have seemed completely repulsive.'

In the first instance, Selina was never compelled to wear one of the plastic (actually rubber) dresses she referred to, and secondly, no one to my knowledge found these attires repulsive. On the contrary, most observers waxed lyrical about the ingenuity and dramatic effect these revolutionary outfits contributed to the merriment of the occasion. Selina's comments, as quoted, did not go down well with me at the time, but on reflection I counted her unconsidered remarks as being part of her forthright character, both amusing and artless in equal measure. Selina is adorably eccentric, with a sense of humour to match. I enjoyed her company when she was working at Quartet, and subsequently when we used to meet in New York. In those days, despite her many creative talents, she had to struggle to make a reasonably comfortable living. New York could and can be a harsh place in which to live on a limited budget. During my frequent trips to the Big Apple, we would go shopping, and, as a concession to Selina's weakness for good food and cakes, indulge ourselves in culinary pursuits – and the occasional shoe-hunting expedition.

Working at Quartet

Selina Blow

I worked for Quartet on Goodge Street from 1987 to 1988. It was a colourful and extraordinary time. Naim ran an eclectic and curious publishing house. The main cornerstone to the firm was David Elliott, with bow tie, wild hair and a great knowledge of books. He often commented with affection and distraction, 'I don't know why I am working with all you debutantes.' Next to him in the running order was Jubby Ingrams, who was very much at the heart of Quartet – vivacious, extraordinary, witty and charismatic. Then came Olive, an accountant from Aberdeen, who sported a grey pudding-basin haircut and ruled the accounts and expenses with a heavy dry humour and an iron fist. The office cat, Saki, had been named after Moussaka, the Greek tavern on the ground floor. Following her various misadventures, including falling out of the window on to Moussaka's striped canopy, she had to wear a surgical lampshade around her head almost permanently. Things were more highbrow in the next building, where the editors were housed. I particularly remember Zelfa Hourani, who spent many arduous hours pursuing the hoped-for publication of her book on the lives of Middle Eastern women. It was remarked that she was so determined to publish it (and she did) that she was already practically doing it herself on the photocopying machine. There were many more equally delightful people making their contribution to the beat of life in this menagerie.

I was a minor in the press office, run by Anna Groundwater. In fact the job involved a lot of time in the post room sending out books. My début, and only, experience of jousting with the press was when a journalist phoned to ask me to comment on a poem written in Japanese for the actress Charlotte Rampling. I had no idea that my remarks were going to appear in the *Evening Standard* that very evening. 'It kind of rambles and I'm not sure what it says,' was the gist of my response. Naim reacted with shock and humour. 'Anna's going to kill you!' he said. After that I was returned to the post room forthwith and left press statements to Anna, who was far more capable of fielding media enquiries with punchy one-liners.

Memories

Every so often, Naim would invite Jubby and me to eat in his swish basement dining-room, where he hosted lunches with bemused but intrigued literary journalists. At these he would cajole Jubby into describing in detail the attentions of her latest admirer. I remember the cheeks of a senior literary editor slowly growing to a shade of crimson as she obliged. Then there was the famous launch of Parfums Namara, where all we girls were given rubber dresses to wear. A slightly troubled journalist asked Jubby, 'Don't you feel humiliated wearing these dresses?' 'No,' Jubby replied, 'it's great. They're free and we can take them home.'

I was also involved in the publication of Naim's massive volume of interviews with women, which created much press attention. (After the book was published, some married 'notables' who featured in its pages became concerned at what local charities they headed were going to make of their views on love, lust and life.) We took *Women* to the Frankfurt Book Fair, where the Quartet stand nestled between Hamish Hamilton and Faber. The fair involved Jubby and me walking the aisles wearing '*Literary Review*' sashes. Mysteriously a heavy book of pop-up German pornography, with machineguns appearing out of every orifice, turned up on our desk. At a dinner with French publicists, and feeling exhausted by the atmosphere of dry air and a diet of frankfurters and apple strudel, I ordered a generous plate of steak tartare, much to Naim's amusement. Back in the UK I enjoyed travelling with Naim to promote *Women*, and ended up at a radio station in Brighton. The interviewer asked Naim, 'Why do you only employ beautiful women?' 'Noo,' he replied. 'There are ugly ones too.' Naim was never one to get tripped up by a snide comment.

With a wardrobe of rubber dresses, crushed midnight-blue velvet dresses and a lot of books I left Quartet. Naim packed me off into normal life with an Asprey knife and fork in fond memory of my steak tartare moment at Frankfurt.

A FRENCH TALE

The story begins at a meeting in Paris that took place early in 1988 with a young author called Elisabeth Barillé, after I had been introduced to her by the French cosmetic journalist Elizabeth Arkus. Elisabeth Barillé's novel *Corps de jeune fille* was just then the latest literary sensation in Paris. She was Parisian born in 1960 and had gained degrees in English and Russian before becoming a freelance journalist contributing to *Paris-Match*, *Dépêche Mode*, *Femme* and *Geo*.

She was currently literary editor of *L'Eventail*. I was entranced by her at our meeting. She had that kind of sexuality which disturbs the senses. I bought a copy of the book and started reading it on the plane back to London. It was a book I could not put down. Its appeal was more attuned to the avant-garde French reading public, but her use of language and the depth of insight into the human condition were impressive. I was determined that Quartet would publish an English version, even though certain expressions she used were going to be hard to translate into English without losing their nuances.

It told the story of twenty-three-year-old Elisa, audacious and sensual, who is accosted by a middle-aged writer in the Jardin du Luxembourg. She is intrigued and troubled by him after he seduces her and says he wants her to be the heroine of his next book. As he interrogates her on her childhood and aspects of her sexual awakening, the tone of the narrative darkens and they begin to play a game in which it is no longer clear who is preying on whom.

The French press had given the book some very positive reviews: 'A revelation ... unpretentious and direct ... truly liberated,' said *Marie-Claire*; 'Gay, tender, biting, playful ... written with enthusiasm and zest,' said *FranceSoir*; 'Vigorous, direct and lucid, sparing nothing and nobody,' said *Le Figaro Littéraire*. The English literary establishment was more ambivalent in its reception of the translated version under the title *Body of a Girl*. It came as no surprise, however, for I had always been aware that its appeal here would be limited. It belonged to a genre that had that intrinsically cerebral quality more consonant with European culture. Clarence de Roch in *Tatler* chose to focus on the book's erotic side. His opening paragraph set the mood of his piece: 'There's a brilliantly funny scene in Elisabeth Barillé's first novel, in which Elisa, the heroine, brings her suitor's amorous *élan* to an abrupt halt by staring at his exposed penis and describing it witheringly (literally so as it turns out) as looking "just like Cyrano's nose!"' Cara Chanteau in the *Listener* was rather more dismissive:

Jane Austen once wrote that in *Emma* she was planning a heroine 'which no one but myself would like': Barillé might, with a lot more justification, have said the same for *Body of a Girl*. It is a problem from which her novel never really recovers ... [But] Barillé has a good and very fluent style; one could wish to see it employed on more searching subject matter. Perhaps the successor to *Body of a Girl* might be a little more sparing with the body and reveal rather more about the girl.

Janet Barron, for the *Literary Review*, found a degree of merit in the book, though she confessed that the use of some words made her blush:

I wouldn't recommend reading some of this in public; try convincing the chap who's peering over your shoulder that 'fanny' is a symbol of women's liberation. Barillé takes the obsessions of male erotic writing and attributes them to her narrator Elisa. The result is often witty. Barillé has a sardonic sense of humour and Parisian bohemianism is given a sarcastic twist.

Rebecca O'Rourke's reaction in the *Guardian* was especially damning:

Elisa's sexual history contains much that is surprising and some that is shocking. It's a joyless account, rehearsing without exploring the idea that women's autonomous sexuality is the province of whores and sluts. The special secret Elisa keeps to herself is compulsive masturbation, fuel to shameful self-hatred. Britain often looks to France, impressed by the latter's sexual freedoms and sophistication. Colette, Violette Leduc and Simone de Beauvoir made enormous contributions to women's writing by pioneering sensual, erotic and sexual themes. On the evidence of *Body of a Girl*, this pre-eminence is now receding.

In late 1990, Quartet published Elisabeth Barillé's second novel, *Marie Ensnared*. This time the author's obsession with prostitution manifested itself even more clearly. The story had the same resonance as *Body of a Girl*, but in this one the heroine began to lead a double life. To summarize the plot, Marie and her husband Luc, a charming and talented architect, apparently make the perfect bourgeois couple. While he provides her with a life of comfort and security, she is his perfect companion and hostess to the cosy, if complacent, dinner parties that are the cornerstone of his success. Then Luc accepts a commission to build a vast palace in the Moroccan desert for a rich megalomaniac Aloui, whose escort is Nalège, a malicious manipulative call-girl. Marie becomes fascinated by Nalège's lifestyle, seeing it as an emancipation from the trap of comfort that is her life with Luc. She becomes her understudy, but when Nalège sends her the obese, alcoholic Aloui, the arrangement ends in a disastrous surfacing of guilt and self-loathing, with Marie now the victim of male cruelty and her own emotional confusion.

When I read *Marie Ensnared* I strongly suspected that the book had an autobiographical basis and that Barillé's fictional account was a clever way of expressing her own dark secrets. Barillé's own explanation for her theme was that, 'Eroticism interests me more than sex. It's the staging of our sexual impulses.' But in the view of Jane O'Grady in the *Observer*, 'chic, pretty Marie' was both 'directing and starring in the film of her life, and Barillé's slim novelette resembles a soft-porn movie minus eroticism'. Neither *Body of a Girl* nor *Marie Ensnared* made the impact I personally had anticipated.

Somehow they failed to catch the mood of the literary public in Britain. *La différance* was once again manifesting itself.

LA DIFFERENCE

Craig Brown was never a great admirer of mine. He lambasted me in the *Mail on Sunday* on the publication of *Women* by penning the most scathing review of the lot. Subsequently he and Bron had lunch with me in Beak Street. It was meant to be a kind of rapprochement, though that was not quite how it worked out by my reading of the situation. Craig was in the same mould as Bron. Both of them felt passionately about things, and particularly about people. Once they had taken against someone, it would be extremely hard to divert them from their target.

Craig's coolness towards me was something I found strange in so far as I could not decipher it. I was a supporter of literature and the arts, spending most of my money bolstering endeavours closely related to them, so even if Craig did feel some kind of antipathy towards me, I could not see why that should stop him being more appreciative. Perhaps I misread where he was coming from and misjudged him unfairly.

His review of *Women* was chosen for special mention in the trade journal, the *Bookseller*, in its regular column, 'Critics Crowner' which sought to round-up the important books and their reviews, compiled by a mysterious personage 'Quentin Oates'. Its tone was so biased a retort was written by David Elliott, a Quartet staff member, pointing out how this had:

> … sought to destroy all credibility for Naim Attallah's *Women*. It was clear he was prepared to use his influence in any way he could to damage the book-trade's opinion of Mr Attallah and his book. I cannot recall any article in the *Bookseller* (and I have been reading

the magazine for over twenty years) ever calling a book 'worthless'. *Women* was sold to *The Times* for a serialization over five days, second serial rights were sold to the *Sunday Mirror* for two weekly extracts and magazine rights were sold to *Women's World*; Australian, Swedish, Dutch, German, Spanish, French and South African serialization rights are sold ... Interviews have already appeared in six major provincial newspapers and two Sunday colour supplements. The author is presently engaged on a tour of Scotland and other parts of England and Wales appearing on regional TV programmes, local radio stations and being interviewed by provincial newspapers.

Any book which generates this torrent of attention and activity usually wins glittering prizes from the trade journals – not so with Mr Oates. With a sniff he dismisses it all as 'hype'. What does he want? Every time any book generates controversy and attention it is good for all the trade. He has ignored the good reviews altogether ...

These reviews were as pleasing and praising as Craig Brown's (quoted at great length by Mr Oates) was nasty and damning. Oates's précis of Anita Brookner's review left out her obvious fascination with aspects of the book and when Deborah Moggach's review for the *Sunday Times* actually praises *Women*, Oates declares he couldn't be bothered with reading it. Precisely, Mr Oates! When Deborah Moggach writes: '... the tone of this book is bracing, honest, highly intelligent and often funny', it does not suit your brief.

Finally the marketplace decides if a book is to sell or not. And this is my real annoyance with Mr Oates and the *Bookseller*. He chooses to deride, in a vindictive manner, a book launched with incredible coverage and attention whilst that launch is still in progress – *Women* was published only two days before Oates's article appeared. Since his name is pseudonymous, I can only imagine his motives, but if the *Bookseller* is to take sides on controversial books, can it do so in a more balanced fashion?

How different it all was in France!

Following the publication of *Women* in October 1987, I was approached by Carrere, the French media group and publishers, with a view to producing a French edition. Their only stipulation was that I should interview an additional thirty Frenchwomen almost immediately. They were in a great hurry to bring out the French-language version in March 1988, a mere six months after the appearance of the English edition. It looked an almost impossible task. They hired a team of translators to work round the clock on the English text while I frantically set about conducting the necessary interviews. The choice of women and arrangements to interview them were all done in conjunction with my own office in Paris. It was just left to me to brush up on my French and plunge into another voyage of discovery with renewed vigour and optimism. Strangely I had remained unaffected by the adverse critical reception I had received in the UK and felt undaunted by the idea that the whole thing might involve a repetition of the experience in France. My new list included writers, bankers, artists and stars of stage and screen, such as Arletty and Emmanuelle Béart, who had recently starred in *Manon des Sources*, the continuation of Claude Berri's hit film based on Marcel Pagnol's novel *Jean de Florette*, with Daniel Auteuil. Also there, among the politicians, was Edith Cresson, who was to become the first woman prime minister of France not many years later.

Despite the shortage of time, the French edition was published as planned and Carrere arranged for a launch party to be held on 22 March at the famous Parisian night-spot, Le Privilège. It was a most glamorous occasion, extensively covered by the French media and attended by hordes of celebrities. I was seated at dinner between Hélène Rochas, the *parfumière*, and Joan Juliet Buck, the American writer and then editor of French *Vogue*. The room teemed with beautiful women. Over the next few days I appeared on French television, discussing the book with some of the stars who featured in its pages. The French critics were unanimous in their plaudits, in sharp contrast with their counterparts in the UK. It was impossible to open a French newspaper without seeing some reference to the book. I felt euphoric at this unexpected show of appreciation and enthusiasm. And to crown it all, the book sold extremely well in France and our efforts were richly rewarded.

Looking through my archives, the retrospective impression is that more was written about the French edition than the already phenomenal amount about the English edition in Britain. The difference in coverage lay in the fact that while the Gallic approach was constructive the trend in the book's home country was certainly destructive. Even after the furore surrounding the original publication of Women in hardback had died down, the appearance of a paperback edition in Britain a year later precipitated the same spitting of venom as before. It was as if those who had missed their chance at first publication now climbed aboard to make their voices heard from the bandwagon. But this was a new wave of women, some not so well known as their predecessors of a year earlier. They entered the fray as if to proclaim solidarity with their dissenting sisters.

In the meantime, a Japanese edition was in preparation. The divergence of opinion between the public at large, who welcomed the book, and the band of its detractors, who did not, posed many questions. Who matters most? Is it the reading public or the self-proclaimed arbiters whose judgement has proved on many occasions to be out of touch with the prevailing mood? Is our cultural life totally dependent on a select few whose opinions seldom reflect the thinking or aspirations of the ordinary man or woman? These questions have continued to trouble me. We seem to be burdened with an élitist literary establishment intent on keeping the myth of its infallibility going at all costs. In saying this I could hardly be accused of 'sour grapes'; I laughed all the way to the bank.

A WONDERFUL COOK

I employed many talented young ladies during my time in my new Asprey offices above Garrard. Being prepared to work hard was always a prerequisite for being part of the team, and a sense of humour was essential. The atmosphere was charged with every kind of excitement. New ideas – often outrageously original – were bandied about. Intoxicating new projects were thought up daily. The buzz was so contagious that each one of the girls had her own theories, perceptions and striking images to contribute. After so many years I still cannot tell whether the energetic environment was the catalyst or vice versa. Each one of them was a character worth describing, either for her singularity or her eccentric disposition. But since I consider food to be one of life's most pleasurable diversions, I will mention my cook, Hattie Beaumont.

Hattie was endowed with exceptional culinary talents and used them with remarkable originality. She improvised almost on a daily basis, creating the most delicious dishes that seemed effortless but always had the required effect. She ranked alongside Charlotte Millward, my cook at Namara House, who likewise never failed to dazzle everyone with her exquisite cuisine. Charlotte herself was not without her eccentricities, but in Hattie it was her skittishness that was her most lovable trademark. Both were cheekily attractive to suit their personalities, Charlotte being more controlled while Hattie was a bit of a loose cannon. When Hattie was on her best behaviour, she had no equal, and conversely, if she was being naughty, her equal would also have been hard to find. She was adorable and exasperating in equal measure. Her exploits were hilarious and sometimes played havoc with her life and ours. But once you loved her, nothing mattered. She became irresistibly addictive and there was no getting her out from under your skin. Her secret was eternal youth, for she looks no different today from the way she looked then: radiant with optimism and joie de vivre.

Work and Antics

Hattie Beaumont

I worked for Naim for several years, moving with him from Namara House to Regent Street, where he then presided as chief executive of the Asprey group. When I look back on those years, I do so with much nostalgia, for they were indeed some of the happiest of my life. We were an eclectic gaggle of girls working for him with a fierce loyalty that we maintain to this day. Most of us agree that he was endlessly forgiving, even when he felt compelled to sack us for chronic misbehaviour, which in my case was not a rare occurrence. But he always relented in the end.

He was more of an indulgent father figure who managed us all charmingly well. Even with so many hormones flying around, we never fell out. In fact we looked forward to every morning breezing into work with a skip in our steps and a smile on our faces that reflected our pleasure in working for such an enigmatic and caring man. Along with the normal workload, we had time for many amusing antics, which we played on our wonderfully patient boss. He would turn the tables on us occasionally, like the time when I was meeting a potential boyfriend at the local pub and he and some of my workmates came to spy on me, after warning me beforehand to play hard to get and not to succumb to any physical temptation in the early stages of the relationship. He had also told me he would easily find out whether I'd taken heed of his advice by the expression on my face next day: a roguish smile would divulge all and I would be in trouble! So it may be imagined how I felt when I saw him and his entourage sitting in the corner of the pub watching my every move. I turned tomato red and wanted to flee, but I was too embarrassed to tell my companion. The following day, when we all gathered in Naim's office to dissect the goings-on of the evening before, there were too many episodes to recount and I suspect they'd be far too naughty to repeat to gentlefolk. In a nutshell, Naim is a man who deserves great respect, who has had a wonderfully colourful life, has not been immune to his share of hard times but has always taken them in his stride with an upbeat attitude. I shall retain these happy memories and consider myself lucky to have had the pleasure to be part of his life.

THIS & THAT

In October 1989 Quartet had announced my forthcoming book *Singular Encounters*, to be published in the autumn of 1990. This time the subject was men. It was to consist of an exhaustive study of twenty-five of them. The interviews, designed to unlock the subjects' innermost secrets, would cover their private and professional lives, their ambitions and aspirations, and would delve into areas that carried the warning: 'proceed at your own risk'. The first assumption made by the press was that it was out to make Anna Ford's recent book on the same subject seem like a toe in the water compared with the murky revelations I would try to uncover. 'It's not going to be yet another book of interviews,' I told the *Evening Standard* firmly. 'I'm doing it for the challenge. My reputation as a writer will rise or fall on the book.'

From the start I saw *Singular Encounters* as a highly ambitious project, one that was bound to determine my future as an interviewer. The men I was seeking to engage were leaders in their respective fields and were unlikely to make any concessions to the fact that I was a novice in this journalistic medium. The women's book was comparatively simple.

My natural affinity with women had been an immeasurable help. I could not as yet advance the claim to have a similar affinity with men. Whether or not the right empathy was there would only emerge with time. Moreover, where the women's book had been, broadly speaking, a compendium of their views on subjects affecting women in general, the men's book must aim to present an individual in-depth study of each participant. As such it needed more background research and a more focused concentration during the interviews.

The difficulties were exacerbated by the slating *Women* had received at the hands of a large majority of critics and commentators. The general tone had been to hold up to ridicule the two hundred and eighty-nine women who had accepted the invitation to appear in its pages. I was anxious that this might now become a discouraging factor, deterring some men from agreeing to a serious encounter with me. Fortunately my fears turned out to be without foundation and most of the men I approached were happy to oblige. A. N. Wilson had his reservations at first, though he soon relented, and they had been on entirely different grounds, as he explained in a 'Diary' piece in the *Spectator*.

> My friend Naim Attallah ... is compiling a volume of interviews with the thirty most important men in the world. I believe it [will include] revealing conversations with Yehudi Menuhin, Lord Goodman, Monsignor Gilbey, J. K. Galbraith and Richard Ingrams. I was flattered to be asked to be of their number. The company is so grand that it really feels better than being given the OM ... I said no at first, because I was frightened that Naim would only want to ask me about sex, but in the event he twisted my arm by saying that if I did not consent there would be no young men in his book. In the event, he did not ask me about sex at all, having covered the subject exhaustively with the others. I was glad to help him out by being the voice of youth.

In fact I got him on to the subject of sex by way of Christianity's disapproval of sex, which brought him out firmly against St Augustine, St Paul and the puritans. But what about the puritan argument that sex was addictive, I asked, and that from addiction comes perversion? 'Obviously, if you're a healthy grown-up person, your sexual impulses go on, but that's not the same as saying something is addictive. To say that is like saying food is addictive.' 'But if you suddenly had three or four women, and you start having sex with them, wouldn't you want to have more and more?' I pressed him. 'What an adventurous life you must have led, Naim,' Andrew replied. 'I'm not qualified to answer that question.' Despite his reluctance to rise to the bait, the riposte was very much vintage Wilson in its sharpness and humour.

Another reluctant target was Mark Birley of Harry's Bar and Annabel's. He procrastinated but in the end agreed as well. Until then he had always refused to submit to any press coverage and his inclusion in the book was a bit of a coup. However, it was a chance I almost missed. On the appointed day I was struck down with flu. If I had cancelled he would no doubt have jumped at the excuse not to reconvene the session at another time. To ensure this could not happen, I rose from my sickbed suffering from a fevered, aching body, swallowed two codeine tablets and phoned Mark's secretary to confirm I would be arriving for our appointment. To my astonishment, as if by a conjunction of fate, she told me Mark had the flu as well but would be willing to do the interview at home if I was happy to make the effort. We ended up sipping champagne together in a state of near delirium and conducting a serious conversation in a codeine-induced haze. The unusual encounter marked the beginning of a friendship that remained strong over the years.

Lord Goodman raised a stumbling block of a different order. I saw him over a lavish breakfast at his London flat, initially to be assessed for my suitability to be an interviewer of this giant among men. I outlined the concept of the book for him and mentioned several people who had agreed to participate, including Lord Alexander QC and Lord

Rees-Mogg. Evidently I passed muster because a month later I conducted the interview itself. Then, a few days later, a letter arrived from Lord Goodman withdrawing his permission for publication on the grounds that Richard Ingrams would be appearing in the same volume: 'It was inexcusable to have lured me with a number of respectable names and to have withheld the fact that Mr Ingrams is to be included in the book.'

I replied with a soothing letter, reminding him of his avowed opposition to censorship and questioning the wisdom of bowing out in vexation. The strategy worked, though his reply was designed to put me in my place: 'In view of your pathetic plea, I am prepared, albeit reluctantly, to allow the interview to appear.'

I heaved a sigh of relief. Lord Goodman, a staunch defender of the cause of the arts, commanded great respect as a legal adviser to both political wings and the establishment itself. He knew nearly everyone in British public life and had been called upon to advise virtually every great national institution. Indeed, he came close to being a national institution himself. It seemed strange that he should have felt so strongly about the one-time editor of *Private Eye*, though the magazine had once allegedly libelled him. He talked only in general terms about libel in our interview. 'I've always deterred people from becoming involved,' he said. It seemed that in the case of *Private Eye* he was unable to follow his own advice. The whole little episode was completely at odds with the image he cultivated of being a sage, invulnerable in his judgement.

Harold Acton made a sharp contrast: though he had the reputation befitting a grand aesthete, I found him easy-going and charm itself. Our interview took place in Florence over dinner at his home, La Pietra, a Renaissance villa that was like a domestic museum full of countless *objets d'art* and priceless paintings collected by his family over the years. I had visited him there many times, mostly for tea or dinner, when he would engage in affectionate gossip about his great friend Tony Lambton, or regale me with the latest scandals making the rounds in the small circle of Florentine society, taking especial delight in any sexual peccadilloes. He considered me an amusing dinner companion – a welcome change from certain other guests, who tended to be academic and whom he labelled stuffy and boring. He often cancelled a dinner date with them in preference for spending an evening of banter with me.

As a student at Oxford, Harold had been well known for flouting convention and mixing in male undergraduate circles where bisexuality was in vogue. His close friends included Auberon Waugh's father, Evelyn, who reputedly used him as a model for some of the more outrageous characters in his novels. I used to tease Harold about girls and enquire if he had ever slept with one. He would put on a show of being greatly shocked at this sudden intrusion into his private life before rolling his eyes and smiling an enigmatic smile. Then he would tap me coyly on the hand as if chastising me for being such a 'naughty boy'. This only encouraged me to urge him on, and on one occasion he told me about an intimate encounter with a young Chinese girl during the time when he lived in China, teaching English at Peking National University in the 1930s. He described the silky skin of her naked body with obvious relish, but that was as far as he ever went. The mystery of whether he actually slept with any girl remained unsolved.

During one of our conversations, he expressed his regret at the way Oxford University had turned down his offer to bequeath them La Pietra with its collection of priceless art works, forty thousand rare books and fifty-seven acres of grounds in his will. They felt they could not have afforded the cost of repairs and restoration. Instead, after he died in 1994, La Pietra went to New York University as a study and conference centre. Although he had an American mother, he would have preferred the legacy to have gone to a British institution. In the years after his death, the estate became the subject of a long-running counter-claim from the descendants of Harold's illegitimate half-sister, with a judge giving authority for the exhumation of his father's body from the family grave in Florence. Happily, it seems there has been no need to disturb Harold's remains, though his father's were reported as confirming the DNA link.

Harold entertained well, but he had one curious phobia about electricity consumption. When I needed to visit the cloakroom he would escort me to switch on the light and linger in the vicinity to make sure it was switched off again after I emerged. It was part of his economy drive to maintain his lifestyle without compromising it with waste. Or that was how he explained it.

John Kenneth Galbraith, the world-renowned economist, was a difficult proposition: he was imperious and patronizing. From the outset he tried to dwarf me by orchestrating every aspect of our conversation, refusing to give me a straight answer when he felt a question might compromise him. Instead he would skirt around it and avoid tackling its essence; or refrain from being specific when challenged. Whenever I tried to insist on a proper response to a question, he brushed it aside with a curt dismissal: 'Move on to the next question.' The tone in his voice made it clear he meant what he said and I knew that, if I stood my ground, I would soon be shown the door. Since he was a name to be reckoned with, I swallowed my pride and moved on under his overbearing direction. Eating humble pie was better than having no portion of pie at all. He was a man totally secure in his self-confidence and impressively grand in his immense knowledge. The experience of meeting him was worth it for the painful lesson it gave me in self-control.

The ennobled Gordon White was another example of someone who made me feel uneasy. This was not because of any display of high intellect, but it had everything to do with the fact that he was a right-wing bigot, bereft of any compassion for the underprivileged and under no compulsion to conceal it. He was without doubt a brilliant market operator, who had found his niche in the United States and been a perfect counterbalance for his partner, Lord Hanson, who was altogether more mellow and less strident.

Lord White was also working hard to re-enact his youth at the time I met him. He had a young girlfriend, with whom he was desperately trying to keep up physically by exerting himself in the gym. His motivation was so transparent as to make it open to ridicule. The adage, 'There is no fool like an old fool,' was particularly apposite in his case. I somehow found myself unable to relate to him at any level. A tone of self-congratulation ran through the interview and even impinged on what he would like to have been if not a businessman – a major figure in the sporting world or an actor. 'I was once offered a screen test,' he said, 'but didn't have the courage to do it. I was afraid of failure. You see, I looked right. I was a very good-looking guy when I was younger.' He was an ardent admirer of Mrs Thatcher, to whom he owed his elevation to the Lords.

With the broadcaster, Michael Aspel, who was introduced to me by Theo Cowan, I had a different kind of problem – one that threatened to blow up into a major row. The interview itself went extremely well. I was particularly struck by Michael's total candour and his willingness to touch on matters that had at certain points blighted his life. His was a story full of pathos and sorrow, and it was indeed moving. The chemistry between us must have worked most effectively and I felt delighted to have extracted from him some gems that would help to make the final version a most absorbing and sympathetic lesson in soul baring. Away from the limelight of his profession, Michael revealed his true self and showed his skills and vulnerabilities in a human light.

A few days later I received a phone call from his agent requesting a sight of the edited interview. It seemed Michael was beginning to feel concerned about certain aspects that he would like to reassess and perhaps omit. Instinctively I felt the agent was angling to doctor the interview and thus fillet out its quality of spontaneity, reducing it to the usual homogenized, polished sort of interview so common in show business – the kind that avoids delving too deeply into inner feelings or dwelling on the frailties of the subject's life. My reaction was not the one the agent had expected. I fought hard to maintain the integrity of the interview as I saw it, while also feeling some embarrassment at the prospect of having to air our views in public with the indignities likely to follow.

Theo Cowan was keen to prevent any falling out and took on himself the role of peace broker. He worked tirelessly to arrive at a solution to avoid a rumpus that was going to benefit no one. Peace was eventually restored, but at a price. Compromise is not always the best way forward. In the event, we ended up with something more like an *entente cordiale*, having had to sacrifice some deeply held principles for the preservation of something called 'image'. That, alas, is more or less the way of the world.

Dominick Dunne became a household name in the United States when, after producing a number of Hollywood films, he turned to being an author and a contributing editor at *Vanity Fair*. A recovered alcoholic, he had tragedy in his background, his daughter having been murdered by her boyfriend in 1983. The impression I had gained on meeting him was that he would have been more at ease doing the interview than being interviewed. He had an irritable impatience and I found it hard going to keep him focused. He did not appear to be interested in any of my questions, but would rather have been formulating his own and then giving what he considered to be appropriate answers. I persevered to the very end without seeming to be rattled. He was not a person I would have chosen to be marooned with on a desert island. I felt that his demons had never left him and he sadly remained a tortured soul. Possibly our encounter was ill-timed, or perhaps I myself was in a state of mental turmoil that I mistakenly projected on to him. All I could remember subsequently was my sense of relief when the interview was over. As I walked away, revived by a light breeze, the sun was shining and New York looked at its best.

Monsignor Alfred Gilbey, the ultra-orthodox Catholic Society priest who resided, till his death a few months after I interviewed him, at the Travellers' Club in Pall Mall, was for decades a chaplain at Cambridge.

He lived in grand style and entertained his guests for dinner at the club with healthy measures of good wine, obviously not believing that abstinence from culinary pleasures was needed to ensure an easy passage to heaven. For the interview, I met him for dinner and then retired with him to a quiet corner to conduct it. He certainly had a rare eloquence and gave the impression of a single-minded individual who was not afraid to court controversy, especially when it came to his views on women. Tackled directly on the subject, he swiftly emerged as a woman-hater *extraordinaire*, nostalgic for the days when universities and other institutions were strictly male preserves. His view, he considered, was 'wholly compatible with the God-given design of women as complementary to men', which was to say they were not the equal of men. I could only feel he was taking an unnecessary risk. What if God turned out to be a woman? What then for Monsignor Gilbey?

The distinguished writer Edmund White remains the most explicit individual I have ever interviewed. Endowed with formidable powers of communication and an elegant prose style, he had the ability to shock while retaining an icy composure. His life was marred as a boy by a violent father and he was later to experience the trauma of losing his male lover to AIDS. Yet his eloquence never deserted him, even when discussing the most explosive of subjects, such as a homosexual son's incestuous feelings for his father.

Many of the homosexuals he had known, he said, 'had strong erotic fantasies about their fathers, and have even slept with their fathers or brothers. It's not unusual ... I definitely had strong erotic feelings towards my father.' An extraordinary story then emerged from his family situation.

> I think the idea was that whoever was sleeping in my father's bed was in a privileged position in the family and would gain power. In other words, my father was a tyrant, and at first my mother was in his bed and a privileged person; then my stepmother became a

privileged person; then my father had an affair with my sister, and my sister was elevated in the family because of it. I didn't know about it at the time, but I sensed it because I once walked in on them when my father was brushing my sister's hair. She had very long blonde hair, and looked quite a bit like his mother, who was very pretty ...

Anyway, my father was brushing my sister's hair, standing behind her and crying as he did so. It was the only time I saw my father cry. I sensed there was something going on, but I wasn't certain to what extent. It was only later, when my sister had a complete breakdown and was in a mental hospital, that I knew for sure. She had tried to kill herself and it all came out, but that was many years later. I guessed she had always had strong guilt feelings about this relationship with my father, maybe partly because she liked it.

I think she had loved him very much. It was extremely dramatic when my father died, because we had a farm in the north of Ohio where he wanted to be buried, and that was terribly inconvenient for everybody because it took hours to get there. We finally arrived in the small town with its little farmers' church, and there he was in an open coffin, which I hated. But my sister went up to the coffin and talked to my father a long time, rather angrily and crying. Then she took off her wedding ring and put it on his finger. She was forty-something at the time.

It was one of the most surprising moments of revelation in the whole book.

I particularly wanted to interview John Updike. He was the American writer of his generation with the most distinguished and prolific output, who had dissected the suburban sexual mores of small-town America. The snag was that he then rarely gave interviews. As André Deutsch was his publisher in Britain, I asked him if he thought he could persuade

Updike to meet me. André said he would do what he could but could promise nothing. Eventually he came back and said Updike would be willing to see me in Boston, but had stipulated that the interview must be restricted to forty-five minutes. I naturally gibed at this impossibly meagre concession, but André said well, it was either that or nothing. I flew to Boston specially and Updike came to my hotel room as arranged. Once he got going, our conversation went on for almost two hours. In his own memoirs he had described himself as malicious, greedy for a quota of life's pleasures, an obnoxious show-off, rapacious and sneaky. This did not really match the public perception of him, I suggested.

I think that anybody who knows me would agree with all those adjectives. I was an only child who never had to compete with a sibling, and my parents were both, in their way, very loving and indulgent. Just the fact that I had the presumption to become an artist is rather ridiculous, isn't it, with no qualifications except that I felt treasured as a child. When my mother died, among the things in the attic was a scrapbook containing many of my drawings done when I was three or four. Not every child gets that kind of attention. The good side of it is that I have a certain confidence, and by and large I've acted confidently in my life and had good results. The bad side is that I like to be the centre of attention.

As for being malicious, I think I am more than unusually malicious. That joy, that *Schadenfreude* we take in other people's misfortunes, is highly developed in me, though I try to repress it. I detect within myself a certain sadism, a certain pleasure in the misfortunes of others. I don't know whether I'm average in this or whether it's exceptional, but I'm interested to a degree in the question of sadism. People who are sadistic are very sensitive to pain, and it's a way of exorcizing the demon of pain.

I'm so aware of my enviousness that I try not to review books by contemporary Americans. I'm not sure that I would really give an honest opinion, and that's sneaky. People who are cowardly and don't especially enjoy confrontation or battle tend to be sneaky. In this unflattering self-characterization though, I was no doubt just doing my Christian duty of confessing sins. Human nature is mightily mixed, but surely all these malicious and cruel aspects are there along with everything else.

I then raised the question of a reviewer of his novel *Couples* calling him 'the pornographer of marriage'. Did he resent this tag, I asked.

> Not too much. I wasn't trying to be pornographic. I was trying to describe sexual behaviour among people, and the effect was probably the opposite of pornographic. Pornography creates a world without consequences, where women don't get pregnant, nobody gets venereal disease and no one gets tired. In *Couples* I was trying, to the limits of my own knowledge, to describe sexual situations and show them with consequences. Without resenting that phrase, I don't think it describes very well what I was trying to do …
>
> I think *Couples* was certainly of its time, just in the fact that it spans very specific years and refers to a lot of historical events. In a funny way, the book is about the Kennedy assassination. It's also about the introduction of the contraceptive pill, the fact that the danger of getting pregnant was almost entirely removed and that a certain amount of promiscuity resulted directly from this technology. It also turns out that it was the pre-AIDS, pre-herpes paradise, so it was a moment that's gone, a moment of liberation which broke not upon a bunch of San Francisco hippies, but upon middle-aged couples, yet was a revolution of a kind. It is very much of its historic moment.

Memories

There was general agreement that Yehudi Menuhin was not only a great musician but also a great human being. I had already been in contact with his father, Moshe, over *The Palestinians*, which Quartet had published, and was interested to hear the son's views on some of the issues involved. My lead-in to the subject was a question about Wilhelm Furtwängler, who had remained in Germany and continued his career as a conductor almost till the end of the Nazi era. As a result he had been much criticized. Yehudi Menuhin's assessment was both eminently sane and full of insight.

> A very great conductor and an absolutely clean man, no question of that. He stood up for Hindemith, he protected a great many Jews, helped many out of Germany, and himself had to escape towards the end of the war. He happened to conduct the orchestra when some of the German leaders were there, but we can't expect everyone to behave in the same way. Sometimes it takes more courage to remain in your country than to leave it. Those who stayed suffered a pretty bad fate, and those who came out, after all, escaped. Yet there was this feeling of superiority among those who escaped, thinking that they showed great determination in leaving it behind. I would say, Jew or Gentile, you can't blame those who stayed, you can't blame those who escaped. It's just the way things went. But Furtwängler himself was a man of integrity.
>
> The anti-Semitism I have seen in my lifetime has had a psychological impact on me only to the extent that I know it is important to maintain the dignity of the Jew and to avoid a kind of behaviour that might prompt a response. The caricature of the Jew is the businessman with the big cigar, who does exist sometimes. They can be charming and interesting people. What bothers me sometimes is that they are a little like desert flowers. When they have only a drop of water they blossom. They make the most of the opportunity, as they did in Germany before the

Nazi days, when they occupied extremely powerful positions. That must have created a certain amount of resentment. Of course, it gives no excuse for anti-Semitism, but you can understand it. The Jew does not stand out in Italy or Greece, nor would he in China, since the Chinese are far cleverer at business than the Jews. There are so many different types of Jew, but traditionally people have fastened on the Jew who is obviously different from them. But there are so many that are in no way different. It's like the problem of the black in the United States. There are almost a majority of blacks that are nearly white, and no one bothers about them.

It is true that the Jews are far too sensitive, though they have perhaps been sensitized by history. They are too ready to imagine an insult; they are not prepared to give enough leeway, even to allow for a certain misbehaviour; and it is part of the psychology. One can understand that too, and one must understand it. They have to compensate for certain established assumptions. If it's not one thing it's another. If it's not religion, it's jealousy or it's race. Yet it's none of these things actually. It's simply that people are nasty and want to condemn anything if they can find a little difference; can say that hair is frizzed instead of straight or there's a detectable accent. Then they pounce on it.

Unfortunately the Jews have come to Israel with the narrow aim of making themselves an independent nation, to a large extent disregarding the environment and the rest of the world. They didn't come to establish a nation with the Palestinians and a wonderful federation (though now they realize that perhaps they should have done). They came instead with the pure desire to establish a Jewish state to the exclusion of everything else. They did it very successfully, but they did it ruthlessly, and probably the sense of fear is equal on both sides. I feel that the only solution lies in a federation, totally equal, as in Switzerland. If both have an equal title to the land, what else can you do? Meanwhile there is something cruel about all of us. We are capable of the most horrid things, especially if we have suffered them ourselves.

Yehudi left an indelible impression on me: a shining example of goodness and humility. He would never have thanked you to feel humbled in his presence, but that was the effect.

In December 1992, three years after my interview with Yehudi, Richard Ingrams, a friend of the Menuhins, asked me to interview Lady Menuhin for the *Oldie* magazine. The interview never appeared for two reasons: first, because of its length there were difficulties over successfully abridging it to fit three pages of the magazine without losing the natural flow; secondly, Lady Menuhin had concerns, as she expressed them to Richard, that some aspects of the interview might cause her embarrassment or even trigger off the kind of controversy that would be extremely harmful to her husband. Richard, not always known for his understanding in such matters, surprisingly refrained from running the interview in any form. I believe Richard took the right decision at the time, but now that the Menuhins are dead it will be enlightening to read some of Lady Menuhin's thoughts on life with Yehudi and the dangers he had faced because of his support for Furtwängler.

As she told it in her own autobiography, Diana Menuhin came from a rigorous background, having had an Edwardian Christian Scientist mother, and a chequered career as a ballet dancer in which you could never afford to be ill, along with a love life that had gained no permanence at its centre. The disciplines she had been through made her, she felt, 'very serviceable for life with darling Yehudi, who prefers to live on cloud nine, which he seems to have rented for most of his life'. She had met him after being in the Middle East during the war and enduring a deeply unhappy end to a love affair.

'When I met Yehudi, my metaphysical attitude to life made me realize that he was my destiny. He fell in love with me, and I was in love with him, but as he was married with two small children I never told him. It took two and a half really terrible years for him to get his divorce, because he was so angelic he couldn't hurt anybody, even if he knew he was not to blame for his first mistake. I may have been his second mistake, but he hasn't found out yet.'

In her book she described her life with Yehudi as 'service in its highest sense'. I'm an incurable, incorrigible worker.

> I think that's what Yehudi liked so much, and he recognized with great relief that we had a tremendous amount in common, that we'd both had aspirations since we were born, that I had enormous experience because I hadn't been protected by wonderful parents who had given up everything for me. He remains to this day the most incredibly modest man, and I think that's what the audience feels. Yehudi's a medium – the music comes through him; he feels responsible to the composer, dead or alive. He was very sad and very lonely when I met him, because his marriage had really broken up, and Yehudi wouldn't admit it; and if he had admitted it, he would have blamed himself. Yehudi never blames anyone else, ever, for anything. He told me that when he first saw me at my mother's house he went away to sit on a pouffe at the end of the drawing-room, and thought, 'I'm going to have her.' I said, 'Don't be ridiculous, it was your daughter's fifth birthday,' for I didn't know then that the marriage was no good, but Yehudi has a way of knowing what he wants, and he gets it.

Before they could marry in 1947, there were two and half 'dark years' while Yehudi was separating from his first wife, but Diana never doubted she was herself doing the right thing.

> I never raised a finger to help him get rid of his first wife. I never told him I was in love with him, because I didn't want him

to feel any obligation towards me. Of course he knew, but I never said it, and when he told his wife about me and mentioned the word marriage, she just said no, although she had God knows how many lovers herself. And Yehudi, who is utterly good and sweet, but can also lack a certain will, blamed himself for everything ...

But I was in love with him, the way I'd hoped to be in love ever since I can remember. I hadn't met his wife, though I had heard rumours of her behaviour and of course I'd seen the results in him. He was completely broken by it and had even decided he would give up playing the violin. I remember saying to him – we spoke mostly in French in those days – 'Yehudi, j'ai peur.' Finally his wife told him that he had to stay with her and the children. It trailed on and on with her promising divorce and then breaking her promise over and over again. Then, thank God, she realized that from a practical point of view it would be better for her to marry whichever lover she had at that time, and so after two years she let Yehudi go.

Attacks on Yehudi in the Jewish press for marrying outside the faith had bothered her not at all.

In any case, the whole of that was not because he'd married a Gentile, but because he had insisted on going to Germany. He has incredible courage, Yehudi, immense courage. He went to Germany and played night and day for every cause, Jewish and German. When we were there we heard that Furtwängler had had to run away in the middle of the night because the Gestapo had come for him. He had done nothing except get on with his job and stay in the country. I knew Furtwängler because my mother had a musical salon to which every musician in the world came, and Furtwängler had lunch with mummy when he was over to conduct the opera; but Yehudi had never even met him. Furtwängler was decent and had helped Jewish members of the orchestra to get to America. He also wrote very dangerous letters from Denmark to my sister – he adored blondes and was mad about her. He wrote: 'When I think I am writing from this country, occupied by my people, it makes me ill.' One night his friends came to him and said, 'Run, because the Gestapo is coming for you,' and he escaped at night with his second wife, the lovely Lizavet. Yehudi was told that the Americans wouldn't give Furtwängler his purification trial, so Yehudi sent off a two-page telegram to America – Yehudi's telegrams are full of notwithstandings and neverthelesses – saying it was a disgrace to the Americans that they hadn't at least given him the chance to clear his name. Furtwängler got his purification trial, he passed a hundred per cent clean, but of course you can imagine what the cabal in New York did about it: the ones who were jealous of Yehudi were heard to say, 'At last we've got Menuhin.' So the press reports were not really because he had married a Gentile but because he had defended a German ...

Before Hitler one didn't analyse Jewishness or non-Jewishness. For example, I realized only afterwards that many of the musicians who came to my mother's house were Jews, but to me they were Russian, or Hungarian, or German, or Austrian. Until the time of the Hitler incitement, one wasn't Jewish-conscious – I had a very broad spectrum, but it was different for Yehudi. His father had sensibly taken him away from Europe when Hitler came to power, but his American experience was very limited because his parents simply didn't go out anywhere ...

When I first married Yehudi, he was more or less estranged from his family because they very foolishly condemned his first wife, the last thing to do to a man who refuses to condemn anybody. So when I first went to California I told Yehudi that no Jew was ever separated or estranged from his family, above all from his mother, and I persuaded him that he should go and visit them. Abba loved America because he felt he could trust people; everywhere else in the world he thought everyone was cheating him. Mamina was a completely emancipated Jewess, totally and absolutely Russian, though she spoke six languages beautifully. When Yehudi made his incredible début at the age of nine or ten, all the Jewish community in New York naturally wanted to claim him as their star. She held them off, which led to a feeling among the Jewish community that she didn't want to have anything to do with them.

Abba was an inspector of Hebrew schools, but they didn't often go to synagogues, and Yehudi was brought up with no sense of what is kosher; there was nothing kosher at home at all. So there was no question of their being ritual Jews. Mamina would never touch Yiddish, and in fact spoke good German, which laid the foundation for Yehudi's assertion that his entire culture came from Germany and Austria. After that the Jews saw their opportunity to murder him. Yehudi's father was only anti-Israel because he had divided loyalties. He was very proud to be American, yet he was of course a Jew, the grandson of a rabbi. When he and Mamina first went to look for rooms in New Jersey when their baby was about to be born, they found a very nice landlady who must have found them an attractive pair – Abba was extremely handsome, blue eyes, blond hair, and Mamina was quite incredibly beautiful, with golden hair she could sit on and Tartar-blue eyes. As they left, the landlady said, 'Well, I'm very glad to have you two young things, because I simply hate Jews, and I won't have them here.' Whereupon Mamina turned and said, 'Well, you won't be having us because we are both Jews.' And as they walked away, she tapped her tummy where Yehudi was prenatally stored, and said, 'This child is going to be called Yehudi, the Jew.' And yet that was the last Jewish gesture she made.

For Abba, the greatest thing on earth was his American passport;

it made him feel that he was somebody, because Mamina certainly didn't make him feel that. Zionism threatened to break apart the feeling of being American; it was going to demand a dual loyalty, so he joined the Philadelphia lot, a group of very distinguished Jews. It was called the American Council of Judaism, and it was made up of all those first- and second-generation Americans who felt that it was terrible to be asked to be less than a hundred per cent loyal to their American naturalization; and this was the basis of his anti-Zionism. Secondly, the Menuhins were Jews who had never suffered. Abba didn't know how important it was for the Jews to have a homeland. I talked to them and explained what it must have been like to have been a Jew in Europe ... The Menuhins didn't know how necessary it was for the Jews to try to escape the pogroms; they had never been through a pogrom.

Yehudi was not really pro-Israel. He hated militant Zionism, yet he realized the necessity for a land for the Jews, while at the same time refusing to talk about it. Yehudi was not one of your pro-Israelis at all, and that is why they tried to kill us when we first went to Israel. With a certain amount of counselling from me, he realized that something had to be done about the Jews, what was left of them, but he never wanted to be a militant Zionist. He played at concerts to raise money for the Jewish fund, of course – that was the least he could do. But because we had already been to Germany, there followed a period [in America] of Jews being told to boycott his concerts. His concerts were always sold out, but only Gentiles were sitting in Carnegie Hall. The Jews were told by all the Jewish newspapers to send their tickets back too late to have them resold, and that Menuhin was anti-Israel. It wasn't true. He was only anti the militancy which was being shouted from the rooftops.

He went everywhere where the Jews had really suffered, where they had been taken out and burned. He even gave a concert in

Berlin for the displaced-persons camp. Unless you've seen what had befallen those wretched Jews who had survived what was done to them by the Germans, you wouldn't believe it. And they came crowding round the car in a wave of hate such as you've never seen. The military police accompanied us into the hall where people were literally hanging on to the players, and the howl of rage was really quite terrifying. But Yehudi has a radiance that makes people suddenly understand what he is trying to be. He got up on the platform, with a huge policeman each side. There was an agent provocateur with a club foot, and he was trying to incite the crowd even more. Yehudi said, 'Let me speak. Let me speak.' And he spoke to them in excellent German, telling them that Jews did not go begging to others because they had been maltreated – 'We are a great race and nothing can extinguish us.' Then they clapped, they applauded, they said, 'Yehudi, Yehudi, you are wonderful ...' He changed the whole mood of the crowd, and when the agent provocateur got up, he was booed. When we left people were crowding round the car, saying, 'Yehudi, please come and play to us again, please.'

It was the most moving thing you can imagine. Yehudi hates talking about this and he may be angry if this comes out, but it was a wonderful moment in his life.

A CLASSIC REVIEW NEVER FADES ...

In a long life spent in the midst of Grub Street, I have known many wicked, stupid and dishonest book reviewers. And now, with the Internet, reading-group blogs, even Amazon reviews, perhaps the well written quality review is now a memory, apart from a few in the 'specialist' press such as the *Literary Review* and the *TLS*. Thinking of this change, I remembered my very favourite review, of my second book of interviews *Singular Encounters*. It still reads well, thirty-two years later.

It was a skit, in lieu of a review, penned by the late Humphrey Carpenter for the *Sunday Times*. It was beyond doubt a send-up, but its wit and hilarity were its saving grace. He constructed it so as to beguile the reader with its originality. I loved it for what it was: a little gem encapsulating the English sense of humour at its best. I wrote to Humphrey, whom I had never met, to tell him how brilliant I thought his piece was and invited him to lunch. It thrilled him that I had taken no offence at his ribbing. I have continued to admire the piece to this day, but to enjoy it means it must be reproduced in its entirety. I hope the reader will appreciate it as much as I have done. It is a joyful piece of writing, skilfully crafted and irresistibly amusing.

HALLOWED BY THY NAIM

1. And the Lord created Naim Attallah and sent him from Palestine to London to be chairman of Quartet Books. And the Lord God said to his servant Naim, Increase and multiply.
2. And Naim Attallah published *The Joy of Sex* and *More Joy of Sex*, and showed his balance sheet to the Lord, and said, Lord, I have increased and multiplied, and done thy bidding. And the Lord God said, That was not quite what I had in mind.
3. And the Lord God said unto Naim Attallah, If thou art going to be a prominent London publisher, then thou wilt have to get thyself a lot of women, so that people will talk about thee. And Naim said unto the Lord, Lord, I will do thy bidding.
4. And Naim Attallah went into the highways and byways of Sloane Square, and hired a lot of young women with double-barrelled names to work for him, and said Lord, I have done Thy bidding. And the Lord God said, That was not quite what I had in mind.

5. And the Lord God said unto Naim Attallah, If people are going to talk about thee, and if thou art going to make the gossip columns, thou wilt have to become intimate with a lot of successful members of the opposite sex. And Naim Attallah said unto the Lord, Lord, I understand, and will do Thy bidding.
6. And Naim Attallah went into the highways and byways and found 318 remarkable women whose common denominator was achievement. And Naim Attallah published the interviews in a book called *Women*, and said unto the Lord, Lord, I have done Thy bidding. And the Lord God sighed and said, That was not quite what I had in mind.
7. And Naim Attallah said unto the Lord, Lord, I am bored and dejected now that the excitement of publishing my book *Women* is over, so I will go and publish a book on men. And the Lord God said, Naim, my servant, why on earth do you suppose anyone wants to read a book about men?
8. And Naim, the servant of the Lord, said Lord, I will call it *Singular Encounters*, because then some people will suppose it to be a sequel to *More Joy of Sex*, but actually, Lord, it will be a book of interviews with twenty-nine remarkable men whose common denominator is achievement.
9. And the Lord said, Naim, didst thou say twenty-nine? Why hast thou not interviewed 318 like last time? And Naim said, Lord, I am not as young as I was, and anyway, I do not like men as much as women, because I was not at an English public school.
10. And anyway, went on Naim, it was very difficult to persuade even twenty-nine men to take part. Most of those I approached, Lord (as I say in my introduction), were over-cautious. But then Richard Ingrams said yes, and encouraged some others, and soon Auberon Waugh agreed too.
11. And the Lord God said, Who is this Richard Ingrams and this Auberon Waugh? And Naim said, Lord, Ingrams is a man whose

daughter works for one of my companies, and Waugh is the editor of the *Literary Review*, of which I am the proprietor. And the Lord God hid a smile and said, I see, I see.

12. And the Lord God said unto Naim his servant, Naim, who are the other twenty-seven that thou hast persuaded to take part? And Naim said, Lord, there is Willie Rushton, Nigel Dempster and A. N. Wilson. And the Lord God said, Who are these people? And Naim said, They have all written for *Private Eye*, as have Ingrams and Waugh. And the Lord God said, Naim, thou dost not appear to have a very big circle of friends.

13. And Naim said, Lord, there is also Sir Harold Acton and Monsignor Alfred Gilbey. And the Lord God said, Who are they? And Naim said, Acton was a friend of Waugh's father and Gilbey is well known unto Wilson. And the Lord God said, That leaves twenty-two to go. Thou hast not covered much ground yet.

14. And Naim, the servant of the Lord, said, Lord there is also Michael Aspel, J. K. Galbraith, Yehudi Menuhin and Lord Rees-Mogg. And the Lord God said, And what made you choose these men? And Naim the servant of the Lord said, Lord, they all great and famous men. And the Lord God said, I see. I was beginning to think they were just chaps you just happen to have met at dinner-parties.

15. And the Lord God said, Naim, what questions hast thou asked? And Naim said, I have asked two of my interviewees whether it is true they have long-running feuds with Gore Vidal. And I have asked Willie Rushton whether he has opened a lot of fêtes. And I have asked the Warden of St Anthony's College, Oxford, what is the secret of his charm. And I have asked …

16. And the Lord God interrupted Naim and said, Naim, how on earth did you think of such daft questions? And Naim not listening went on, And I have asked André Deutsch about his disagreement with Tom Rosenthal and I have asked Lord Lambton why young

journalists find Margaret Thatcher sexually attractive. And the Lord God said, I do not believe this.
17. And Naim, the servant of the Lord, smiled and said, Maybe, Lord, but I have featured in magazines and have made the front page of the Style section of the *Sunday Times*, and I have never had such coverage before in my life. So maybe, Lord, I know what I am doing after all.
18. And the Lord God nodded, and said, Naim, my servant, maybe you do.

LORD LAMBTON

In the late 1970s, George Hutchinson had introduced me to his friend Charlie Douglas Home, who subsequently became editor of *The Times*. Charlie was a down-to-earth gentlemanly character, warmly disposed towards his fellow men and bereft of any pretensions. His upper-class background in no way affected his relationships with those who came from other sections of society. Because of these qualities, I found myself drawn to him and felt quite at ease in his company. In the years before I met him he had been battling a drink problem, not uncommon in members of the journalistic profession. Only by resorting to total abstinence did he manage eventually to lick it. Whenever we met for lunch, usually at his office, he would unselfishly offer me a drink, which I then ceremoniously turned down as a gesture of solidarity. Charlie was always easy going and prepared to be a listener, liking nothing better than to engage in light humorous gossip about people we both knew. One thing that fascinated him about me was the way I had become integrated into British society. He thought it quite an achievement, given that I had arrived in the United Kingdom as a student of limited means and had had to make my own way in an environment that must have been harshly alien.

During one of our lunches he had mentioned his cousin, Tony Lambton, now living in Italy following his resignation from his post as a junior defence minister after being secretly photographed smoking cannabis in bed with two prostitutes. It was a public scandal that contributed to the collapse of Edward Heath's Conservative government nine months later. Tony Lambton only came into the conversation because Charlie wanted to find out if, as a publisher, I would be interested in reading the manuscript of a satirical attack his cousin had written in the form of a novel. The subject was George Weidenfeld, loathed by Tony with an intense passion. Weidenfeld was certainly no friend of mine in that epoch; in fact he was my most consistent adversary. His uncompromising Zionist ideology and his blind support for Israel whatever the circumstances placed us in diametric opposition. It therefore intrigued me greatly to have the chance to read the Lambton manuscript, though I was doubtful whether it could ever be made publishable. The word in publishing circles was that it had been going the rounds for a while and had been rejected by various imprints as too antagonistic and probably legally actionable.

Once I had read the manuscript I realized why. Not only could it be interpreted as libellous, but the fact that it was mainly fired by Tony's splenetic loathing of his subject came over more strongly than the storyline. The flaws in the novel rendered it unworthy of its author's talents, which were clearly discernible. My conclusion was that Tony would have better prospects in establishing himself as a fiction writer with a text free from such shortcomings. These views I communicated to Charlie, stressing that my rejection should not be seen as closing the door to other possibilities and that I would be interested in becoming Lambton's publisher, though it would have to be with the right manuscript.

Before very long the right manuscript arrived. It was called *Snow and Other Stories* and heralded a remarkably original début by a storyteller with a calm, laconic eye for the odd and the ordinary alike: as Christmas approaches, a London housewife begins a leisurely diary of her daily life – leisurely, that is, until the snow arrives and its proverbial whiteness turns into a vision of the apocalypse; in 1918 a Russian aristocratic landowner of utopian persuasion is slowly and unwittingly delivered up to the very different utopia of the Bolshevik revolution; an Englishwoman in Italy has premonitions of disaster and prays at the ancient shrine of Minerva, pagan goddess of handicrafts – and of violent conflicts. These were the themes explored in the author's first collection of short stories. Harold Acton wrote of it: 'This illuminating ... brings to mind an eclectic art collection in which oil paintings, pastels, watercolours and etchings are discriminatingly displayed on the walls of a spacious gallery ... One rubs one's eyes before the revelation of a fresh literary talent.'

The launch party for *Snow and Other Stories* was a grand occasion attended by over three hundred guests who flocked to the Arts Club to celebrate the event. I was anxious to mark the author's return to the London scene in his new role as a writer rather than as the budding politician he had once been. Lambton was spoken of as having had the makings of a future prime minister, had it not been for the scandal that wrecked his chances. He was still considered a most intriguing and charismatic figure. Nearly tout Londres was there to greet him, attended by the usual turnout of gossip journalists, anxious to find some mischievous story to fill out their columns. The large number of his friends who were milling about included Angus Ogilvy, Lucien Freud, Lord and Lady Harlech, Woodrow Wyatt, Lady Melchett – as ever in the company of Sir Hugh Fraser – Lady Falkender, Guy Nevill, Auberon Waugh, Taki, Nigel Dempster, Tracy Ward, Katya Gilmour, Valentine Guinness, Liz Brewer, Nicholas Coleridge, Charlie Douglas Home, Lady Liza Campbell, Minnie Scott and Domenica Fraser.

All of Lambton's five daughters were present, as was his son and heir, who arrived with his new bride Christabel (née McEwen). His estranged wife Bindy, with her arm in a sling, was looking rather baffled and out of place, while his long-time mistress, Mrs Claire Ward, was clearly enjoying the party. Lambton himself was in his element, as if to say (to adapt the words of General MacArthur), 'I have returned.' The evening was judged a great success, not only as a public-relations exercise but also for the number of copies of the book sold. Lambton's first published venture as a storyteller was to prove triumphant, and to lead on to even more accomplished and ambitious work.

In 1985, we published Tony Lambton's epic novel, *Elizabeth and Alexandra*. We considered this to be a potential bestseller, and planned the campaign with the precision of a blitzkrieg on all fronts. The launch party was to be hosted by the Marchioness of Dufferin and Ava and myself at the Dufferin London home in Holland Park, where guests could spread out and drift in the neoclassical garden. The invitation card was so heavily embossed that, as some journalists remarked, it must have broken half the thumbnails in London. Catering was arranged by my cook, Charlotte Millward, aided and abetted by Charlotte Faber. Both were talented cooks and artists and the sublime ideas they introduced achieved a new high in buffet presentation. The sumptuous cocktail they devised had pieces of real gold leaf floating on the surface of each drink. The Quartet girls were provided with specially designed, slightly transparent, flowing evening dresses in lilac to wear while circulating among the guests, their exquisitely toned, gold-painted bodies shining through from underneath. The concept and stage management of all this were down to the two Charlottes, whose creative imaginations knew no bounds. Among the Quartet girls was a new recruit, Richard Ingrams's daughter Jubby, who was already making her mark, both within the ranks at Goodge Street and in the world beyond. Jubby was a free spirit whose sense of fun was to find a place on the London scene, though sometimes to the dismay of those encumbered with a stuffy outlook. Her impishness had a whimsical appeal for the literary set as well as for the young ravers who clustered around her, always on the lookout for mischief.

At the party itself there were four hundred guests from every walk of life. Aristocrats were there in hordes to celebrate Lambton's first major novel, including his family. Lady Lambton (Bindy), unmissable because of her imposing presence, was seen chatting to Lady Soames. She stood at a distance from his companion of many years, Claire Ward, the mother of the film actress Rachel Ward. The tension between the two women seemed to be allayed by the grandeur of the occasion. Sir Jack Colville and old political colleagues like Lord Jellicoe and Viscountess Lymington mingled with the group round Lady Sylvie Thynne, who was drawn in turn to the *haute art* set, among them Lucien Freud and Kasmin. Princess Michael of Kent and Nicky Haslam were engaged in good-humoured conversation. Others busy circulating included the satirist John Wells, the novelist A. N. Wilson and the columnist Nigel Dempster; Auberon Waugh and Richard Ingrams; John Saumarez-Smith from the Heywood Hill bookshop; Lord Durham, the Earl of Wilton, Emma Soames, Susan Ryan, Countess Fitzwilliam, Arabella Weir, Roc Sandford, Lady Delves-Broughton, Lynn Arial, Ari Ashley, Dennis Walker MP and Mrs Walker, Nigella Lawson, Laura Faber and Amanda Lyster, to pick names from the guest list at random. The Quartet girls looked stunning and entertained the guests with their usual social aplomb. In his account of the party Auberon Waugh waxed lyrical, describing Lambton as 'the great swordsman turned novelist, being fêted by the most glittering people in England and the most beautiful young women'.

Tony Lambton was definitely back in the limelight, but this time in triumph rather than for reasons of political disgrace. The scandal that had wrecked his political career was relegated to the past and no longer mattered. His emergence as a first-class novelist was a clear sign of a new dawn for the man who had once been a rising politician. The difference was a change in direction, and in his new role he would excel. Significantly hidden behind dark glasses, he was delighted to see the large number of celebrities who had answered his invitation call. Among the crowd of people who were keen to shake his hand were David Dimbleby and Diana Rigg. His indiscretions had clearly been forgiven by the establishment, while to the bohemian section largely made up of the young set, many of whom referred to him as Uncle Tony, he remained a hero. Possibly they admired his wicked sense of humour, which could be biting indeed, and a disregard for conformity he tempered with a certain aristocratic fastidiousness.

Elizabeth and Alexandra was well received by the critics. *The Times* wrote that, 'Antony Lambton shows himself to be a considerable novelist, deftly handling a large cast of characters from Queen Victoria to Joseph Stalin.' The *Listener* called the book 'a good solid read'. The *Daily Telegraph* concluded that, 'Antony Lambton's research has clearly been prodigious, and his description of the stifling atmosphere of the Russian court is memorably convincing.' In line with that opinion, the *Observer* considered 'it accumulates respect ... by sheer archival industry'. And the *Literary Review* called it 'a massive achievement'. The book attained the bestseller status we had anticipated for it. Quartet's promotional campaign proved highly effective.

THEATRICAL SWINGS & ROUNDABOUTS

The theatre has always exercised a hold over me. One evening, in 1982, I went to the Half-Moon pub theatre in Islington to see a play that I heard was enjoying an enthusiastic audience response: Claire Luckham's wrestling-ring marital allegory, *Trafford Tanzi*. I loved it instantly for its originality. It had a rough edge that made it simultaneously dramatic and entertaining. Howard Panter, the impresario, with whom I had earlier collaborated on Donleavy's *The Beastly Beatitudes of Balthazar B*, agreed we should join forces to bring the play to the Mermaid Theatre and ensure it an extended run.

Staging it at that venue meant a radical remodelling of the auditorium, but the Mermaid had been dark for months, leaving us a free hand to revamp it. We subjected it to much ripping out and rebuilding to form four ringsides and increase its seating capacity by a hundred to seven hundred and ten. A bar was also installed at the back of the auditorium to add to the wrestling-hall atmosphere. With licensing regulations overcome, the audience, clutching their glasses of bitter in authentic fashion, would be able to watch Noreen Kershaw as Tanzi hurling her stage family about in the ring. When the show opened in October, they also found themselves caught up in a degree of audience participation as the actors were liable, at unscripted and unscheduled moments, to come hurtling through the ropes, as happens during real-life wrestling matches. It was this sort of realism in the action, coupled with its feminist orientation, that brought the audience to its feet. The *Evening Standard* reported how their man, sitting in the front row, had enjoyed an even more direct experience of participation when one of the actresses, Victoria Hardcastle, appeared from nowhere in fishnet tights and clambered aboard his lap. Miss Hardcastle, whom he considered to be a most comely creature, predisposed him to a new appreciation of feminism. He concluded by describing how I was dressed for the occasion as a 'wrestling promoter'.

Trafford Tanzi was playing to capacity houses in December when two members of the cast took exception to the promotion and sale in the foyer of three Quartet titles, namely Jean-Paul Goude's *Jungle Fever*, featuring on its jacket the naked Grace Jones in a cage, Helmut Newton's *Sleepless Nights*, a recent collection of photographs strong in erotic suggestion, and Janet Reger's *Chastity in Focus*, a celebration of the exquisite lingerie she designed to make women more desirable. The objectors were Victoria Hardcastle and Eve Brand, who spent most of their time in the play in the ring, wrestling men into submission. Victoria rang me up and requested a meeting. In really quite a sweet-natured way, she suggested that the books on sale were unacceptable from her feminist perspective and she would rather I withdrew them from the theatre. It was her gentle persuasion that ultimately won the day, quite apart from the fact that I did not relish the prospect of having to settle the issue in the wrestling ring. When the press came on the line to ask for confirmation of the story, I simply said, 'Since it was the women in *Trafford Tanzi* who objected, how could I be expected to fight?'

The production got a new lease of life in March 1983 when Toyah Wilcox took over the lead. She had to spend several weeks beforehand in training with a bruiser by the name of Howard Lester to cope with being pummelled, arm-locked, sat upon and thrown around in the ring. The following month it was scheduled to open on Broadway, with Debbie Harry, the lead singer from the pop group Blondie, reprising Toyah's role. Debbie was being trained by Brian Maxine, who had been responsible for instructing the London cast in the ungentle art. With a deluge of unanimously favourable critical comment behind it, there was every reason to anticipate an equal triumph for *Tanzi* in America.

The *Sunday Telegraph* had called it 'A rare show', and the *Daily Telegraph* described it as the 'most original, refreshing, surprising, exhilarating and fierce drama to reach London for years'. 'Claire Luckham,' wrote the *Daily Express*, 'has not only written a musical, but a contest that had us going wild in the aisles for feminism', while its competitor, the *Daily Mail*, called it a 'play which brings new meaning to the term action-packed'. The *Guardian* reckoned that 'It's a message you don't forget', and the *New York Times* labelled it a 'feminist play to end all feminist plays'. *Cosmopolitan* magazine thought it the 'most innovative and entertaining show in London', while *Options* went overboard by saying, 'It is, quite simply, unique in the history of the British theatre. Glorious ... liberating.' The *Tatler* simply said, 'The best night out in London.'

With the critics unanimously on side with their superlatives and the public flocking to see the show, Quartet rushed into print with an illustrated large format paperback containing the history of the production and an unabridged script. It went on sale in the theatre and to the wider book trade. The success of *Tanzi* made it one of the highlights of my theatrical career. Through it I learnt a great deal about the theatre and what makes a production click with the public. It was also very timely, with feminism becoming such a burning issue.

Then the curtain went up on the Broadway production and I travelled to New York to attend the first night. There was a vast contrast with the London experience and it failed miserably in seducing either the critics or the public: as the saying goes, it closed as soon as it opened. Everyone had agreed at the time that Debbie Harry would make a most refreshing choice in the casting, but in fact she looked uncomfortable in the role. There seemed to be none of the rapport between performers and audience that was the key to its success in London; no sign of the zing and vitality that characterized the Mermaid production. Fortunately we had sold the American rights outright. *Trafford Tanzi*'s failure on Broadway did not involve us in any financial responsibility.

A TRUE PRIMADONNA

One evening in 1988 Princess Dina (see page …) introduced me and my wife, Maria to her friend Dame Margot Fonteyn, the famous ballerina revered for her art and considered to be a saintly figure for the way she tended her husband, Roberto Arias, after he was confined to a wheelchair following an attempt on his life in 1964. Arias had been a former Panamanian ambassador to London. I found Margot's aura was as magical in an ordinary setting as when she was performing on the stage. I was so captivated that I practically monopolized her all evening, while she, in turn, seemed to appreciate my focused interest. After our meeting I sent her many books, and we corresponded for a while.

Her public had seen her as a delicate even ethereal figure, so it came as a shock to many some years after her death when facts emerged to change their perception of her. Intimate friends revealed how sex had been her driving force; she had had many affairs and even lost a baby fathered by her dancing partner, the bisexual Russian Rudolf Nureyev.

I did not feel so surprised. I have always believed that extraordinary talent and strong sexuality walk hand in hand. There seemed to be a definite correlation between the two. God in his infinite wisdom had evidently chosen to fuel genius with a generous helping of libido – and in some cases with a pronounced leaning towards a deeper sensuality. It is a theory to conjure with in the case of those whose disapproval of physical gratification may explain their failure to bequeath any outstanding creative legacy. Damnation may be seen as a small price to pay for leaving the world with works of art and science without which all our lives would be poorer. I felt gratified that lust had shed its ugly side and an enchanting being had risen above it, emerging unscathed through her passion for the physical fulfilment by which her art had been enhanced.

In their different ways, Margot Fonteyn and Princess Dina were two remarkable women of their time. Maria, my wife, and I were to see very little of Dina in her final years. Her failing health was one reason, and she died at a grand old age some years after Margot Fonteyn. Both remain more absent friends, vivid in their cherished memories.

AN OVERRATED SEXPOT

A recent *Sunday Times* puff for a new biography of Angela Carter suggests her fervent sexual appetites and unconventional thoughts on feminism contributed to her legendary reputation, and even quotes Salmon Rushdie's generous description of Carter as a 'benevolent witch queen.' My memories of her are somewhat more guarded.

Quartet had just published her short story collection *Fireworks* in 1974, a few months before I bought the then struggling publisher and though I had little to do with her at the time, the sales staff told me of how shabbily she had treated them. She had even stubbed out a cigarette onto the back seat of Quartet's sales manager's company car! She had few friends and supporters in the company that was for sure, and when she opted to join the trendy Virago feminist publisher, then at the height of their fame and influence, no tears were shed at Quartet.

Later, I would interview her for my book *Women* and found her unsympathetic, not especially pleasant, lacking any intelligent insight and frankly, conventional to a fault. To her credit, she never tried to seduce me. Perhaps she found me lacking in that department.

Her only interesting if somewhat bizarre observation was when I asked her about her sexuality she retorted:

> One of the big reports from Masters and Johnson said it is just as well that women have never culturally realized their full sexual potential, because men would never be able to cope, and I'm sure it's true.

I have never understood why she retains such a reputation amongst a certain strata of the metropolitan elite and is even taught in secondary schools, but that may well be my loss.

I can't help feeling, however, that the fairy story she most represents would be *The Empresses' Clothes*.

REMEMBERING CHRISTINA FOYLE

In January 1991 *Publishing News* reported that Christina Foyle, a favourite of mine, had just finished reading *Singular Encounters* and found it quite diverting. Christina and I had got on remarkably well when I interviewed her for *Women*. She told me how she had adored her father and how much she had learned from him.

> My father was really rather a gambler. He was always up to something. Once, coming back from America, he kept playing

cards with some rather sharp people. First of all, he won quite a lot, about a thousand pounds a day – this was in the 1930s – and then he lost it all and a lot more besides. He told these men – they were real sharpers – that he couldn't pay, but they accepted a cheque. Then I had to get off the boat very quickly at Southampton to stop the cheque. He used to give me all those sorts of things to do. And then there was a lot of money owing him from the Soviet Union, with all kinds of bad debts, and he sent me over there to collect them. I went to Russia, by myself, when I was twenty-one. I went all over Russia, but most of the people who owed us money had either been executed or gone to Siberia. I didn't have much luck.

Christina was very entertaining and a good raconteur:

When I first came to Foyle's, it was a wonderful time. There were very many great writers about: Bernard Shaw and Wells and Kipling, Conan Doyle. They all used to come into the shop, and they were charming to me. That's why I started my luncheons, because customers used to say you're so lucky, you meet all these great people, I wish I had your opportunities. So I said to my father, we ought to give a luncheon and let our customers come and meet these writers. So my father said, well, you've nothing much to do, why don't you arrange it? That's how our luncheons came about. But I found that, although I was so young, they never patronized me or talked down to me at all. I used to go round and call on these people, asking them to come and speak, and they always said yes. And we've had them from that day to this. The first lunch we gave was for Lord Darling, the famous Lord Chief Justice and Lord Alfred Douglas came, who had been involved in the Wilde affair years before; and then our most recent lunch was for Jeffrey Archer, who wasn't born when we started them. So it's been marvellous, and I can hardly think of a time when I've had any unpleasant experiences.

She was a woman to whom I could relate. She often invited me to a Foyle's luncheon, usually held at Grosvenor House Hotel, and invariably seated me next to her. She was worldly and gossipy and it was enchanting to be in her company. On one occasion she told me how Colonel Gadaffi of Libya would send Foyle's a cheque for two hundred and fifty thousand dollars and ask her to choose the books for him. She loved her profession and she loved people. The two strands were completely interlinked in her life.

TWO SPECIAL PEOPLE

Susie Craigie Halkett, who hailed from Scotland, was disarmingly engaging, with a smile that blended sophistication with natural diffidence. She went about her work responsibly and with diligence. Her low-key approach to things endeared her not only to the Quartet enclave but also to those on the outside she had to deal with in discharging her duties. Her unassuming presence was charmingly unencroaching and that was in essence the secret of her popularity. Looking back, I remember being struck by the way she conducted herself and glided through life, seemingly unflappable. I wanted to discover more about her. It was not simply her beauty that aroused my interest but an instinct that told me there was more to her than was visible to the casual eye: there was an intriguing depth to her that I was determined to plumb. In pursuit of this aim, I arranged for her to accompany me to New York on two occasions, and once to Frankfurt to attend the book fair. On all of these trips she stayed with me and I found her company both stimulating and relaxing. The differences in our characters produced from time to time some innocuous ripples but these never lingered on to have any destabilizing effect on our working relationship. Her time at Quartet as editorial assistant and publicist was remembered with great affection. I retain fond memories of our travels and am certain Scotland could not have sent forth a better child to enchant and capture the English.

Meanwhile, at my Regent Street office, a new light appeared in the form of Jess Collett, a young, attractive blonde who could have dazzled the socks off any red-blooded youthful male, let alone a man of my age. Her presence enlivened the atmosphere, and in her own words she sums up that time with a stylish cheekiness.

Getting Away with Murder

Jess Collett

When I walked into the marketing department of Mappin & Webb in 1995 as office skivvy, the only thing I knew about Naim was that he and my dad used the same hairdresser – and still do, what class! I was surrounded by nubile young ladies accredited with brains, looks and charm. The only man to be seen in the office, apart from Naim himself, was the postman!

I seemed to fall into position of youngest (who gets away with murder) with extreme ease, and was soon known affectionately as 'Blondie'. On Naim's bad days I hopped on to his knee to cheer him up, and on his good days I did the same. After a month, I was presented with a beautiful watch for my services. I might have left at this point, pawned the watch and got the money I needed for going to Mexico. But I didn't. Instead I had the most exciting, amusing and of course instructive six months. I met some lovely people, posed in a very short pvc skirt, modelled thousands of pounds' worth of jewellery and watches up my arm, sat at the wheel of a couple of Ferraris in Bond Street, drank fine champagne in Winston Churchill's underground cabinet war rooms and stuffed a lot of envelopes. So, as my only experience of working in an office (I am now a milliner), I would say it was a very good advertisement.

BLOND ON BLOND

There was an important development at Quartet in August 1987 when the publisher Anthony Blond and I joined forces to form a partnership that according to the London *Standard*, under the headline 'Terrible Twins!', had 'all the incendiary potential of a latter-day gunpowder plot'. Blond's own company, Muller, Blond & White, had gone down earlier in the year, having reached the point where, as he said in his autobiography *Jew Made in England*, 'We couldn't even pay the grappa bill from the friendly neighbourhood Italian restaurant.' Although he had managed to clear all his debts, he no longer wanted the hassle of refinancing and starting up again from the beginning. He was considered to have brilliant flare as a publisher but less acumen as a businessman. Now he was seeking a home within an established publishing house, from where he could operate and supply ideas for projects, in return for which his name would appear in any books which might materialize. It was his wife Laura who suggested he give me a ring and I invited him to Namara House.

> I climbed the four flights of stairs to Naim's offices. There I encountered a macho lair, strewn with tiger skins and occupied by young ladies who supplied his occasional needs, like a glass of water or a pullover when the air-conditioning became too intense.

I explained I only needed 'walking money' – an expression employed by the late Dominic Elwes.

'How much?' asked Naim.

'Ten thousand.'

'Too much, that would upset the others.'

'OK, then five thousand.'

'No,' said Naim, 'six thousand.'

And so it was.

My relationship with Anthony Blond had always been warm, a warmth strengthened by recognition of the support he gave me in my early days as a publisher when I was being sneered at and referred to as a 'cowboy' in the trade. He defended me when others stood aside and took no part in the furore that followed the publication of *God Cried* and Roald Dahl's subsequent notice of it in the *Literary Review*. While he personally condemned the book, he refrained from using any intemperate language and was deeply unhappy about the torrents of vitriol that flowed from many of the commentators. Throughout the crisis he remained staunch in my defence, rejecting the accusations of anti-Semitism being levelled against me in certain quarters and arguing that free speech should never be sacrificed to suit any particular ideology or viewpoint. He never questioned my entitlement to publish material sympathetic to the Palestinian cause and considered my rights in this to be equal with George Weidenfeld's when he published similar material in favour of the Israelis. Each of us was conducting a crusade of our own and affirming the democratic right of free expression in our society.

I did not always agree with Blond, but our disparities and our different ethnic backgrounds proved a strength rather than a weakness and we forged a good working relationship. I am a Palestinian Arab, while he was an English Jew from a distinguished assimilated background. Even our sexuality was of quite a different kind in its orientation, he being drawn to both sexes whereas I was passionately heterosexual. He became a practising Jew at the time when my Catholic faith was wavering. He drank and smoked heavily while I hardly ever touched alcohol and had given up the latter many moons before. In an interview with *Publishing News*, Blond said he and I in fact had a lot in common, he even went so far as to describe us as kindred spirits. We both liked pretty, well-heeled girls with double-barrelled names from aristocratic families (his wife Laura was a daughter of Colonel Roger Hesketh, whose father-in-law was an earl). Of his Quartet tie-up he said:

> It's a wonderful arrangement. I'm not much of a dab hand at admin or finance, but I am good at acquiring. So I'll just get on publishing around a dozen books a year. Naim and I both believe in eccentric rather than category publishing. It will be anything from the official biography of J. R. Jaywardine, president of Sri Lanka, to a book version of Muran Buchstansangur. I also have in mind books from two new English novelists. It's such a relief to feel all these jewels are no longer unwanted.
>
> I trust Naim fully to take care of all the financial arrangements. He is very pro-Arab of course, and I'm a Jew, but Naim isn't anti-Jewish, he's anti-Zionist. I used to be a Zionist, but now I'm one of the Jews for Peace. I'm for a multi-racial Israel.

In addition he argued that these factors could be seen as bringing an extra piquancy to our working relationship. 'But it's an irrelevance,' he added firmly. 'The kind of irrelevance I enjoy ...' *Private Eye* put its usual more jaundiced spin on events:

> Veteran publisher Anthony Blond is certainly down on his luck. Not so long ago he had to wind up his publishing company Blond & Briggs [sic] and last year he even resorted to the catering trade, accompanying his wife, the former Laura Hesketh, as she distributed cold sandwiches to office workers in the City. Now,

however, he has had to accept the most ignominious fate in the world of publishing – a job with the crazed pro-Arab publisher Naim Attallah. A press release announces that Blond has been offered his own private imprint and list within the Quartet empire. He will liaise with Attallah's main editor, the leery Stephen Pickles, author of *Queens* ...

Of Blond's proposed list, *Private Eye* commented that the official biography of the president of Sri Lanka – 'more hagiography than biography' – should 'sit easily alongside the tedious memoirs of obscure Middle Eastern politicians that Attallah is fond of publishing'. Anthony described his new workplace thus:

Quartet Books occupied two adjacent rickety houses in Goodge Street, between which, it was always being mooted, a door would one day be breached. To the young ladies who clattered and chattered up and down the two flights of stairs, I was presented by Pickles as 'seasoned timber' and by David Elliott, the sales director, known as 'dump-bin Dave', as 'a living legend'. The young ladies, however, were understandably more interested in stealing each other's boyfriends on unmonitored telephones than talking to me. The circus mistress of the *salle de manège* was Jubby, daughter of Richard Ingrams, who cracked a condescending whip and outlasted them all. She was to look after me. Jubby was the Saint-Simon at the court of King Naim, registering his movements, moods and reactions.

On one occasion Anthony tried to set up a television interview with Simon Raven at the Reform Club in their library, which he felt to be 'the most splendid room in London'. He received a curt no to the idea of any television cameras entering the portals of the Reform, the reason to emerge being that Jubby once hired the Reform for a photo shoot and subsequently the secretary was horrified to be sent a copy of *Playboy*, to which surely neither he nor the club subscribed. I am sure the magazine featured a naked girl standing on one of Sir Charles Barry's horsehair sofas, next to the bust of the young Queen Victoria, in the marbled atrium.

'I was never allowed to attend editorial meetings,' Anthony recorded, 'though my modest suggestions were nearly always agreed to.' The partnership produced a handful of titles, including biographies of Hugh Montefiore, the former bishop of Birmingham, who had been bar mitzvahed at Blond's own synagogue, as he reminded him, and Justin de Blank. It was odd, he reflected, 'that these titles, from a Jewish editor, should emerge from a publisher who is Arab'. He almost had one coup in introducing to Quartet Jennifer Patterson, of future 'Fat Lady' best-selling-cookery-books fame, but unfortunately his letter of recommendation, advising that we might get her 'cheap', was sent to Jennifer by mistake and she went to John Murray instead. Jennifer, a fellow Catholic, was to become one of my dearest friends. Without fail on the morning of every first of May she would ring me to sing 'Happy Birthday' over the phone.

In the end Anthony Blond decided to go and live in France, though I continued to pay his honorarium for a while. We also published his book *Blond's Roman Emperors* but, 'Eventually he [Naim] wrote me a most elegant letter of farewell.' Blond was widely known for discovering many novelists, his most outstanding protégé being Simon Raven, whom I interviewed some ten years later. Raven was perhaps the most outrageous writer of his generation, frowned on by the whole establishment, defying convention and writing explicitly about his own bi-sexuality. Blond had an enduring reputation as a publisher and retained an admiring and faithful following. As a preface to *Jew Made in England* he printed his own obituary, full of honest self-appraisal.

Muller, Blond & White had gone bankrupt after publishing 'a lavish volume on the Sistine Chapel, on every copy of which the company contrived to lose money'. Of his coming to Quartet he wrote:

> Although an energetic spotter of talent, Blond lacked the discipline and temperance to make a good businessman, and was, according to his friends, trusting and gullible. He was now bereft, having regarded an imprint as a form of self-expression. Blond attempted to secure work through his extensive network in what he liked to call the 'publishing game'. No one wanted to know: and Blond was quoted as saying, 'None of my best friends are Jews.' Nevertheless, he was taken up, out of charity, by the Palestinian Arab Naim Attallah, as a consultant to his firm, Quartet.

THE ENIGMA OF LENI RIEFENSTAHL

Leni Riefenstahl may have been slight in build, but she was big in everything else. She was a giant of her generation, with so many talents it was hard to conceive of their all being in one person. Before the advent of the talkies, she had been a silent-film star in Germany; prior to that she had been a brilliant dancer. She then went on to become a formidable sportswoman, an amazing photographer and a film-maker of prodigious scope and ability. She always had a highly perceptive eye, was a stickler for the minutest detail and a perfectionist in whatever assignment she took on. Her single-mindedness could be both a strength and an irritation. Difficult to handle, impossible to shift from any set course, she embodied the Aryan discipline with a steely resolve to have her own way, whatever that might entail.

The first time I set eyes on her was at the Frankfurt Book Fair, in the German section. Many years before that chance encounter I had tried with no success to make contact after seeing some of her films on television. The impact of her work had completely bowled me over with its artistry and power. Tracking her down turned out to be an extremely difficult process. Eventually, through a highly reliable German source, I did secure an address for her in Munich. But though I wrote, I received no reply. This was perhaps not surprising, but when I saw her in Frankfurt and introduced myself, her eyes flashed as she casually informed me she remembered getting my letter. No explanation was forthcoming as to why she had never replied, but she was friendly and suggested I submit a written proposal for what I had in mind. With that, our cooperation began, and led in due course to the publication of her memoirs, *The Sieve of Time*, on her ninetieth birthday. It was edited and in part translated from the German by Jennie Bradshaw (now Erdal). 'My aim,' wrote Leni, 'was to tackle preconceived ideas, to clear up misunderstandings. I spent five years working on the manuscript; it was not an easy task since I was the only one who could write these memoirs. The book did not turn out to be a happy one.'

In fact, to mark her seventy-fifth birthday back in 1977, Stern magazine had wanted to write up her life story, but Leni Riefenstahl had refused to sanction the project in the belief that she was the only one who could do justice to her own life. Her career began on the stage in the early 1920s, working as a ballet dancer for Max Reinhardt among others. Her début as a film actress came in 1925 with *Der heiliger Berg* (*The Holy Mountain*), filmed in the Alps by Arnold Fanck, her mentor, who was the father of the vaguely pantheistic mountain cult in Weimar cinema. In the late 1920s, Riefenstahl became the high priestess of this cult, starring in, among other films, *Die weisser Hölle vom Piz Palü* (*The White Hell of Piz Palu*, 1929), directed by Fanck in collaboration with G. W. Pabst; and *Stürme über dem Montblanc* (*Storm over Mont Blanc*, 1930), directed by Fanck. Her last film with Fanck was *SOS Eisberg* (1933), but a year earlier she had laid the foundations for her own company and co-authored, directed and produced, besides playing the leading role in, *Das blaue Licht* (*The Blue Light*), which the critic

David Thomson has called 'the pre-eminent work of mountain mysticism'.

Hitler admired her artistry, and despite her loathing for Joseph Goebbels and the fact she was never a party member, commissioned her to make a film record of the 1934 Nazi rallies at Nuremberg. Premièred in Berlin in 1935, *Triumph des Willens* (*Triumph of the Will* – Hitler had suggested the title) won a gold medal at the Venice Film Festival and established Riefenstahl as Germany's foremost film director. The next year she filmed the 1936 Olympic Games in Berlin. This was not a Nazi party commission, but came from the International Olympics Committee. The gala performance of *Olympia* in Berlin in April 1938 marked Hitler's forty-ninth birthday, and it took the prize for best film at Venice. The power of the imagery in these two films and the virtuosic way they were cut and assembled make them unforgettable, though, given their historic context, their aesthetics were destined never be disentangled from the political polemic of their background. In the words of David Thomson, Leni Riefenstahl became 'arguably the most talented woman ever to make a film', but was 'still neglected in an age of feminist militancy'. Jean Cocteau had hailed her with the words, 'How could I not admire you, for you are the genius of film and have raised it to heights seldom achieved?' The pioneer of the British documentary movement, John Grierson – a committed man of the left – gave it as his opinion that, 'Leni Riefenstahl is one of the great film-makers in history', likening his salute to the one Churchill gave to Rommel:

> Leni Riefenstahl was the propagandist for Germany. I was a propagandist on the other side ... I took Leni Riefenstahl's films and cut them into strips to turn German propaganda against itself; but I never made the mistake of forgetting how great she was. Across the devastation of the war, I salute a very great captain of the cinema. There has been only one true masterpiece of the Olympiad and that is of course Leni Riefenstahl's in 1936.

On a trip to New York, I was invited to lunch by Tina Brown, who was then editor of *Vanity Fair*. During the course of our conversation, I happened to mention the proposed memoirs of Leni Riefenstahl. Sharp as ever, Tina wasted no time in extracting from me a commitment to give a *Vanity Fair* contributor, Stephen Schiff, the first exclusive coverage of the book prior to its publication in the UK, by arranging for him an interview with Leni. In my wild exuberance at the prospects of gaining a heightened profile for the book, I readily agreed but omitted to ask Tina for any kind of financial consideration. Unbeknown to me at the time, the *Sunday Times* had already interviewed Leni under the impression that their interview would be run as an exclusive prior to the book's publication. While Leni acknowledged that she gave the interview to someone she knew at the *Sunday Times*, she was adamant she had never given the newspaper the right to publish it before the Vanity Fair article. The Sunday Times then became equally entrenched in their position and a legal battle ensued that cost Quartet a great deal of money. In this Quartet found itself having to protect what were essentially the interests of *Vanity Fair*.

By the time the litigation was over, and *Vanity Fair* had published their long-awaited interview ahead of the field, Quartet found itself deeply out of pocket for having kept its word to the magazine. Yet when I applied to *Vanity Fair* for reimbursement of the legal fees incurred on their behalf, they washed their hands of the matter completely. The affair, they claimed, had not been of their making and consequently they admitted no responsibility. Given that *Vanity Fair* had not paid Quartet any fees for what were, essentially, first serial rights, I was in my view justified in feeling aggrieved. My goodwill gesture towards Tina Brown had misfired badly on this occasion, and I resolved afterwards that journalistic favours were hardly ever likely to bear fruit. In retrospect the magazine was guilty in my opinion of unethical behaviour, and I have often wondered whether Tina was aware of the turn taken by events after she had extracted my promise. I was too proud to broach the subject with her, for I have always believed in the honour of a commitment irrespective of any commercial consideration.

The launch party for the book was held appropriately at the Museum of the Moving Image on London's South Bank. A comprehensive invitation list was sent out, but very few people turned up for the occasion. Those who stayed away did so as a sign of protest, claiming that Leni had been a Nazi who collaborated with the Third Reich, and that having any truck with her would compromise their own strongly held anti-fascist convictions. They were not even prepared to be attracted by the extraordinary fact that she had just returned from diving in the Maldives to film underwater in her ninetieth year, and that her next stop would be New Guinea. 'The only dangerous animals are the journalists who turn up,' she said.

Among the guests were Auberon Waugh, who happily posed with Leni, the newscaster Gordon Honeycombe, and Claus von Bulow, who was sporting a newly grown beard. Von Bulow stalked around the museum, the *Sunday Telegraph* reported, casting a quizzical eye at the television screens that were showing clips from some of Leni's work. 'These films have extraordinary power,' he said, 'but now some of them send shivers down my spine. They make such horrible things seem so attractive.'

Notwithstanding the general boycott of the launch party, the book itself received phenomenal review coverage, Celina Sippy, Quartet's publicity manager, having done a fabulous job with the promotion. None of the critics could resist the urge to write about the book and Leni's picture was splashed across many a front cover, including that of *The Times Literary Supplement*. Both critics and media observers were almost unanimous in acknowledging her genius as a film-maker, but the label that claimed she had been a propagandist for Hitler and his ideology continued to stick in general. Her denials that she had simply been pursuing her artistic endeavours fell on deaf ears and failed to convince any of them. She was to remain the *bête noir* of the media until her death at the age of over a hundred.

The historian Ian Buruma was allotted the task of assessing the book for *The Times Literary Supplement*. He began by looking at some of her main claims: that she had never been a Nazi, that she had never heard of Hitler before 1932, and that she had no idea what happened to the Jews until she was told in 1945. Yet, he said, this was Hitler's greatest propagandist, who when she heard of his death 'threw herself on her bed and "wept all night"'. Perhaps she had been lying for so long that she believed 'her own fibs'. Nevertheless he was prepared overall to give her the benefit of the doubt, granting credence to a 'rich, poetic inner life'. 'But the mind that looks in, naturally sometimes fails to look out, and is bound, therefore, to miss a few things – the rise of Hitler, for example, or millions of people disappearing into cattle-trucks.'

> [With] her experience of rapturous mountain films, starring pure, clean, heroic German youths seeking the sublime on moonlit nights, the step towards becoming Hitler's propagandist was not a big one. She was, one might say, exactly the right woman in the right place at the right time. Was she an opportunist? Let us say that career and faith formed a seamless whole. The reason she continues to fascinate us is that she lifted Nazi propaganda to something approaching excellence.

Buruma's feeling was that her claim that *Triumph of the Will* was not propaganda, but purely and simply a documentary, was absurd and did not bear scrutiny. She had repeated the assertion that it had 'nothing ideological in it' to Gitta Sereny in an interview in the *Independent on Sunday*, but this too was 'nonsensical'.

> In speech after speech, the Nazi ideals, woolly and murderous, are extolled. If Riefenstahl missed the point of her own most famous work, her boss certainly did not ... The film, Hitler wrote

[in a preface to a book called *Hinter den Kulissen des Reichparteitag-Films (Behind the Scenes of the Nuremberg Rally Film)*], was 'a totally unique and incomparable glorification of the power and beauty of our movement'.

If Riefenstahl really thinks that her film is nothing but a dispassionate chronicle, her simulation of great passion, indeed worship, is the product of a deeply cynical mind, or else she is the truest of coins, the believer in whom the faith simply is reality. Again my inclination is to give her the benefit of the doubt. Triumph of the Will is a work of passionate engagement. Riefenstahl is intoxicated by the sheer beauty of it all.

A fellow film-maker, Lindsay Anderson, added his comments in the *European*, saying that even more memorable than *Triumph of the Will* was *Olympia*:

Its power and poetry have never been surpassed. Riefenstahl's account of its preparations, shooting and above all editing, shows the meticulous concentration of the true film artist. It won the Grand Prix at the last Venice Festival before the war. But its identification with the Nazi myth cast a shadow over its director for the rest of her life. And it put an end to her career as a film-maker.

One cannot help feeling that this condemnation and the continual repression that went with it were largely unjustified. Riefenstahl was naïve and certainly unwise to accept Nazi patronage. But she was not the first artist to sacrifice her good name for the opportunity to practise her art.

Helena Pinkerton wrote a very level-headed notice for the *Jewish Chronicle*.

That these two films, *Triumph of the Will* and *Olympia*, were also the artistic masterworks of a huge talent might not be seen as a redeeming factor. Yet her hefty book of memoirs, timed to coincide with her ninetieth birthday, portrays a woman whose greatest sins were political naïveté, self-absorption and a measure of cowardice. She was never a Nazi party member. Nor, she says, did she share the Nazis' views on race and Aryan supremacy ...

And an objective viewing of *Olympia* leads to the conclusion that its most exalted star is the black American athlete Jessie Owens.

Why, therefore, had she not left Germany when the Nazis attained power, but stayed on 'despite the repressions which she claims to have abhorred'? Here it had to be remembered that many stayed 'who could and should have left, including indeed many Jews, who had better reason that Riefenstahl did to jump ship'. These had stayed 'because they felt themselves to be, above all, Germans'. Her book was worth reading to correct the many misconceptions there had been about her, for 'hers was an independent artistic vision', though she 'did allow her art to serve an evil master, and for that she must take the rap. She was certainly not heroic. But how many were?'

During an interview for *The Times* with Christian Tyler, he suggested that, 'like Marlene Dietrich, she could have gone to America'.

Riefenstahl corrected me. Dietrich had to go to the US for her career and denounced the Nazis from there because she had been better informed of the truth by her circle.

Riefenstahl's own Jewish friends – they loyally defended her later – had initially been impressed by Hitler and had advised her not to leave Germany, she said.

'You could have followed your instinct and kept away from those men. But it was too late.'

'Riefenstahl is a tough old bird,' concluded Philip Purser in an article in the *London Review of Books*.

> When nearly sixty she began a new career as a photographer specializing in anthropological studies, notably of the Nuba people in the Sudan. At seventy-one she qualified as a scuba diver and added underwater photography to her portfolio. She has never been short of professional admirers ... Nor, of course does she lack detractors; the latest has been Susan Sontag, who traced a line of fascist exaltation right through the *oeuvre* ... Obsessed by these extremes of approval or censure, Riefenstahl seems unable to look back on the things she did with any objectivity or even to recognize ordinary cause and effect.

In a review in *The Times*, Mark Almond said Riefenstahl was a film genius, but predicted that her 'overlong self-defence', as represented in the memoirs, would 'do little to lift the shadows from her reputation':

> It fits too easily into the catalogue of gifted Germans who went along with Hitler, preferring to promote their own careers and genius under his patronage and remaining wilfully ignorant of the nature of his regime until too late ...

Her films will remain her legacy, arousing ambivalent admiration.

Although she had written her memoirs 'to tackle preconceived ideas and to clear up misunderstandings', Janet Watts found in an interview conducted for the *Observer* that she was not proud of the result, admitting that she was 'not gifted in writing'. She had felt it was a necessary duty, and sure enough 'the book has already been rubbished'.

Yet many people have loved Leni Riefenstahl, too. The Nuba people of the southern Sudan, for example: and they have played a part in her survival. When she finally admitted (after many struggles) that her film career was over, she went to Africa, discovered the Nuba and – almost by accident – began a new career by photographing them ...

In all her tribulations, Leni Riefenstahl vibrates with life. For many people she will never be able to pay for her great mistake ...

'I am not happy. But if I have not an interview ... if I have nothing to do with the press ... If I see my Nuba, if I dive ... I fight against depression. Even if it is hard, I say to the life, yes.'

Quartet was to publish two more books of Leni Riefenstahl's. One of them, *Olympia*, covered the 1936 Olympics in Berlin. The other was *Wonders of the Sea*. Both were photographic books to take the breath away. *Olympia* was all in black and white, its stunning photographs documenting the spectacular games for future generations. *Wonders of the Sea* contained photographs she had shot in beautiful colour at the age of eighty-five during spectacular dives she made in the Red Sea, the Caribbean, the Maldives and the Indian Ocean. These images of great natural beauty depicted the fantastic variety of marine life: minuscule prawns, sponges, bivalves, coral in bloom and the wonderful world of fish. The splendours of their shapes and colours were again caught on film for posterity. Leni's patient, tireless efforts had resulted in a photographic collection of outstanding beauty, each intricate composition as delicate as a painting.

With her death at the age of a hundred and one in 2003, the world said farewell not only to a remarkable woman who had made her mark on history, but also to one who had evoked in unforgettable imagery the time when Germany's colossal renewal of power was poised to inflict human misery and slaughter on an unprecedented scale. Her detractors understandably continue to argue that her work is a celebration of that power – unwittingly perhaps, but undeniably. When, however, her creative contribution is viewed through an artistic perspective, devoid of its moral equivocacy, then it seems to transcend these considerations.

There was no doubting that Leni herself continued to struggle with her inner demons till the end. She survived a helicopter crash when she was ninety-eight, on her last trip to visit the Nuba. The film-maker Ray Müller visited her in hospital and asked what in her life she regretted. There had been many, many mistakes, she said. What mistakes did she mean, he asked. 'Well ...,' she responded, 'I mean, this relationship with the Third Reich.' For a film he made in 1993, Müller had previously made the point bluntly to her: 'I feel this country [Germany] is still waiting for you to say publicly: "I made a mistake, I'm sorry ..."' Leni replied:

Being sorry isn't nearly enough, but I can't tear myself apart or destroy myself. It's so terrible. I've suffered anyway for over half a century and it will never end, until I die. It's such an incredible burden that to say sorry ... it's inadequate, it expresses too little.

A TALENTED YOUNG MAN

Stephen Pickles was a talented young man of some distinction who had worked for a number of years at a classical record shop in Great Marlborough Street, round the corner from Namara House. I used to buy my classical CDs in the shop and in due course a kind of friendship grew up between us that resulted in his joining Quartet to oversee the editorial department. The first personal contribution that he made to Quartet was his book *Queens*, a brilliant study of some of those who inhabit the London gay scene. Glamorous and sordid by turns, it described, among many characters, 'The Northern Queen', 'The Opera Queen', 'The Screaming Queen', 'The YMCA Queen' and 'The Rent Boy'. The elements of drama, documentary, diary and monologue were brought together to create what was the first mainstream book to chart the labyrinths of gay metropolitan life. It combined sympathy with acid comment and was both an anatomy of a subculture and a virtuosic celebration. *Queens* received critical acclaim while also achieving commercial success.

Pickles was a formidable character, gifted with prodigious talent and singularity of mind. His mood swings could sometimes seem bewildering and contradictory and he was uncompromising in his judgements. In that respect he resembled Auberon Waugh: if he got a bee in his bonnet about someone, his dislike would manifest itself in no uncertain terms. My own relationship with Pickles was consistently cordial and warm, and I do not recall any discord between us during the time he remained with Quartet. Anthony Blond, in his autobiography *Jew Made in England* (Timewell Press and Elliott & Thompson, 2004), described him as someone who had influenced my musical tastes, coaxing me from Tchaikovsky to Bartók. He then went on to paint a little word picture of Pickles:

> Delicate in stature and address, with big swimming eyes, he passed so much of his life propping up the bar in the Coach and Horses in Romilly Street that I warned him he might get clamped. Pickles was tricky and touchy, a militant homosexual with an air of having been scarred in some terrible romantic battle. He loved Naim and glowed ... when complimented by him. Naim, on the other hand, when accused by a not totally sober Pickles of homophobia, one evening at the Frankfurt Book Fair, just smiled.

The office Pickles occupied at Goodge Street became like a Chinese opium den of the nineteenth century, but filled with books and personal treasures rather than narcotic fumes. It always remained locked, for it was his very private domain where no chance intruder might trespass. The contribution that Pickles made to the eclecticism of Quartet's list in giving it a more emphatic literary orientation was tremendous. During his years as editorial director he lifted the imprint's literary output to place it on a level with the likes of the Penguin Modern Classics.

The Encounters series grew to the point where it contained over a hundred titles, representing on the British publishing scene an unprecedented selection of European novels of outstanding merit. It was a brave attempt to bring European twentieth-century literature to a wider audience at a time when the political link with Europe was becoming an actuality. Commercial success eluded us, it is true, but perhaps that was because we were ahead of the field. The critical acclaim was resounding and established Quartet's image as an imprint that left no avenue unexplored in its search for innovative ideas.

The *Daily Telegraph* wrote how, 'Since 1985, Quartet publishers have been doing their bit to promote a free market in European writing with the "Encounters" imprint, which offers translations of work by distinguished, and sometimes neglected, modern European authors.' 'The best of world writing in translation, Quartet Encounters has an editorial policy of real vision and imagination. Long may it flourish,' wrote Gabriel Josipovici. John Banville in the *Observer* said, 'Quartet are to be warmly commended for their courage and enterprise in making available to English-speaking readers so many modern European authors'; and Michael Tanner wrote, 'Quartet Encounters strikes me as one of the most enterprising and worthwhile ventures in contemporary publishing.' 'Not only extraordinary variety,' said John Bayley, 'but remarkable quality too. A comparativists' paradise.' The *Spectator* was even more fulsome in its praise: 'The series as a whole is a landmark in responsible, original and stimulating publishing.'

Pickles also acted as mentor to the host of gifted young men and women who flocked to Quartet to exercise their talents in an environment free of conventional humbug. There was no doubt he could be brutally frank on occasions when his tolerance wore thin, but his influence was far-reaching and enduring.

Memories

The Quartet Encounters list continued to grow prodigiously. It kept to its literary focus in the main, though widened its scope to bring in other items of international cultural interest. Lou Andreas-Salomé's *The Freud Journal* (translated by Stanley W. Leavy and introduced by Mary-Kay Wilmers) was a personal view of Freud's studies and relations with colleagues against the background of a literary coterie that included the poet Rilke; Rilke himself was represented by *Rodin and Other Prose Pieces*, he having at one time been secretary to the great sculptor (translated by G. Craig Huston and introduced by William Tucker), *Early Prose*, which included memories as well short fiction pieces, and his *Selected Letters 1902–1926* (translated by R. F. C. Hull and introduced by John Bayley). Gaston Bachelard's *The Psychoanalysis of Fire* (translated by Alan M. C. Ross and introduced by Northrop Frye) was an idiosyncratic exploration of ideas concerning fire in human evolution and their symbolic and subconscious connotations.

Bruno Walter's *Gustav Mahler* (translated by Lotte Walter Lindt and introduced by Michael Tanner) was an indispensable source book for any study of the composer, coming from the foremost interpreter of his music, who had been deeply and personally involved in realizing much of it in performance. With over a score of other titles to choose from, the following list can only be highly selective, but will show the consistency of quality achieved by Pickles. Hermann Broch, the son of a Jewish textile manufacturer in Vienna, was an industrialist, mathematician and philosopher who came to literature reluctantly as the only way of expressing his thoughts and feelings. *The Guiltless* (translated by Ralph Manheim with an afterword by the author) was a book he called 'a novel in eleven stories'; it portrayed a group of eleven lives in the pre-Hitler period. *The Sleepwalkers*, one of his major achievements (translated by Willa and Edwin Muir and introduced by Michael Tanner), was a trilogy that traced from the 1880s the social erosion and dissolution that culminated in the Nazi era. Another Viennese novelist of stature was Heimito von Doderer, who was an active Nazi up to 1938. His vast trilogy, *The Demons* (translated by Willa and Edwin Muir and introduced by Michael Hamburger), explored every strand of life possible in Vienna, both comic and tragic, where the 'demons' concerned arose from people's minds in the tumultuous years between the two world wars. Thomas Bernhard was born in Holland but grew up in Austria and wrote in German, becoming, George Steiner considered, 'one of the masters of contemporary European fiction' in the post-war years. *Concrete* (translated by Martin McLintock and introduced by Martin Chalmers) was a story in his 'black idyll' style about a writer who goes away to start a project but finds himself obsessively following an altogether different line of inquiry set off by a tragic memory. *On the Mountain* (translated by Russell Stockman with an afterword by Sophie Wilkins) showed him working in parallel with themes to be found in Kafka and Beckett in a novel written as one sentence. E. M. Cioran had been born in Romania in 1911, but had won a scholarship in Paris and subsequently made the decision to live in France and write in French, though he said he had no nationality – 'the best possible status for an intellectual'. He was regarded as a foremost contemporary European thinker, the heir of Kierkegaard, Nietzsche and Wittgenstein, who wrote incomparable, elegantly styled essays on the state of man in the modern world. Five of his collections found a place on the list (four of them being translated by Richard Howard): *Anathemas and Admirations* (introduced by Tom McGonigle), in which incisive estimates of literary figures were interspersed with caustic aphorisms; *A Short History of Decay* (introduced by Michael Tanner), whose theme was the 'philosophical viruses' of the twentieth century; *The Temptation to Exist* (introduced by Susan Sontag), a 'dance of ideas and debates' on 'impossible states of being'; and *The Trouble with Being Born* (introduced by Benjamin Ivry), which started out with the proposition that the disaster of life begins with the fact of birth, 'that laughable accident'. The fifth title (translated and introduced by Ilinca Zarifopol-Johnston) was *On the Heights of Despair*, a youthful work, written in Romania, which showed him to be already a 'theoretician of despair'.

Representing Swedish literature was, first, Stig Dagerman, whom Michael Meyer thought to be 'the best writer of his generation in Sweden and one of the best in Europe'. *A Burnt Child* (translated by Alan Blair and introduced by Laurie Thompson) was set in Stockholm in a family where the mother has died, the drama being played out between the husband and son and, respectively, the father's ageing mistress and the son's timid fiancée. *German Autumn* (translated and introduced by Robin Fulton) gave a documentary portrait of the Germans in defeat immediately after the fall of the Third Reich which courageously saw them as suffering individuals. *The Games of Night* (translated by Naomi Walford and introduced by Michael Meyer) was a collection of stories showing his versatility. *The Snake* (translated by Laurie Thompson) was a tour de force where the threads of disparate stories, arising from a conscript army camp, are brought together in a denouement. Then came Sweden's Nobel Prize-winning Pär Lagerkvist who had two titles in the list: *The Dwarf* (translated by Alexandra Dick and introduced by Quentin Crewe), a dark historical tale of a Machiavellian dwarf at the court of a Renaissance prince; and *Guest of Reality* (translated and introduced by Robin Fulton), a set of three stories linking the growing of a boy into a young man. A major novel of social concern from Sweden was Per Olov Enquist's *The March of the Musicians* (translated by Joan Tate), which told about the political uprising of the workers in a remote northern part of the country against their exploitation by sawmill owners and browbeating by hellfire preachers on Sundays; the author's profound empathy with his characters gave this small episode in Sweden's labour history a universal resonance.

Gabriele D'Annunzio was a leading writer of the so-called Decadent school. *The Flame* (translated and introduced by Susan Bassnett) was his scandalous novel about a passionate affair between a young writer and a great actress, in which they battle for supremacy in love and art; it was scandalous because based on his own relationship with Eleanora Duse. *Nocturne and Five Tales of Love and Death* (translated and introduced by

Raymond Rosenthal) was a selection of his prose fiction demonstrating what a formidable pioneer D'Annunzio had been as a writer. Equally pioneering was his compatriot and contemporary Luigi Pirandello, known mainly for his experimental plays, though his short stories were also among the greatest in literature. Those selected for Short Stories (translated and introduced by Frederick May) showed his concern with the masks people use socially and their interplay with the reality behind them. Elio Vittorini was a writer from Sicily who aimed for 'neo-realism' in his work and produced an undisputed masterpiece in *Conversations in Sicily* (translated by Wilfrid David and introduced by Stephen Spender): first published in 1939, the censorship it was constrained by gave it an underlying power in the story of a young man's journey back to Sicily to console his mother after his father had deserted her. From the next generation, Pier Paolo Pasolini was seen primarily as a film-maker of originality in Britain, though in his native Italy he was regarded rather more as a poet, critic and novelist. Helping to rectify our view were *A Dream of Something* (translated and introduced by Stuart Hood), a story about three friends from northern Italy whose search for money takes them abroad, though they return home to political violence and an end to their carefree roistering; *Theorem* (translated and introduced by Stuart Hood), which was written in tandem with the making of a film of the same title, in which Terence Stamp played the young man gaining a sexual, emotional and intellectual hold over a rich bourgeois family; and *Roman Nights and Other Stories* (translated by John Shepley and introduced by Jonathan Keates), a selection of five stories from Pasolini's miscellaneous writings that reflected the cultural changes taking place in post-war Italian society.

Yevgeny Zamyatin chose exile from Soviet Russia in 1931, foreseeing the clash between writers and the state that lay ahead. *A Soviet Heretic* (translated by Mirra Ginsburg and introduced by Alex M. Shane) was a collection of his writings on fellow writers and the condition of literature in the Soviet Union, as well as his letter to Stalin, seeking voluntary exile, and his letter of resignation from the Soviet Writers' Union. The status of Osip Mandelstam as the pre-eminent Russian poet of the twentieth century gave him no protection from murderous NKVD brutality. *The Noise of Time and Other Prose Pieces* (collected, translated and introduced by Clarence Brown) was a selection from the range of his writing, including a work of invective and outrage against the state's official campaign against him. Yury Tynyanov's *Lieutenant Kijé & Young Vitushishnikov* (translated and introduced by Mirra Ginsburg) were two glittering novellas by a Russian master satirist about abuses in the eighteenth and nineteenth centuries which allowed him to be obliquely critical of those of the Soviet regime. Abram Tertz, the nom de plume for Andrei Synyavsky in his samisdat publications (that won him hard labour and exile), wrote *Little Jinx* (translated by Larry P. Joseph and Rachel May and introduced by Edward J. Brown) as a black farce containing the line: 'Were we not guilty, neither Hitler nor Stalin could have surfaced among us.' *The Fatal Eggs & Other Soviet Satire* (translated, edited and introduced by Mirra Ginsburg) was a famous subversive anthology by seventeen boldly comic writers, including Mikhail Bulgakov, Ilf and Petrov and Zamyatin. There were also the stories of Aharon Appelfeld, with their subtle and profound recreations of life in Europe's Jewish communities as they moved into the gathering shadows of the Holocaust; and Giorgio Bassani's artistic account of the impact on a Jewish family in Italy as Mussolini's fascism geared up the anti-Semitic component in its laws under pressure from Nazi Germany. Another important aspect of the Quartet Encounters list was the way it demonstrated the importance of literature in delineating the dimensions of human experience and suffering within the history of the twentieth century's traumatic events. While this summary of the list has not by any means been comprehensive, it is enough to show there was a spirit of adventure at work in Goodge Street for which it would have been hard to find an equivalent elsewhere in British publishing at the time.

A GRAND OLD MAN

In April, 1993, I interviewed the Duke of Devonshire at his London home in Chesterfield Street, Mayfair, for the *Oldie*. I found him to be congenial, a true English gentleman with a disarming honesty. I did not want the interview to end, for I enjoyed being in his presence and was struck by his down-to-earth view of the world. He had none of the patrician arrogance of his class. On the contrary, he showed the kind of humility normally associated with great sages as they delve into the incomprehensible. The following vignette appeared in the *Daily Telegraph* under the heading 'Peerless':

> It seems there are occasional bleak moments at Chatsworth, seat of the Duke of Devonshire. Interviewed by Naim Attallah in the *Oldie* magazine, he announces he could rub along quite well without a handle.
>
> Devonshire, asked about the future of the House of Lords, says he would be sorry to see it go, 'although I wouldn't in the least mind losing my title and being called Andrew Cavendish. I'd mind very much if my possessions were taken away, but my title, no.' Attallah proceeded to ask Devonshire if he gets on well with his son. 'I get on very well with my son … He also gets on well with his mother and stands up to her too, more than I do.' Is the Duchess 'a strong character'? Devonshire replied: That would be an understatement.'
>
> The Duke seems to have been on good form. At one point he told Attallah that 'when I was young I used to like casinos, fast women and God knows what. Now my idea of heaven … is to sit in the hall at Brooks's having China tea.'

There was no question he refused to answer. His honesty came to the fore when I suggested that his image had been rather tarnished a few years earlier when he revealed, in the Old Bailey witness box, a side of his private life that at the time many people would have considered rather disreputable. He replied that being in the witness box and speaking on oath was a salutary experience, 'and it was very painful for my family. The only consolation was that I didn't attempt to lie. My private life isn't all it might be, but it would only make it worse to lie about it.' At this point I asked him if he ever repented. Again he was forthright: 'I find repentance very difficult, particularly if you are aware that you may do the same thing again … one has to be very careful of repentance.'

Years later his wife, the formidable Debo, told me that the interview I conducted with the Duke was the best he ever gave. I was flattered and surprised, for I thought she might have minded my intrusive questions about his private life. In fact she seemed relaxed about it. She rose even higher in my estimation and we occasionally corresponded. With her sister Diana and her other Mitford siblings, she belonged to an aristocratic family that has become something of a legend.

A NOTE ON BILAL

In the mid 1970s I had the privilege of meeting the Irish poet H. A. L. Craig who lived in Rome and who, with the late Mustapha Akkad, the producer and director of the film *Mohammad – Messenger of God*, was also the scriptwriter of the film.

Craig, during the course of his research, was encouraged by Akkad to write a book about Bilal which Quartet first published in 1977. Here is a note on Bilal which Craig wrote as an Introduction to his book.

Bilal is remembered for the love people felt for him.
He inhabits the heart. But, by the same token, Bilal was
so loved and so present in people's affections that few
felt the need to write down much about his life. It was to

them sufficient to say that he was there, always beside the Prophet Mohammad, and loved by him. In the few paintings of this historic moment, usually backward glances in manuscript decorations, Bilal is always easy to recognize. Bilal was black.

The few facts known about Bilal can be told quickly. He was born in Mecca, the son of an Abyssinian slave called Rabah; in a city of idol-worship, he was tortured for his belief in one God; he was bought and freed from slavery by Mohammad's close friend, Abbu Bakr; he was made the first muezzin, the caller to prayer in Islam; he had the responsibility for the food supply of the first, small armies of Islam; he was so close to the Prophet that he had the duty of waking him in the morning. After Mohammad's death, Bilal's legs, in his grief, failed him. He could not climb up the steps to make the call to prayer again. He died in Syria, probably in 644, Twelve years after Mohammad's death.

*Not much to base a life upon – although, from the day of Bilal's conversion, every event in Mohammad's life was an event in the life of Bilal. Moreover, the two pillars of his memory, the love he had from all who knew him and his nearness to the Prophet, are enough for a writer who shares the first and is awed by the second. The Black Muslims in America have renamed themselves the Bilali. Bilal is also a patron saint, to use a Christian description, of Moslem Africa.
Mohammad (peace be unto him) called Bilal 'a man of Paradise'.*

Memories

With the current misinterpretation of Islam's message, *Bilal* is a book of peace and fraternity that everyone should read. The world will be a much safer place as a result. For peace and goodwill has never been so threatened throughout the globe.

JO CRAVEN

During 1993 a new recruit had begun to grace the offices of the *Literary Review*. Her name was Jo Craven. She was a delightful young lady with heavenly looks, who enlivened the atmosphere and became one of Bron's favourites. Her recollections of the time she spent there give a further insight into what Bron was like, both at home and in the office. The piece that follows illustrates yet again the reason why Bron was loved and revered, especially by the young.

Saved from Spiritual Death

Jo Craven

When I first walked through the door of the *Literary Review*'s Beak Street office, in 1993, straight from university and fresh off the train from Yorkshire, I was amazed to be greeted like a long-lost friend by a beaming Bron Waugh, whose first words were, 'How long can you stay?' Never one to miss an opportunity, I dived in with, 'As long as you like.' 'Good,' he said in a very pleased way, looking around the room at the other two staring members of staff for confirmation. It would be some time before I would witness him wave vaguely at his own daughters and mistake many another stranger for an old friend. But it would never occur to him to go back on his word and I stayed for the next five years.

Within weeks Bron had invited me to stay in his Brook Green flat, taking pity on my penniless state and constant flat-hopping. At that point I was working for free as 'a slave'. I couldn't have been luckier and quite enjoyed my friend's taunts about our 'special relationship'. My part of the deal was to make sure there was always plenty of loo roll and Bran Flakes, and occasionally arrange a party with food from Lidgates. Bron's son and girlfriend would also move in, his daughter for a period, and then my boyfriend, and then the deputy editor. It was open-house for the impoverished.

In the overcrowded office I would package up books, type in copy, eventually commission reviewers and generally be in the same room, at the same lunch table as Bron, his other editors and some of the most fascinating figures in British literature. I've never been so drunk in all my life. I loved sharing a couple of bottles of wine over lunch – Bron always paid from his own pocket – and often in the afternoon, over a game of bridge, I could never remember the rules, probably because of the port we'd sip, and maybe thanks to lunch. Then there'd be more boozing after 6 p.m., downstairs in the Academy Club, from where I'd stagger back to the flat; and late at night in Brook Green, Bron would often suggest a nightcap of sweet gin, half gin and half red Martini. It was revolting, but I'd do anything to please this kind generous man for saving me from spiritual death in an ordinary office. By the following morning, I honestly thought no one noticed as I sat at my computer, nestling a can of Coke to cure the worst of my hangover.

I always knew I was lucky to be part of this wonderfully ramshackle universe, so removed from the regular working world. I was one of the last in a long tradition of girls who either worked at Quartet Books, waitressed in the Academy Club or slaved on the magazine. Most had already gone off to find fame. Of course one day it would come to an end: the rickety buildings heated by plug-in radiators, doing everything by hand, paying only £25 for reviews – many writers framed the beautifully handwritten cheques rather than cash them – and top writers being paid with wine from Bron's cellar. It couldn't last. Every few months reality would come knocking. Naim Attallah, the endlessly benevolent owner, would apologetically announce that he just couldn't keep supplementing us while we failed to make any money. Bron would go into a spin. He most of all didn't want anything to change and was always the first to say how much we had to be grateful to Naim for. Naim in turn was hugely fond of Bron and was only doing what any rational person would when the debts kept coming. Selfishly the rest of us found it hard to understand that twenty-first-century accounting had a part in our lives. We were used to being paid terribly and producing a brilliant magazine, and having so much fun that we didn't want anything to change. For me, the moment of departure came when I finally gave up on the notion that someone would headhunt me as a brilliant literary editor, and decided £7,000 a year could be improved on. Two years later Bron died, but the *Literary Review* lives on with its present proprietor, Nancy Sladek, who keeps Bron's flame burning and the spirit of Naim's commitment.

AN INTERNATIONAL INCIDENT

In early June 1991 a lunch took place at the *Observer* newspaper with Donald Trelford, the editor, at which I was one of the guests. Its after-effect was an international political row that soured Britain's relationship with France. I had known Donald for a number of years, particularly during the period when the Observer was owned by Tiny Rowland. Our paths crossed periodically in a number of ways, socially and otherwise. When we met we would discuss general topics of the day, including his own remarkable entente with Tiny, who was hard to handle and rather unpredictable in his choice of friends and business associates.

At the time Donald had a television slot on BBC2 in which he appeared in conversation with political leaders. He was contemplating an interview with Edith Cresson, who had recently been appointed prime minister of France by President Mitterand. *En passant* Donald asked me whether, in my diverse activities, I had ever met her, faintly hoping I might contribute to his research process. As it happened, I had met her, before there was any talk of her becoming prime minister. Some four years earlier I had interviewed her for my book *Elles* – the French edition of *Women* – but had never been able to use the interview as I had missed the deadline for its inclusion. The interview had been in French and remained unseen by anyone, having subsequently lain dormant in one of my files. Donald asked whether he could see it, notwithstanding the fact that it was conducted in French. He would have it translated, he said, and return it to me as soon as he had had the chance to read it.

Three days later an excited Donald came on the telephone. The interview, he reckoned, was sensational, and with my permission he proposed to publish it in a world exclusive as the cover story for the 'Review' section of the newspaper the following Sunday. At the same time he would negotiate worldwide syndication rights, for which I would receive half the total benefits in addition to a substantial fee for its UK publication. I said yes without hesitation.

The interview had all the impact Donald anticipated and more. The majority of people were appalled by the ill-considered statements Madame Cresson made about Anglo-Saxon men. She tossed statistics into the air without their having the least basis in fact. In my opinion, she had shown herself to be vain, arrogant and full of her own importance. She kept looking at her watch all the time we were talking, warning me my time was up, but then carrying on with her pontifications regardless. Everything to do with her was studied, and she failed to convince of any sincerity. What was beyond doubt was that she came over as an attractive woman in her prime who was highly intelligent and confident. Her movements and gestures were all part of her repertoire. There was no doubt that without much effort she beguiled Mitterand, who was not at all immune to feminine wiles.

Edith Cresson's sex appeal was of the sort that men would fall for then try to master and subdue. I felt it as I was talking to her. Her delusions of superiority stirred one's animal instincts sexually, though I would have been far too embarrassed to admit it. In different circumstances I could see myself falling prey to this egocentric woman were it not for her contrived haughtiness, which overrode and negated every other consideration. But before analysing the furore that followed the publication of the interview and making a considered judgement, it is essential to quote the passage that triggered off the whole controversy. I asked her why most men preferred the company of men in Anglo-Saxon countries:

'Yes, but the majority of these men are homosexuals – perhaps not the majority – but in the USA there are already 25 per cent of them, and in England and Germany it is much the same. You cannot imagine it in the history of France. Traditionally the image of Frenchmen has been heterosexual, an image given to them by men of power, by the kings, etc. Frenchmen are much more interested in women; Anglo-Saxon men are not interested in women, and this is a problem that needs analysis. I don't know whether it is cultural or biological but there is something there that isn't working – that's obvious. Moreover, I remember from strolling about in London, and girls are making the same observation, that men in the streets don't look at you. When you do this in Paris, the men look at you; a workman or indeed any man looks at passing women. The Anglo-Saxons are not interested in women as women; for a woman arriving in an Anglo-Saxon country it is astonishing. She says to herself, 'What is the matter?' It is a problem of education and I consider it something of a weakness. A man who isn't interested in women is in some way a little maimed.'

The *Observer* of 16 June summarized the interview under a front-page heading: 'French PM: One-in-four Englishmen gay':

Continental people have sex, it was once written: the English have hotwater bottles. As if to prove the point, France's first woman prime minister, Edith Cresson, has bared her soul in a remarkably candid and controversial interview on the subject of men, sex, power, discrimination – and the supposed amorous failings of the Anglo-Saxon male.

The fall-out was immediate and it went round the world. On Monday morning the *Daily Telegraph* reported: 'A certain *froideur* has befallen Anglo-French relations after a decidedly undiplomatic attack on British manhood by Mme Edith Cresson, the French prime minister. The fifty-seven-year-old mother of two, whose quick temper and sharp tongue are renowned in Paris, has suggested that the Anglo-Saxon male at best lacks the passion of his Gallic counterpart, and in one in four cases is homosexual. 'The remarks were made four years ago to the publisher Naim Attallah, but surfaced in yesterday's *Observer* to ripple what might be left of any *Entente Cordiale* … Not since one of Mme Cresson's predecessors, M. Jacques Chirac, dismissed Mrs Thatcher's remarks as *couillons* during a European summit has a French prime minister been quite so disparaging about the British. But as diplomatic rows go it was perhaps somewhat short of the lamb wars or a single European currency. "I don't think we have a position on this one," the Foreign Office confessed yesterday.'

The *Telegraph* also included a few ill-informed assumptions of its own, stating that the book *Women* had 'featured conversations with more than 150 unsuspecting women, frequently over lunch, and containing remarks they would never have made had they known they were on record'. These women had been furious, alleged the *Telegraph*, 'but none more so that Mme Cresson, who was apparently too boring to make the book'. The next day the *Telegraph* printed an unequivocal apology:

Mr Naim Attallah assures us, and we entirely accept, that all the 289 women he interviewed for his bestselling book *Women* were aware that their remarks were being tape-recorded for inclusion in his book.

> Therefore the statement in yesterday's Daily Telegraph that they were unsuspecting and said things they would not have said if they had known they were on the record is without foundation.
>
> We also accept his assurance that, contrary to our statement, none complained to him, orally or in writing. In particular the interview with Mme Edith Cresson, now the French prime minister, was conducted only for the French, not the British, edition and did not appear in the French edition because of the publisher's schedule. Therefore our statement that she was 'too boring to make the book' is unfounded.
>
> We apologize sincerely to Mr Attallah for the misrepresentations in our news story and for those reflected in our leading article.

When I met Max Hastings, the editor of the *Daily Telegraph*, at a Downing Street reception, he greeted me with the words, 'You are a gentleman. I shall be writing to you a personal letter of appreciation.' And he did.

For Edith Cresson the whole *affaire* came to the fore as another diplomatic contretemps was brewing over the campaign of remarks she had been making against the Japanese from the moment she became prime minister a month earlier. These were aimed at Japan's export policies, despite the fact that one of France's great success stories in recent years had been its luxury-goods export trade to Japan. Among her accusations were that Japan wanted to conquer the world, and had already taken over the world's photographic industry, forced its own people to pay high prices at home to finance cheap exports and sealed off the domestic market to foreign competition. According to her, the Japanese were too busy plotting against the American and European economies to be able to sleep at night. They were 'ants … little yellow men who sit up all night thinking how to screw us'. Japan was the 'aggressor', she claimed on television, and 'lived in a universe different from ours, a universe of domination'. In reaction to her pronouncements, far-right groups in Japan were already organizing protests outside the French embassy in Tokyo, but she was showing no sign of backing down. Later in July, on a visit to America, she gave an interview on the ABC network repeating that the Japanese 'work like ants, live in little flats and take two hours to commute to work'. On 14 July, Bastille Day, the demonstrators in Tokyo guillotined her in effigy.

Her immediate reaction to the publication of the interview was to say she had no recollection of ever meeting me, let alone of being interviewed. An aide denied, moreover, that she had ever made the 'gay' remark. This inflamed the situation even further. When the media sought my reaction to the denial, I was able to produce the evidence by exhibiting the tape. The French authorities, having been given 'not only the date – Wednesday, 27 September 1987 – not only the place – at her then office in the Boulevard St Germain – but also the time of the interview – 11.30 a.m., sought to establish that she had been misrepresented, allegations which did not survive the briefest study of the tape transcript', as John Sweeney wrote for the *Observer* from Paris on 23 June. He gave a graphic description of their official disgust:

As slowly and stately as Montgolfier's gondola, the left eyebrow laboured heavenwards: "Disgusting." The right eyebrow the same. "Evil. *Stupide*." His hair, cut *en brosse*, bristled with distaste. His stomach, an overwrought shrine to the magnificence of French cuisine, shuddered in pain like a Sumo wrestler with tummy ache. The eyebrows climbed ever more upwards and now the lips were brought into play, squeezing together until opening to create a small explosion of compressed air, exactly mimicking the Paris Métro hiss. "We would never do a thing like this."

He paused to work the gondola eyebrows, sumo tummy and Métro door some more. "This rubbish. Trash. Garbage. It is always the English that play these games. Always Great Britain." He pronounced "Great Britain" as if it were not a country but a particularly nasty form of sheep apoplexy.

Jean-Philippe Atger is the French Bernard Ingham, the man charged with handling press relations for the new French prime minister, Madame Edith Cresson. With delicate disdain, he held a photocopy of a *Sun* story between finger and thumb; its headline, slotted on page three to the right of a pair of breasts, screamed: BRITS BLAST POOFTER JIBE FROM MRS FROG.

It was all the *Observer*'s fault.

Last week Atger was breathing garlicky bunkum and balderdash at your hapless reporter after our paper brought Anglo-French relations to a new low by disclosing that 'MRS FROG', er, Mme Cresson, believes that one in four Englishmen is gay and, more, they lack all interest in women.

Madame Cresson's fall-back position had subsequently become that the *Observer* story was not in the tradition of *le fair play*. "If this conversation took place," she told the listeners to a French radio programme, "I was not only not prime minister, I was not even in the government." She claimed she did not remember meeting me, but, 'Maybe I had a conversation with an English journalist because I had a lot of conversations with English journalists. All I know is that if the conversation took place, and if he found the things I said interesting, he would no doubt have included them in his book. I have nothing to add to this interview that has been taken out of a drawer.' When pressed about her allegation that a quarter of Englishmen were homosexual, she simply stirred the pot again, saying, 'It's difficult to produce a statistic.' The inference was that she remained unrepentant.

The tabloids, with the *Sun* in the vanguard, certainly spotted in the story a green light to let fly with a few blasts of chauvinism. Under the headline 'Brittany Fairies' the *Sun* said:

> Edith Cresson, France's first woman PM, claims one in four Englishmen is homosexual. That's a bit rich coming from the leader of a nation where most men carry handbags and kiss each other in public. They don't call Paris *Gay Paree* for nothing, you know.

Julie Burchill in the *Mail on Sunday*, sharpening up her gift for delivering a provocative insult, asked how it was that, if France was so straight, it had an 'AIDS rate higher than in most African countries and higher than any Western country apart from the USA (which is really a Third World country anyway)?' She found Mme Cresson's claim that British men did not look at women in the street 'incredible'. 'Because back here in dear old Blighty, the problem that personable women have to face is not too little male attention but too much ... Men who not only look at you in passing but indeed look at you as if they were trying to pick you out of an identity parade of suspects who might have done in their dear old mother ... In fact how very pleasant to be as plain and past it as Mme Cresson – an honorary man, no less! And if it is true, as she claims, that Frenchmen still ogle her – well, is it worse for a quarter of men to be homosexuals, or for the majority to be shameless, perverted gerontophiles?'

Mr David Jones of Bolton, Greater Manchester, suggested in a letter to the *Observer* that for Mme Cresson's next state visit to Britain he could envisage a 'guard of honour of scaffolders at Heathrow, ready to receive the premier by ceremoniously intoning, "Cor, I bet she does the business."

Marjorie Proops, in her column in the *Daily Mirror*, turned the theme into a case for exhortation: 'Maybe it's not a bad idea to keep your heads up, lads, and take a keener and closer look at the passing talent. Somehow we've got to go on breeding good, strong, silent Britons – and it can't be done without your cooperation.'

There was also the inevitable facetious question raised in the House of Commons, which brought a welcome interruption to the business of serious politics and reduced the chamber to hilarity. The Conservative MP Tony Marlow said that, in view of Mrs Cresson having 'sought to insult the virility of the British male because the last time she was in London she did not get enough admiring glances', he wished to put down a motion saying: 'This House does not fancy elderly Frenchwomen' – but was ruled out of order by the Speaker.

With Mme Cresson's remarks rebounding in various directions on other matters besides these, it began to seem to many commentators that Mitterand's judgement in appointing her as prime minister might soon be seriously called into question. Julian Nandy in the *Independent* on 20 July commented on how her predecessor, Michel Rocard, had been criticized for his reluctance to speak out on current issues during his three years in office, but there had been no such problem for Edith Cresson in the two months she had been in the job: 'She talks, what she says gets into print and, more often than not, it boomerangs. It has become known as *parler cru*, or talking raw. In the meantime her popularity rating has zigzagged, while President François Mitterand – who appointed her – has publicly backed her bluntness. Last week, however, her popularity, after falling 16 per cent in seven weeks, began to rise. In the weekly *L'Express* a poll showed that she had picked up seven points ... The poll was published just as Mrs Cresson made unfashionably frank comments on illegal immigrants, stressing that laws requiring their expulsion should be applied more strictly.'

An assessment by Robert Cottrell in the *Independent on Sunday* of 21 July put more detail on the situation: 'But to question Mrs Cresson's wisdom is, in effect, to question that of Mr Mitterand. He put her there. So had he since come to think, as he was asked during his annual 14 July television interview, that this was *une fausse bonne idée*? Mr Mitterrand insisted not. "After fifteen years of technocratic language," he said, "I find it healthy to have a prime minister who speaks clearly." The people of France, he said, "have a living language. Mrs Cresson has a living language ... It is true that Mrs Cresson upsets people. Well, some people are against her. I am for her. She is rather charming, don't you think?" Since you cannot say "No" to the president of France on live television, the question was left hanging.'

Edith Cresson failed to serve a full year as prime minister, though this gave her time to plumb new depths of unpopularity before she resigned after a poor showing by the Socialists in the elections. I have sometimes since wondered whether, in some indirect way, I contributed to her demise as prime minister. The aftermath of the interview showed her, I thought, in a silly light and made it clear she was quite incapable of reining in her loose tongue. There were even persistent rumours that she had formerly been Mitterand's mistress, leading her to feel the presidential backing she received was his way of appreciating the favours she had bestowed on him over the years; and, this being so, that her vulnerability was well protected.

Under Mitterand's patronage, she went on to be the European Commissioner for Education, Research and Sciences in Brussels. One of her first actions was to appoint her own dental surgeon, René Berthelot, as her personal adviser on HIV/AIDS, a subject of which he knew little.

After two years – though eighty-five thousand pounds the richer – Berthelot had produced a total of twenty-four pages of notes later deemed to be unqualified and grossly deficient. Another project she generated, known as the Leonardo da Vinci Vocational Training Scheme, which she claimed was the best administered programme in Brussels, became implicated in massive fraud, and the company she had chosen to run it was stripped of its five-hundred million-pound contract. Investigations uncovered a whole nest of falsified contracts, forged handwriting and embezzled funds, leading to the resignation of the entire Santer Commission in 1999. Allegations that she had personally gained from any wrongdoing remained unproven, though the Commission inquiry said she had 'failed to act in response to known, serious and continuing irregularities over several years'. Though the Advocate General of the European Court of Justice recommended that she be stripped of half her forty-seven-thousand-euro pension, she was allowed to escape the imposition of any financial penalty. 'Maybe I was a little careless,' was the extent of her public admission.

PAULA YATES

There seemed to be no stopping Quartet in 1981. Children's books were a specialized market that conventional wisdom said was better left to those experienced in the field. Nevertheless two illustrated books appeared: *Liza's Yellow Boat* by Bel Mooney, the well-known Fleet Street journalist; and The *Adventures of Chatrat* by Venetia Spicer, whose father was a director of Lonrho. Despite both titles achieving reasonable sales, Quartet took a policy decision that this line of publishing was not really their forte. The experiment had been well worth the effort but the possibilities were not pursued. The only exception to the rule was made in 1983 for a charming book by Paula Yates, illustrated by Sophie Windham, called *A Tail of Two Kitties*. It told the story of two cats, Porky and Rowdy, thrown together by fate in the Clapham home of the Yates family. Porky had been rescued from a cats' home whereas Rowdy, a white-haired Persian feline, had been acquired from a smart pet shop in Bond Street. Rowdy at once became the family favourite, thanks not only to his good looks but also to his ingratiating behaviour. All of this inevitably irritated Porky, who always got the blame for Rowdy's escapades. It was an amusingly entertaining tale of the trials and tribulations in the lives of two cats.

I had known Paula Yates since she was fifteen, having met her at the home of my friend, Michael Deakin. Michael and I were planning to collaborate with her father, Jess Yates, also known as 'The Bishop', on producing a musical extravaganza for the famous Casino du Liban in 1974. Jess was out of work after having been discredited by scandal following his antics in Spain with a buxom blonde at the same time as he was fronting the religious television programme 'Stars on Sunday'. In the end, our efforts came to nothing, partly because Jess's frame of mind was in total disarray and he was feeling the pinch financially. Scandal continued to stalk him when four years after his death in 1993 it emerged that Paula's biological father was not in fact Jess but Hughie Green of television's 'Opportunity Knocks'.

I followed Paula's career over the years. In 1978 she posed for Penthouse magazine, and in the 1980s became widely known as a co-presenter, with Jools Holland, of the Channel 4 pop-music programme 'The Tube'. In 1986 she married Bob Geldof, whom I first met in New York through Sabrina Guinness. We remained in touch until two years before her tragic death, but I will always remember her as an impish teenager with a sharp cheeky tongue, always full of mischief. She was a child of her generation, out to try anything to create a sensation yet invariably great fun – a gifted extrovert whose zany personality endeared her to her many friends.

QUENTIN CREWE

In September 1991 I attended a party at the Queen Anne Orangery in Kensington Gardens to celebrate the publication of the memoirs of a very dear friend, Quentin Crewe. The title he gave them was *Well, I Forget the Rest*. This remarkable sixty-four-year-old writer had been for more than half his life confined to a wheelchair, from which he greeted the friends and former wives who turned up to salute him. The *Evening Standard* covered the event as follows:

> Naim Attallah, something of an authority on these matters, confessed his unbridled admiration for Crewe's romantic endeavours. 'He is the greatest seducer,' he said. 'I don't know how he does it. There's no way I could have achieved any of the things he has if I had those disabilities.'
>
> Lord Snowdon, who invented Crewe's first electric wheelchair, disclaimed any part in such goings on. 'I don't think it has anything to do with my chair,' he told me. 'And if it has, it's a peripheral thing. It's his sheer strength and will of personality.

Quentin was a truly extraordinary man. As well as being a successful journalist and writer he was also a determined adventurer who had defied his disabilities by travelling through some of the most difficult terrain on earth. His exploits were legendary, but his powers of conquest where women were concerned remained the aspect of him I most admired. I saw it happen at first hand when his daughter Candida brought him to have lunch at Namara House. While waiting for me to come down from my office on the fourth floor he went to kill a few minutes browsing in the bookshop on the ground floor. It so happened, at the time, that a twenty-six-year-old model with stunning looks was working in the shop between modelling assignments. Before I could get down to greet him, Quentin had engaged her in conversation. Two months later she was his lover, accompanying him on a long journey through India. When I saw them together on their return, the girl was so besotted that she could not keep her hands off him. She hugged and caressed Quentin with a tenderness that belied the difference in their ages or any *impuissance* arising from his handicap.

Despite his disability, Quentin had three wives, five children and lovers aplenty, but his was no straightforward tale of triumph over adversity. When he was a boy his mother's nightly admonition was, 'Keep your hands above the sheets!' It was advice he never heeded. He continued to delve beneath the covers even after a Swiss governess had shown him a cautionary Victorian illustration of the madness and degeneration that lay in store for those who failed to take note. Using all the authority of her position, she pointed to the perpetrator of such shameful acts, explaining that the consequences of his wickedness had come about because *il joue toujours avec sa quéquette, comme toi*. Later, in view of what happened to Quentin, it was as if the governess had been a genuine Cassandra figure, a real prophet of doom, for he was struck down at an early age by muscular dystrophy, a cruel disease that had him confined to his wheelchair for the rest of his life.

When I interviewed him for *Singular Encounters*, I mentioned to him how his reputation for attracting beautiful young women was fabled. Did the secret lie in his combining being such a great raconteur with an irresistible charm, or was there some inherent sexual chemistry that attracted feminine beauty and youth? His response was typically diffident:

It gets less easy, but I think they're intrigued by something different – that is to say, somebody in a wheelchair. The only explanation I can think of is that those who seduced me wanted to discover what it was like to go to bed with somebody disabled. Or there is always the other possibility, that one is less frightening to them, that one isn't a great beast who's going to leap on top of them and beat them. Whatever it is, I've been very lucky.

His explanation seems quite plausible, especially in the light of a more recent instance where the publisher of the *Spectator* reportedly said she had slept with former home secretary David Blunkett to find out what it was like to sleep with a blind man.

Quentin was one of my heroes, and his death, like that of Auberon Waugh, has left a gap in our society that can never be filled. One hopes that these two men, who loved women with a true passion, are receiving their rewards in heaven from celestial creatures even more beautiful than those who dazzled and beguiled them in their terrestrial lives.

A SUMMING UP

Back on 22 January 1988 two items had appeared in the press announcing the resignation of David Elliott from Quartet. The *Bookseller* reported that David, 'who had worked for Quartet for ten years, intends to take an extended sabbatical' and that 'no date has been set for his departure, which he and Naim Attallah describe as "entirely amicable"'. *Private Eye* put an entirely different twist on the story:

> Crisis has struck at Quartet, the publishing arm of Naim Attullah Disgusting's business empire. Hot on the heels of the acquisition of the tired and emotional Anthony ('Fine old piece of seasoned timber') Blond comes the resignation of David Elliott, the publishing director. Known in the book trade as 'Dump-bin Dave', Elliott was the only person at Quartet with any grasp of publishing. His departure, which follows a major row with Attullah-Disgusting, is likely to throw the firm into turmoil.

Over the years I had known David our relationship was such that, no matter what occasional disagreements we had, the bond between us remained steadfast. We had a deep understanding that was not easy to define. David's mode of work and mine sometimes clashed, but the infrequent eruptions that followed were soon forgotten. Each had a soft spot for the other and the possibility of a rift was out of the question. Our close comradeship created unrest within the group. At Quartet our playfulness was considered juvenile, with David being referred to as 'the spy'. We regarded all this with a degree of insouciance that was beyond the comprehension of others.

An argument with David arose as a result of his sanctioning one of the Quartet reps to accept the return of some copies of *Women* from Liberty's book department. Rightly or wrongly I felt I should have been consulted before such a decision was taken. A flare-up was understandable. The barrage of negative publicity surrounding the publication of *Women* had brought nerves to snapping point and it needed the least provocation to set tempers rising. It was then, in a sudden moment of pique, that David decided it was time for him to depart the fold – at least in terms of his physical presence. He left Quartet six months later to act as adviser to two small publishing outfits while remaining on the Namara payroll for a few further years. While his role with us had outwardly changed, in essence it remained the same. Whatever function he fulfilled from then on, it was as if the watchful eye of Namara never left him. Today, after an even longer passage of time, the camaraderie and friendship we shared retain their original freshness and we are as close as ever.

The Chairman Publishes

David Elliott

Some time ago I wrote a book about the book trade, including my years at Quartet. It was an attempt to tell of my experience during what seemed to me was the greatest change to our cultural ethos since the first industrial revolution: the wanton destruction of sustainable work by technology, and the worship of the market.

I do think it lucky I was able to enter the book trade when editorial staff still told their salesmen what was expected of them. I was lucky when Claude Gill Books was bought by a US conglomerate and I saw the last great flowering of the US trade, after the seminal influence of the European *émigrés* who had fled Nazi Europe transformed American attitudes. I was lucky to run a chain of aggressive metropolitan bookshops able to challenge Net Book Agreement certainty and antiquated retail practices. And, most of all, I was lucky to work at Quartet and The Women's Press.

It was a very special atmosphere. Years later, I still rejoice that I shared such good times with so diverse an assortment of people, all trying to publish books: radicals and wide boys; captains of industry's daughters; toffs, wastrels and debutantes; feminists and celebrities; earnest and not so earnest writers; intellectuals, wankers and raving loonies. Each day was different, but everything that happened hinged on the attitudes and opinions of the man I called 'The Chairman'.

Anthony Blond, in his memoir *A Jew Made in England*, likened 27 Goodge Street to the court of Louis XIV. He had a point.

Naim once published a brilliant account of life at the Ethiopian court of Haile Selassie – *The Emperor* by Ryszard Kapuscinski – yet always denied its description of the intrigue and chaos as having any similarity to the dramas and tensions of Goodge Street or the feminist retreat in Shoreditch. Not that the dramas ever interfered with the parties.

I remember being driven terrifyingly fast into a dark German forest by a beautiful princess to drink champagne by a floodlit swimming pool; eating Sunday brunch at Elaine's; being asked to leave the Plaza for wearing inappropriate clothes; watching a man in a gorilla suit doing something rude with a banana in an Amsterdam night club; seeing the sunset over Manama having eaten so many huge lobsters I was ill; my first Broadway show; Covent Garden in the early hours, after a party where champagne and caviar had been consumed by over five hundred guests; telling the Chairman I thought he was nuts not to let Ruby Wax interview Leni Riefenstahl; driving to the Frankfurt Book Fair, and back, in a London taxi cab; escorting Lady Stevens of Ludgate to tea at the Ritz or lunch at the Four Seasons (and she was a Hungarian aristocrat, to boot!). And there are, to paraphrase Bennett Cerf's fine publishing memoir, just some memories at random.

Cerf wrote an obituary for Horace Liveright. Now long forgotten, Liveright was a gambler and autocratic publisher whose New York list was one of the most vibrant around in the 1920s. He did change things, founded The Modern Library, but destroyed himself in the process. After a somewhat ambivalent account of Liveright's career, Cerf concludes he 'had an amazing faculty for winning the unquestioning loyalty of a great number of fine men and women. They love him still. They probably always will ... [He had] a rare love of life and a reckless generosity they could not resist.' Like Horace Liveright, the

Chairman led a disparate team into many adventures. I remain convinced the real achievement of that unique time was the diversity of talent which was published. Quartet and The Women's Press produced some extraordinary books.

Years later, when a memoir portrayed Naim to be an illiterate bully, incapable of empathy or compromise, written by a woman who had been part of Quartet and whose life, she claimed, had been wasted and abused by a monster, all of us old Quartet staff signed a letter to the *New Statesman*, which had hailed the book as wonderful. What pleased me the most about this action, apart from the chance to rebuff the book's vicious sentiment, was the spontaneous manner in which we all sought to contact each other, reunite and nail our colours, yet again, to his remarkable mast.

TROUBLE IN STORE

A vital part of my working life involved my relationship with the Asprey family and the iconic Bond Street store that bore the legendary name and reputation for luxury. During the late 1990s, worrying events were taking place at Asprey's. I was particularly concerned about a deteriorating relationship between John Asprey and Ronald Lee, of R. A. Lee (Fine Arts) Ltd, which had been precarious at the best of times.

John, who was a marvelous salesman, with a charm to match, could nevertheless show a regrettable lack of deference when aroused. He also displayed impatience with people whose methods of working differed from his own. As a result, he tended to leave behind him a trail of disaffected individuals. Impulsiveness can have its merits, but a pause for reflection may sometimes make a better alternative. Ronald Lee, who was eighty-one, found John very difficult to deal with and there were many occasions when I had to intervene to lower the temperature. They were like chalk and cheese and a parting of the ways seemed likely to occur sooner rather than later. *The Antiques Trade Gazette* reported the incident that broke the camel's back. It concerned a failed attempt to purchase two historic panel paintings from the thirteenth century for the British Museum. They had come up for sale at the Bristol Auction Rooms, and Ronald was acting as under bidder on the museum's behalf. To his astonishment, he saw them being 'knocked down to Asprey (bidding on behalf of an anonymous British-based collector) for £120,000'.

> 'The long-established Lee family business was taken over last summer by Naim Attallah's Asprey Group. Son Charles continued as a director and Ronald was retained on a consultancy basis. Asprey maintain that, so far as they were concerned, Mr Lee was bidding in a private capacity and managing director Timothy Cooper described the incident as 'an unfortunate misunderstanding'. However, Ronald Lee described his position as 'untenable', and the eighty-one-year-old dealer added: 'I call it "quietly retiring", but it is a resignation.'

The old boy retired amid some bitterness. I tried to defuse the atmosphere as best I could, but John was beginning to show signs of petulance, another development that caused me unease. Our relationship was the key to the success of the Asprey group. We were different but complementary. Lord Rothermere (Vere), who was my friend, and even a member of the Academy Club, set an example as a very astute operator. A true press baron, well aware of his own limitations, he appointed David English to run his empire. It was a wise move that paid dividends. The secret of their success was that each adhered to his own area of responsibility without encroaching on the territory of the other. The fruits of this cooperation came with the emergence of the Daily Mail and General Trust as one of the most profitable press conglomerates in the United Kingdom. The same principle had so far applied to the Asprey group, John being chairman and the salesman par excellence while I was group chief executive.

This pairing worked extremely well until the group grew in size and stature; then cracks began to appear in the fabric of our relationship. At the instigation of his friends, and a number of members of his family, he began to interfere in areas where his competence was perhaps not up to the mark. He started issuing instructions to other sectors of the group, and while these were seldom fully implemented, they set off ripples of discord. None of this went down well with the senior management in the group, who invariably reported John's aberrations to me with a degree of apprehension. John would then in most cases deny the incidents concerned and matters would stabilize for a while. But these were danger signs portending a more serious situation ahead.

To move the focus from Asprey's internal problems to fashion, Tomasz Starzewski had been actively preparing for British Fashion Week, under the auspices of the Asprey group, as reported in *OK* magazine, with Baroness Izzy van Ranwyck as one of his patrons. His creations were displayed at the Natural History Museum in the British Fashion Council Tent. 'Tomasz's brand-new collection is fashionable, stylish and fun and his show was appreciated by a discerning audience.' My relationship with Tomasz was also great fun. Within the Asprey group he was directly responsible to me, and we had a close working partnership as a result of this proximity. It was certainly not bereft of its lighter moments. We both, as bon viveurs, liked to escape on occasion from the pressures placed upon us by our different roles. Our sexual orientation might not have been exactly the same, but we both loved women for a variety of reasons. In that domain the disparity worked in ways that were quite complementary and consolidated the relationship further. We undertook a few promotional trips abroad, accompanied by a small entourage of exquisite young ladies, who not only carried out their assignments with immaculate precision, but also brought colour and glamour to the proceedings. Life at the top end was undoubtedly good and we were determined to savour the delights while they lasted.

The Asprey Era

by Tomasz Starzewski

I had reached a point in my career when I needed to be part of a large parent company. A friend of mine mentioned Naim. I remember saying to him, 'I think I'm the wrong sex,' because Naim had always been known for supporting and encouraging quite a lot of my women friends over the years. But my friend said, 'He could still be the one, you ought to meet him.' I can't remember exactly how the interview was instigated, and unbeknown to me Naim was married to a Polish woman. I think that was a lucky connection and a good omen at that. From Naim's point of view, another advantage was the innocence of my ways, my unbounded enthusiasm plus an extraordinary clientele, which he reckoned would be a great asset to Asprey.

He made it very clear from the outset that we were not going to get old-fashioned management. It became as though we lived in a crazy, spontaneous though not reckless arena of activity; but each of us in the team knew that as far as the group was concerned the question was how Naim had managed to do something so impossible as set us up in this unique situation. We also knew that the way to get to him was through his PA, whoever the PA happened to be at the time. It was important for us to find out his mood and his thoughts, or whether we needed to orchestrate a campaign to win him round. I also knew he had fundamentally banned men from his floor. However, I was quick to work out that my worth would be greatly enhanced by tantalizing him with the latest acquisition of tender young staff with good credentials. Dealing with Naim was an education in itself.

Early in our association I told Naim I needed a managing director to look after the commercial aspects of the business and to keep a tight purse. One day I asked him if he remembered a pop/folk duo called Nina & Frederik. 'Well, their daughter is coming to see me,' I said. She had been working in Rome for Valentino and had moved to England because she wanted to be near her current beau, the ex-husband of a great friend of Naim's. I then met this incredibly beautiful, chic girl, Anna Maria van Pallandt, who looked just like her mother, Nina, used to look, but who was also relatively icy and distant. Naim interviewed her as well to see if she'd make part of the team, though it never occurred to me she might be material for a managing director. I may therefore have said something out of order when Naim announced, 'This is your new managing director.' Against all expectations, she turned out to be highly efficient and sensible. She took in her stride the responsibility of seeing that money kept coming in. My main concern at that point was to design clothes to sell and not to bother myself with accounts.

Eventually my team was headed by this beautiful Dutch girl, Anna Maria. My press attaché was Sophie Hedley and Fiona Sleeman looked after the customers admirably. They were all great girls. With Anna Maria it took time to earn her friendship as she was very reserved. She came from a colourful upbringing, her parents having been very much part of that swinging seventies mad calypso crowd, gravitating between Lisbon and Ibiza on their yacht, the Sir Leonard Lord. Yet their offspring was a very focused and serious young woman, protective and sensible. Soon after the wonderful Sophie Hedley was promoted by Naim to be the new PR of the company, I found a crazy French assistant designer who produced incredibly spectacular illustrations and had learnt English through watching television. It was a time of constant laughter. We were always in fits as we tried to work out how to sneak into Naim's office to get what we deserved – or thought we deserved. The process would be me saying, 'I do need a new watch,' or Sophie saying, 'I quite like that ring,' knowing full well Naim's unbelievable generosity. This always provoked the complete annoyance of the rest of the group, bar Tania Foster-Brown, who was then Naim's head of marketing and had that same wicked sense of humour. She was the one who taught me the works, because the other young woman belonging to Naim's inner sanctum at the time was Julia Ogilvy, whom I found completely terrifying.

It was a heady period. When I look back at it, I appreciate Naim's acquisition of Tomasz Starzewski even more than I did at the time. It was quite a controversial decision for Asprey. I remember sitting at a dinner party with some great friends of mine, and my hostess taking me aside and saying, 'I've placed you next to this person, because I think you ought to know there are some members of the Asprey family who deeply disapprove of you being part of the group.' And I remember being sat next to this unbelievably frosty Frenchwoman, who stuck her nose up at me and just said, 'Who are you?' then ignored me.

Naim showed great courage in bringing me into the fold, which at that point was really about jewellery and applied art, whether watches or pictures. It may be thought that fashion can be a logical extension of all that, but in fact it is quite a distinct sort of proposition. I don't think we ever realized how protected we were from Bond Street by Naim in Regent Street, who ensured the non-interference of the hierarchy. In the end it seemed the little group of us all working together somehow managed to charm its way through. Ultimately we were able to pacify the parent company, though of course we continued to shock. There was a very concentrated, sexy period when everything seemed to get bigger and greater than it probably was, but it was also a period of immense calm – though that, of course, was only a transient moment in one's life to be appreciated much later. Then Asprey was sold and the magical group of people who had all been working together disappeared and went elsewhere – but it had been an exhilarating experience.

I know there's a preconceived idea about fashion designers not needing to work hard, but that was never the case with me. I think I gave even slightly more than expected, though my curiosity was not just about what was happening with us in our sector, but what Naim was up to in publishing. Some of it consisted of the most exciting books of the day. I was fortunate to be able to lay my hands very quickly on a copy of anything that took my interest. Naim would send one round straight away. Another thing that made it a very exciting period was flying to New York to do a recce with a view to consolidating and enhancing our international reputation; or, on two or three occasions, travelling with Naim to Milan and to Paris, along with Anna Maria and Sophie, when a great time was had by all.

The best way for me to summarize that part of my life is to say it was an indelible era of spontaneity and mischief, though also very naïve and innocent. I'm not sure it could exist in today's context, because we probably thought we were being naughty and wicked when in fact it was underpinned by good intention and had a rather beautiful quality about it. I consider that says a lot about the people involved. And in a way we were never shaken up or brought to heel. I can recall Naim losing his temper only once, and it wasn't anything to do with work. We hadn't actually done anything wrong in the office – it may have been something we never told him. We were given unbelievable trust and that was truly magical. That's really it.

SELF PORTRAITS, NICHOLAS COLERIDGE AND I

Nicholas Coleridge's recent best-selling memoir reminded me of many things, and here's just one. In the autumn of 1993, the painter and portraitist Emma Sergeant was interviewed by Celia Lyttleton, the art critic, for an article Jane Procter, the editor of *Tatler*, had commissioned. The subject was society's promising young painters. The feature had to be accompanied by a good example of the work of each artist by means of a coloured transparency of their choice. Emma's preference – a large portrait of me which she had painted in 1991 – was sent to Celia, who in turn presented it to Jane Procter. The latter saw red and refused point blank to entertain its inclusion. Emma telephoned me to enquire whether I knew what lay behind her opposition. Naturally I was taken aback and at the same time perplexed. Although the reason for this bizarre turn of events was never given, informed sources attributed Jane's intemperate behaviour to my having made her husband, Tom Goldstaub, redundant following Asprey's acquisition of Mappin & Webb, where he had been the head of marketing.

As it happened, my relationship with Jane's husband could not have been better. Now, as managing director of Fintex, the fine-cloth merchants in Golden Square, he was always perfectly accommodating and I subsequently became one of his most regular customers. I therefore felt at a loss to understand his wife's action, given the importance of the Asprey group in the luxury-goods market and its close association with Condé Nast, principally as advertisers. Jane's throwing down the gauntlet, I could only conclude, was a deliberate attempt to humiliate me and one to which I had to respond. My reaction was swift. I suspended all advertising contracts for the Asprey group with Condé Nast until such time as the incident had been properly investigated by Jane's employers and a satisfactory explanation produced.

A few weeks later, when tempers had cooled, a conciliatory top-level meeting took place at Condé Nast, chaired by their managing director, Nicholas Coleridge, whose first book Quartet had proudly published. Present at the meeting was myself accompanied by Tania Foster-Brown, who had once worked at Vogue House but was there this time acting as a peace broker. A weepy Jane Procter was summoned to the meeting and tried to bluff her way through with some cock-and-bull story that made little sense. A suggestion that Emma Sergeant was stirring the pot went down badly with me and almost brought the meeting to an abrupt halt. At this point Procter changed her tactics, becoming apologetic and managing to placate her employer as well as myself with the claim that she was possibly the victim of circumstance. A few months later the whole truth had come out and Procter and *Tatler* had parted company.

After meeting for the first time in 1982, Emma Sergeant and I got on so well that our encounter led to a friendship that remained close over the years that followed. Her first portrait of me was done in charcoal the year of our meeting and hangs today in our house in the Dordogne. It is a moody picture, strongly expressive of character and conveying a lean and hungry look. Emma must have captured me at a phase in my life when those characteristics were dominant. It was also the time when Rupert Birley and I, having met at Emma's, took to meeting up regularly at her place for coffee in the early mornings. These were gatherings that I sorely missed after Rupert's tragic disappearance on a beach off West Africa. He was undoubtedly the embodiment of that cliché 'the heartthrob of his generation', whose good looks, poise, charm and outstanding intellect combined to set him apart from his peers. All those who knew him well and grew to love him – among whom I count myself – were shattered by his loss, which happened when he was at the zenith of his youth with a life full of promise ahead of him.

In January 1994, I wrote a foreword to mark an exhibition of Emma's work at Agnew's. It took the form of a tribute which best encapsulates our friendship and gives an insight into her background and her work as an artist. For that reason, I reproduce it in full.

Orpheus and the Underworld

Emma Sergeant, 1994

I first met Emma Sergeant twelve years ago at a Quartet Books party. Emma was then in her early twenties and exuded an energy and zest for life which sent out shock waves to those around her. Her youthful beauty was untarnished by the levy of life and when she moved about the room, eyes followed her.

In those days it was often alleged that I employed only beautiful and desirable young women who graced the London social scene and attended my publishing parties: if Emma had possessed mere beauty alone, she might easily have merged into the general glamour of the occasion. But she had other qualities: a sublime smile, a musical resonance in her laughter, an impish elegance and a light in her eyes which one sensed was linked to her vision of the world. All this, and much more, made her stand head and shoulders above the rest.

As I came to know Emma Sergeant I discovered that her

artistic talent was outstanding. From the outset she had been determined to succeed and had worked very hard to ensure a steady progression in her oeuvre, at an early age demonstrating the boldness required to push back the boundaries of modern art. As a result the evolution of her work is truly remarkable. There is nothing preordained about it; it does not follow a set pattern; it possesses enormous power and the ability to surprise, even to shock.

She studied for two years at Camberwell and then at the Slade, graduating in 1983. In 1981 she won the Imperial Tobacco Portrait Award for her painting of Lord David Cecil. This resulted in commissions to paint Lord Olivier among others.

In 1986, an exhibition of her paintings and drawings of Afghanistan was held at Agnew's to raise money for UNICEF to help Afghan refugees. In 1988 she exhibited "Faces from Four Continents", again at Agnew's. She has had many commissions to paint portraits, which include Imran Khan, Lord Carrington, the Earl of Verulam and Roani, Chief of the Kayapo Indians.

A RUMBLE FROM THE JUNGLE

Of the many photographic books I published, *Jungle Fever* retains a special place in my heart. Its publication in 1982 precipitated a whirlwind of controversy. The first published collection of photographs by Jean Paul Goude, then unknown to most Englishmen (and women come to that), its cover featured a naked Grace Jones (also then unknown in this country) as a caged creature, her sharp glistening teeth eager for the kill. Across the top of the cage was a notice that read: 'Do not feed the animal'.

The feminist lobby condemned it as the most humiliating and demeaning portrayal of a woman ever published. It could perhaps also have been said to be the most extraordinary portrait ever of a woman by her lover; the artist asserted that it was he who had caged the beast. Some years later Jean-Paul was quoted as saying of their relationship, 'I was Svengali to Grace's talent. As long as I seduced her, and she was in love or infatuated with me, I could do anything I wanted with her creatively, because I was constantly admiring and paying tribute to her. It all ended dramatically when she felt I had started to love the character we had created more than I loved her.'

They remained friends, but he regretted the way the relationship had, in his view, ended prematurely, the crunch having come when Grace read the chapter he wrote about her in *Jungle Fever*. She was 'so angry and felt so betrayed that we couldn't go on. Creatively, it was just impossible.'

Jungle Fever was a dazzling trawl through the international underworld of beauty, humour and eroticism. Jean-Paul Goude, the uninhibited graphic genius behind the manipulated images, was once aptly described by Esquire magazine as 'The French Correction'. Through his surrealist-influenced techniques, placed at the service of high-profile advertising campaigns, the public probably became more aware of his work than of his name. In many ways, he was always ahead of his time, going beyond kitsch to produce new configurations of images to stretch the imagination afresh.

His aim was to make nature conform to his fantasies, as the collection in the book illustrated. Besides Grace Jones, it included Kellie the Evangelist Stripper, Sabu, Gene Kelly, Zouzou, Little Beaver, Judith Jamison, Russ Tamblyn, Toukie, Radiah, the Sex Circus of Eighth Avenue and the nocturnal *flore et faune* of 42nd Street. The only thing these disparate fantasies had in common was Jean-Paul Goude, but even so, as the blurb explained, they formed 'a very special community: they have been made perfect to fit the world as Goude wants it to be – there are stilts for Radiah, a new ass for Toukie, a crew cut for Grace Jones'. To give an adequate account of Goude's artistic range, his 'work must be considered that of a painter, photographer, sculptor, musician, dancer, couturier, stage director and set designer – all of these and none of them. "To say the truth," Goude says, "I see myself as an artist who uses the best means available to get a point across. What comes first is the necessity to communicate 'my world'. Through the use of different media, I am able to show what to me is important."' He scornfully dismissed a plastic surgeon who refused to follow his design for a girlfriend's new nose. '"After all, I am an artist," Goude says. "What does he know?"'

It was the ultimate effect that concerned him: 'the extension of a limb, the padding of a flank, a nip here and a tuck there – and suddenly the fantastic people and places of Jean-Paul Goude have become his forever and hopefully the reader's too'. *Jungle Fever* sold extremely well, and was destined to become a collector's item. Copies can now sell for hundreds of pounds on the Internet.

GILLIAN GREENWOOD

Gillian Greenwood was the editor for Robin Clark, a small paperback imprint I had bought, specialising in literary reprints. She took over the editorship of the *Literary Review* from Anne Smith, presiding over the journal during the most turbulent part of its history. In 1984, however, she decided to join the team for Melvyn Bragg's *South Bank Show*, fulfilling a wish she had always expressed to make a career in television. The opportunity came and she could not pass it by. I was thrilled at the prospect of her finding the niche she was seeking. I had grown very fond of her and admired her courage and tenacity under fire. During the inflated controversy over *God Cried* (see below), she stood resolute and fought her corner, refusing to be intimidated when the onslaught was at its most vituperative.

She wrote of her time with me, calling the piece:

Bumpy Rides and Gentle Days

Gillian Greenwood

I first met Naim Attallah in the early 1980s through the late Patrick Cosgrave, a right-wing journalist and former contributor to the magazine *Books and Bookmen* (where I had been assistant editor – my first proper job – until its sudden bankruptcy). Patrick presented me to Naim as a contender to run a small paperback imprint of Quartet Books, Robin Clark. I knew something about books, but little about publishing. None the less Naim decided to give me a go. People have implied that Naim's employment policies were based on the social status of the applicants. That wasn't so in my case, and I like to think it was my ability that he recognized as well as Patrick's recommendation.

… Twenty-odd years later I have a recurring dream that I am recalled to the *Literary Review*. It is always a pleasant dream and is indicative of the magical time I and all those other young (mainly) women had in Naim's employ. I spent three years editing the Literary Review and they were exciting and very happy times, even with the occasional bumpy ride, and I will always be deeply grateful to Naim for the extraordinary opportunity he gave me.

At first our offices were in the Goodge Street rabbit warren, later in a beautiful building in Beak Street. The Literary Review office had been Naim's at one point and he had left behind a magnificent chair and desk which I sat on and behind, much to the amusement of my contributors, many of whom liked to visit regularly. In the case of the male contributors this was probably in part because, particularly in the Goodge Street days when we shared premises with Quartet, it must have been like visiting some exotic girls' finishing school. Naim liked young women – that is self-evident– but my recollection is that most of them were clever and efficient. Many of them were also well connected, but their presence wasn't because of some desire on Naim's part to be connected to the British upper classes but a canny understanding of how publicity and the establishment can be worked when cash is short. And cash was short since the whole publishing enterprise was underwritten and, certainly in the case of the magazine, heavily subsidized by Naim. We were very fortunate in having Bridget Heathcoat-Amory as our business manager. She ran a tight, if unprofitable, financial ship, her contacts were spectacular, and her party skills (I have a memory of lethal White Lady cocktails) devastating. Between us (and Kathy O'Shaughnessy, the deputy editor) we managed to persuade all sorts of wonderful establishment novelists, writers and journalists to write for the *Literary Review* for almost nothing.

The bumpiest moment of my relationship with both the magazine and Naim was over a review by Roald Dahl of a book about the plight of the Palestinians, *God Cried*. It was a Quartet publication. Naim had been introduced to Roald Dahl and they had discovered a mutual sympathy for the Palestinian cause. Naim phoned me to suggest that Dahl should review the book. It was unusual for Naim to involve himself with commissioning, but I wasn't going to look a gift horse in the mouth. Roald Dahl was a coup for the magazine. When the piece came in we were aware it was provocative and there was much debate about publication. We consulted our lawyer and mentor, Michael Rubinstein, who assured me that in his opinion the piece was anti-Zionist but not anti-Semitic. I was reassured. We published. All hell broke loose. Dahl, it turned out, had been accused of anti-Semitism by Christopher Hitchens. Editorials were written.

Lobbies were mounted. Naim found it challenging and exciting. I found it confusing and stressful, but together we faced it out.

… But this moment of high political drama was not the norm. It was a gentle life of reading and commissioning and trips to the printers, interspersed with magnificent parties, hot tickets in a journalistic pool, presided over by Naim, who stood beaming over the social scene like some Anthony Powell creation. Life in the London of the 1980s would simply have been much duller without him. Above all else, it was fantastic fun, and how rare it is to be able to say that these days about a job. It was a privilege to be a part of it. I left after three years because, although I loved literature and the magazine, I wanted to make films. But I still dream.

KATHY O'SHAUGHNESSY

Kathy O'Shaughnessy has become one of our leading cultural critics, but she was very much the delightful ingénue when I first met her:

Life at the Literary Review

Kathy O'Shaughnessy

I hadn't spoken to Naim for years, when out of the blue came a phone call, asking me to write a piece about the *Literary Review*. Within minutes I was experiencing his personality in full, just like in the old days. He was telling me not only I could write anything I liked, but – 'If I was a monster, you can say I was a monster!'

(voice rising to an excited, already indignant little scream).

'Only a very benign monster,' I replied, but I was laughing away, as Naim's enthusiasm and un-English lack of restraint took me back twenty years. He was far and away the most enthusiastic employer I ever had, with a generosity, theatricality and warmth that was extremely endearing, and a long way from corporate publishing as it is today.

I was twenty-three when I went to work for the *Literary Review*. I had abandoned my post-graduate degree at Oxford on Byron ('See you at the end of the term,' my supervisor had said on day one, somewhat dispiritingly) and begun writing book reviews for *Time Out* and the *Spectator*. Shortly after that I heard about an impossibly perfect vacancy – deputy editor at the *Literary Review*. I applied and was interviewed by Gillian Greenwood, the editor, who seemed at once interesting, funny, lively – the sort of person you'd like as a friend, let alone to work for. Happily she took me on, and the next day I went to meet the already legendary Naim. 'Welcome to the family!' he said, as he vigorously shook my hand. My eyes were wandering, however, to the far end of the office, where a stupendously good-looking blonde had materialized as out of nowhere; and this was to be a recurring feature of working for Naim: beauties popping up in doorways and offices and desks like hallucinations, each more splendid than the last.

The *Literary Review* offices were above a hairdresser's and a strong-smelling restaurant: you had to climb three flights of rickety stairs to get to the two rooms in question – one for editorial (Gillian and myself), one for business (Bridget Heathcoat-Amory). And that, beguilingly, was it – so small-scale, so DIY, so very hands on! On one trestle table lay the books ready to be reviewed. Gillian sat at the large leather-topped boss's desk; I sat at a suitably smaller desk facing the traffic of Goodge

Street, and so began my career in literary journalism. (So, too, my intense career as a passive smoker, as all of the magazine's editors smoked with a will, a few feet away from me; yet I have to admit to a nostalgic fondness for that smoky office of the past, with its piled-up books and tottering, over-spilling ashtrays, redolent of a more relaxed and less health-'n'-self-obsessed era.)

It was a dream of a job for a twenty-three-year-old. Each morning began with a pile of post: cardboard-encased books, which, like a cluster of presents, looked all the more promising for being wrapped; and the copy – typewritten, of course. It was a thrill to open the envelope and discover the copy. The typewritten pages had a presence and shadowy sort of character that today's computer print-out could never aspire to – maybe the n's didn't print properly, the page might be clotted with inky crossing-outs; the very letters bore the imprint of effort expended. Then, if the copy was unexpectedly funny, or clever or just felicitous, you had the feeling of treasure-in-the-making. If it was flaccid or lacklustre – well, cutting and editing could accomplish a lot. This was my editing apprenticeship, and I loved it.

Gillian was my first and main boss at the *Literary Review*. Like most fine editors, she was herself a gifted writer, and I learnt all about editing and commissioning and putting a magazine together from her. It was a tiny operation, just the two of us, and it felt lucky to be part of this two-man or rather two-woman team – the job so enjoyable it was like being a child in a sweetshop. I soon began writing for the magazine myself, as well as helping with the commissioning. But then we had to do everything: sometimes even driving round London and dropping off batches of the newly printed issue at the not-so-many booksellers that took it at the time; and always spending one exhausting but satisfying day a month putting the magazine to bed at 'the printers'. The printers were in fact a husband and wife team, Ken and May, operating out of a small house in Chatham, Kent. There we spent many hours in the dank and indeed dark basement correcting the final proofs as the magazine went to film. It was a bonding experience and we became close friends.

Part of the job was of course meeting the writers. Broke! solitary! talented, not so talented – satirical – worthy – brilliant – the whole gamut passed through the doors of the *Literary Review*; and if they didn't pass through our office they very likely appeared at Naim's parties or at his dining table in Poland Street, where you might meet Ryszard Kapuscinski on one day, J. P. Donleavy on another, Hilary Mantel on another, and so on. In the early days our contributors included, to take a random sample from the time: Francis Wheen, David Profumo, A. N. Wilson, Colin MacCabe, A. L. Rowse, John Lahr, Carlo Gebler, Max Egremont, Geoff Dyer, Sheila MacLeod, John Orr, Christopher Hawtree, Martin Walker, Antony Beevor, Richard Williams, Christopher Hitchens, Grey Gowrie, Lucretia Stewart, Neil Berry, Kyril Fitzlyon and others. For their pains, they were paid the princely sums of £10 or £20! But the world of books was different then: there was less money around, marketing was less to the forefront, and those mergers between the publishing houses were still an evil mirage on the horizon.

The magazine's offices were in Goodge Street, busy and lively with its sandwich bars, Italian delis, shoe shops, bikers dashing in and out with their important packages, and Charlotte Street with its restaurants round the corner (the Spaghetti House being our top budget outing). It was a short walk from there to Naim's office, where we would either have lunch (his cook Charlotte was a maestro of the kitchen as well as a beauty, *ça va sans dire*); or debate the perennial problems of circulation, advertising and distribution; or receive Naim's advice, and above all, almost intravenously it was so intense, his enthusiasm. Clapping his hands, exclaiming, he would tell us his idea for a mischievous article that would stir up controversy, and so help the magazine's ailing circulation; and indeed circulation was part of the aim, but so, it must be said, was Naim's badly concealed and infectious joy in taking on the British establishment.

At a certain point the *Literary Review* moved its offices to 51 Beak Street, future site of the Academy Club. But wherever we were, the spirit of Naim was always hovering around. He would ring up on the telephone, and somehow his voice lingered in the office, with its rolled r's, and his favourite phrases – 'at the end of the day' – or, my particular favourite, the exclamation, 'Bobby's your uncle!' In short, the experience of working on the *Literary Review* could not be disentangled from the experience of working for Naim, because you were always conscious of the increasingly wide-ranging activities of your unpredictable impresario boss, who had this protean fund of energy and will, to the point of metamorphosis. One moment he was publishing books, the next he was launching perfumes with the titles Avant l'Amour and Après l'Amour, unmistakable variations on a certain theme, and doubtless there would be a party held in some splendid arena such as the Reform Club or the Travellers' Club. As Naim held one party after another, London seemed to open its doors to reveal an endless number of potential party venues.

The *Literary Review* filled a niche determined in part by its competitors. The *London Review of Books* clearly occupied the intellectual high ground; *The Times Literary Supplement* had its firm allegiance to matters academic; and so the *Literary Review* was there to be perhaps more comfortably on the ground, not highbrow, but not lowbrow either; distinctly lively; drawing on journalists as well as writers. The writers ranged from the famous to the little known, and that was one of the pleasures of working on the magazine – coming into contact with many relatively unsung writers who wanted to bring their particular sensibility and encounter with literature to paper in some form. It always seemed to me that this 'middle ground' gave the *Literary Review* freedom to run, for example, exhaustive interviews with writers that went at a serious ruminative pace, giving place to all kinds of unshowy detail that was nevertheless of literary interest.

Gradually the *Literary Review* became a home for maverick columnists such as A. N. Wilson or Cosmo Landesman, where humorous or odder and more free-wheeling sentiments could be expressed in pieces that were short but piquant; later on, when Auberon Waugh became editor, this bent, the sense of the magazine's character as idiosyncratic, was to become more developed, as Auberon Waugh stamped his own exceedingly British and in some ways divinely eccentric personality on it.

There were three editors at the Literary Review during the period I worked there: Gillian, Emma Soames and Auberon Waugh. I shall always be grateful to Gillian or Gilly for taking me on. Gilly had diplomacy, patience, sensitivity and an unerring feeling for whether or not a piece worked. We ran early pieces by David Sexton (two particularly good ones I still remember, one on Tolstoy's diaries, another on father and son in fiction, focusing on the Waughs), Paul Taylor and Andrew Graham-Dixon, and many others. The magazine was going from strength to strength when she left, to go to the *South Bank Show*, and a new editor was appointed, Emma Soames.

Emma was confident and instinctively clever in her judgements, and gifted with wit in abundance (certain jokes still make me laugh – 'TAXI!' to be shrieked when you want to get out of a situation). The magazine began to take off in new directions: we changed its typeface and logo, got in a very funny cartoon from Nick Newman and Ian Hislop, thought up the anonymous column 'Scrivener' (usually about the nefarious goings-on behind the scenes in newspapers); I persuaded Richard Curtis to do a television column, which was hilarious, and which he later passed on to Stephen Fry, who, perhaps less funny than Richard, was nevertheless an elegant, fluent and reliable contributor. In a relatively short time Emma had made her decisive mark as editor, and we had become great friends (we really did have a lot of laughs), but change was afoot again. Anna Wintour had come back from New York to edit *Vogue* and was claiming Emma as her features editor. Once more the editorship was vacant and this time Naim appointed Auberon Waugh.

I had met Bron, as he was universally known, at a *Spectator* lunch, but nevertheless his columns at the time, which could be so provocative, filled me with apprehension. The *Literary Review* was an extremely small ship. As deputy you sat about five feet away from the editor, and all day you shared an office, just the two of you in the one room; if one of you was on the telephone, for example, the other heard everything you said. In short, it was essential to get on.

However, when Bron did appear, wearing that memorable hat, I liked him immediately. It was in fact impossible not to. He was courteous, kind, considerate, but none of these words (though true) get what was fun about him, which was his drollery, his immensely discerning eye, his effortless dry intelligence – which he wore, almost as a point of honour, lightly. Nor was he ever affected. I couldn't imagine him ever adopting a sentiment that wasn't truly his. He had an original interesting mind, and was without fail interesting to talk to.

I think Bron was grateful for my help because of course it was new to him, running a literary magazine. But it was clear to me that he viewed me sometimes as a sentimental leftie. We always tried to run a short story and we were inundated by short stories, most of which were, to put it bluntly, screamingly terrible. But I remember one on the slush pile depicting a mining community devastated by pit closure. It seemed to me a moving story, that felt authentic, even though the treatment of the subject was in no way surprising; and I showed it to Bron. He read it and was horrified by my suggestion that we run it, seeing it as predictable in the nth degree. I suspect we both had a bit of a case.

As a team, we had our comic moments. I remember that if I arrived and Bron had got there first, perhaps even just fractionally earlier than me, and was sitting ensconced at his desk, I would feel extremely guilty, as if his silent diligence were a reproach. Later, as we became more relaxed colleagues, it turned out that he experienced the identically persecuted sensation if I had preceded his arrival.

With such a small staff there was always a great deal to do. There were proofs to correct and re-correct, proofs to be sent out to authors, authors' corrections to transfer, 'shouts' on the cover to be decided, illustrations from publishers to be chased up, short stories to read, and so on; and it was characteristic of Bron that shortly after arriving he advertised for a 'slave' to work gratis in the *LR* office, on the grounds that this menial apprenticeship would be the gateway to future triumphs. I was sceptical if amused, but sure enough, the next month found Grub Smith, whose very name seemed to beggar belief, like some fantastic projection of a Dickensian imagination, sitting at an exceedingly small and low table, almost child-level, below the intercom phone near the door, our slave for the immediate future. Bron was proved right.

Auberon Waugh did to a degree re-mint the magazine in his own image, with his opening column 'From the Pulpit', and that was very good for the magazine's profile. At the same time the magazine became more hospitable to a strand of literary activity that was in some ways proudly anti-intellectual (I always remember him saying that Proust would have written a good book had he kept it to one volume), yet in other ways deeply committed to the concept of the literary, even if it came to that notion by ranging it against a partly exaggerated foe, the too-intellectual or the narrowly academic. Perhaps this battle too found its secret expression in Bron's commitment to placing, at all costs, the word 'sex' on the cover (no dry magazine this). Thus it became a running and well-known joke: even if this month's literary offerings refused to yield anything involving sex, there might be a piece by David Sexton, that would then get cover billing, as in – 'David SEXton on Kingsley Amis', and so on. And then obviously there followed all sorts of things like the 'Bad Sex' competition, all of which earned the *Literary Review* more publicity. But by this time I had followed Emma to Condé Nast, to edit the arts and books section of *Vogue*.

During all this time Naim was the kindest and most supportive of bosses. Although he sometimes got a mixed press, being often depicted as a very sexist employer, the truth is that Naim defied simple labelling. In the world of British publishing he always seemed to me to be something of an innocent who, like all essentially good-hearted people, expected the same in return – windfalls of goodwill. One has to remember certain things about Naim: that it was he who also owned and funded The Women's Press, and published an imprint like Quartet Encounters, run by Stephen Pickles – a less commercial, more riskily high-minded list would be hard to find.

When I came to leave the *Literary Review*, I helped Bron find a successor (pointing him in the directon of Kate Kellaway, for which he was always grateful). But before then various candidates came along, including the sadly late Linda Brandon. Linda – who was to die tragically young – was extremely intelligent, with an exceptional CV. She had also become a lesbian, and wore short hair and dungarees. Accordingly we had an interview: Naim, Bron, Linda and myself. Bron, who was usually utterly unlike the persona of his more extreme kind of column, behaved briefly like the said invented persona – as soon as Linda had gone, he dismissed her completely. Naim on the other hand was perplexed by the single-mindedness of Bron's response. All he could see was this incredibly impressive CV, and her pleasantness as a person. Naim and I argued for her, but Bron was resolute.

That was typical of Naim, who had a disinterested open-minded respect for achievement, and at the risk of stating the obvious, an appreciation of women above and beyond their appearance.

Well, to be fair he liked that, too. But then, to recycle that great last line in cinema, nobody's perfect.

A WONDERFUL GESTURE

By the end of September 1984, I had made my peace with Carol Rumens, the poetry editor of the *Literary Review*, who had left because of her strong disapproval of Roald Dahl's review of *God Cried* [see above]. I was utterly moved when I discovered that a poem she had written about the Arab-Jewish conflict was dedicated to me. It appeared in the *New Statesman* in their issue of 30 September. The poem, which was a cry for peace, was so beautifully worded and full of sympathy for both Jews and Arabs, that it deserves today, as it did then, as large an audience as it can reach. It is as relevant now as it was at the time and I am proud to include it here in full.

Carol Rumens

A NEW SONG
(for Naim Attallah)

'Thou feedest them with the bread of tears, and givest them tears to drink in great measure.' (Psalm 80)

>Silence of old Europe
>Not even the Shofar
>Can utter: Maidenek,
>Mauthausen, Babi Yar –
>
>Death of the innocent being
>Our speciality,
>Let us add Lebanon's breaking
>Sob to the litany.
>
>So many now to mourn for,
>Where can the psalmist start?
>Only from where his home is
>And his untidy heart.
>
>We pluck our first allegiance
>With a curled baby-hand
>And peer between its fingers
>To see our promised land:
>
>Yours on a hillside clouded
>With olives; mine a cot
>In a London postal district,
>Its trees long spilled as soot.

Memories

On a late wartime morning
In Northern Europe, my
First breath seems implicated
In yells of victory.

But it's the quieter voices
That keep on trying to rhyme,
Telling me almost nothing
But filling me with shame.

Germany in the thirties
And half my family tree
Bent to an SS microscope's
Mock genealogy.

Duly pronounced untainted
For his Aryan bride,
My uncle says it's proven,
There are no Jews on his side.

Ancient, unsummoned, shameless,
The burdens of prejudice –
All through my London childhood
Adults with kindly eyes

And sharp throw-away phrases
Like bits of shopfront glass
(Grandfather: 'He's a schneider' –
Frowning and treadling fast.)

Later, the flickering movie:
Greyish, diaphanous
Horrors that stared and whispered,
'God has forgotten us.'

Naim Attallah

Oh, if our unborn children
Must go like us to flame,
Will you consent in silence
Or gasp and burn with them?

It is so late in the century
And still the favourite beast
Whines in the concrete bunker.
And still the trucks roll east

And east and east through whited
Snowfields of the mind
Towards the dark encampment;
Still the Siberian wind

Blows across Prague and Warsaw,
The voices in our head
Baying for a scapegoat:
Historians gone mad,

Thugs on a street corner,
The righteous Gentile who
Pins Lebanon like a yellow star
To the coat of every Jew.

Silences of old Europe,
Be broken; let us seek
The judgement of the silenced
And ask how they would speak.

Then let the street musician
Crouched in the cruel sun
Play for each passing, stateless
Child of Babylon

Memories

Conciliatory harmonies
Against the human grain,
A slow psalm of two nations
Mourning a common pain –

Hebrew and Arabic mingling
Their single-rooted vine,
Olives and roses falling
To sweeten Palestine.

GOD CRIED

I had an uncanny premonition that 1983 would be a difficult year. So far my new career as a publisher had been bumpy but without too much discomfort. The controversies of the past twelve months had left my fighting spirit intact. My wife Maria maintained that I always courted trouble because basically I enjoyed adversarial combat. It was my way, she said, of reassuring myself that I was capable of defending what I felt to be right, whether ideological or political. There was an element of truth in that, I had to admit. I function at my best under pressure and relish the art of tactical manoeuvring. I never seek conflict for its own sake, and I would rather win a contest through debate or highly charged negotiation. To pit one's intellect against that of an opponent and win is far more satisfying and morale boosting than entering into some vulgar spat that is undignified for both winner and loser. While I am prone to flare up at the least provocation, I try to leave matters to simmer down before I react.

The start of 1983 was benign enough. The attentions of the press seemed to become focused on Sabrina Guinness, who was causing a great deal of speculation following her appointment to head a book club affiliated with the *Literary Review*. The announcement of the launch party led to various cheap asides in the press questioning her suitability to run such an enterprise. The gossip writers had a field-day delving into her background and claiming she possessed the less serious attributes of a social butterfly. Some reported that she was presently engrossed in books to bring her up to the mark in her new job; others held more cynical views. Sabrina herself showed great reserve, refusing to let her feathers be ruffled by this onslaught of adverse publicity. She proved to have an impressive measure of resilience in coping with the situation and rose above it all with dignity.

Sabrina organized the launch party, which was notable for the rich mixture of people it assembled. The literati were there in force, alongside the gossip mongers who could not resist the chance of picking up more material for their columns. The usual crowd of book-event attenders chattered with delight as they circulated among the beautiful young women there to show their solidarity with Sabrina, whom they considered one of the gang. Roald Dahl, who reputedly never attended a publishing function unless it was to do with one of his own books, had responded to a personal invitation from Sabrina. He was there with his daughter Tessa, who had had a small part in *The Slipper and the Rose*, the film I had produced with David Frost.

Roald Dahl and I began our conversation with his asking me in which part of Palestine I was raised. He knew the country well, he added, having been stationed there as a fighter pilot with the RAF during the Second World War. Their target at the time had been the Vichy administration in Lebanon. When I told him my home town was Haifa, his face lit up. The mention of it brought back poignant memories, he said. He described how the Arab peasants would wave to signify good luck as the fighter planes flew over Mount Carmel on their outward sortie, and waved to welcome them back when the pilots made a safe return to base. As he was speaking a sudden thought shot into my mind. Quartet was about to publish a book, hard-hitting in its views, on Israel's invasion of Lebanon. Perhaps we could ask Dahl to write a piece about it for the *Literary Review*.

The title was *God Cried* and the author was Tony Clifton, a well-known and respected journalist who worked for *Newsweek*; his collaborator was Catherine LeRoy, a veteran French war photographer. The book described, in harrowing detail, by way of its words and pictures, the violence and destruction inflicted by the Israeli armed forces on West Beirut through shelling and bombing and the harsh realities of their occupation. Its title derived from a piece of Palestinian black humour circulating in the Middle East at the time, it being said that God had agreed to answer one question each from Ronald Reagan, Leonid Brezhnev and Yasser Arafat. The American president asked his question first, wanting to know when an American would become leader of the whole world. 'In fifty years,' said God. And Reagan cried. When God asked him why he cried, he said, 'Because it won't happen in my lifetime.' Next it was the turn of Brezhnev, who wished to know from God when the whole world would be communist. 'In a hundred years,' said God. And Brezhnev cried for the same reason as Reagan. And when it came to Arafat, he asked God, 'When will my people have a homeland of their own?' And God cried.

Before I could broach my idea for a review from Dahl, I needed to observe the protocol between proprietor and editor and consult with Gillian Greenwood on whether she would agree. Hers was the last word editorially on what went into the magazine and the choice of contributors. I tracked her down in another corner of the launch party and put the question. She gave me the green light at once. Returning to Roald Dahl, I asked him whether he might be interested in writing such a review. His reaction was abrupt to the point of hostility. He received many requests from publishers to review their books, he told me, and never agreed to do one, irrespective of the book's merits. He would certainly make no exception to the rule on this or any other occasion. Dahl could display a rather intimidating side if he was roused and I stood there dumbstruck. The earlier warmth of our conversation evaporated instantly. I mumbled a few meaningless phrases and retreated politely, under the pretext of not wishing to monopolize his company.

After recovering from the shock of this sudden embarrassment – not because of his refusal to write a review but because of the manner in which he had expressed it – I went to seek Tessa Dahl to protest at how I was mortified by her father. She was not in the least surprised to hear my tale, being quite accustomed to his brusque moods. Would she be able to persuade him to change his mind, I wondered, given his interest in Palestine? If we sent her a copy as soon as the book became available, she suggested, she would try her very best to cajole him into a change of heart. I held out very little hope of her succeeding, but sent her *God Cried* even so, just for its promotional value.

Hardly a week had passed before a letter from Dahl arrived enclosing a comprehensive review and informing me that he did not wish to receive any payment for it. I was thrilled until I started to read it, and then my spirits fell in semi-horror. It was couched in language unhoned by diplomacy and without the least regard for the art of gentle censure. Dahl was bold and unrelentingly scathing in his condemnation of Israel for its brutal opportunistic incursion, which had taken its army all the way to Beirut. I knew at once that publication of the piece would send the influential pro-Zionist lobby into a frenzy of rage. It was addressed to the editor of the *Literary Review*, and since the decision on whether to print it would have to be Gillian Greenwood's, I passed it on quickly.

Gillian shared my concerns and we agreed we must first check it out with our lawyer, Michael Rubinstein, whose advice and suggestions would be pertinent since he was himself Jewish. To our utter surprise, Michael liked and approved of Dahl's review. Apart from editing out a few of the more intemperate expressions, he urged us to publish it. The reason he gave was that criticism of Israel should not, when it was deserved, be silenced by those who chose to see only one side of the equation. Michael was a liberal and an ardent champion of the oppressed and dispossessed. His last words to Gillian and myself were: 'Publish and be damned.' We did publish; and we were damned.

The reaction to the review was far more extreme that we had anticipated. Apart from the overreaction of the Jewish lobby, the friends of Israel in the media became virulent in their onslaught on Dahl, myself and the *Literary Review*. The attacks came in from every side, even reaching a pitch where many journalists and politicians of high standing called for a boycott of the magazine and anyone connected with it. Every day something more vicious than the day before appeared somewhere, with accusations of anti-Semitism becoming more strident and preposterous as the campaign to discredit Quartet and the book gained momentum. Dahl did nothing to help matters by growing even more combative and being provoked into making outrageous, inflammatory responses. He was not in the least chastened by all that was being said about him. On the contrary, he expounded on his views and riled the press by being abrasive and dismissing their questions out of hand. There was no way of putting a gag on him and no point in asking him to cool things down. He had the bit between his teeth and nothing would stop him giving our adversaries all the fuel they could have wished for to keep their engines firing.

Time after time I was asked by the press to comment on one or other of his utterances and found myself at a loss for an appropriate response. He was still my contributor and I could not let it seem I was being unsupportive of his right to hold his own views. It was a difficult situation that had gone beyond control. Although we were fighting from the same corner, our temperaments and perceptions of how to get a grip on things were vastly different. In a way, he had dug himself into a hole from which he could not extricate himself without sustaining some damage. When the whole uproar began I had, in fact, been away for a break in Italy, visiting Lord Lambton, who had invited us for the first time to stay at his villa outside Siena. The holiday was constantly interrupted by the latest reports from London as the drama began to unfold. On the way back to England we travelled via Florence to meet Harold Acton. He had asked us to tea at his famous palazzo overlooking the city, and afterwards took us to walk in the extensive historic gardens, insisting on having his photograph taken with my wife. From that rarefied and civilized experience I plunged into the explosive turmoil back in London, generated, first, by the publication of *God Cried*, and secondly by the furore that was continuing over Dahl's review. Rather than showing signs of blowing over with time, the row seemed to be gaining strength. The entire British press gave the impression of having ganged up to condemn us unjustly– given that in every dispute there are two sides to the issue.

To make matters even worse, Jeffrey Bernard, in his 'Low Life' column in the *Spectator*, went way beyond the bounds of decency by proposing that, as a retaliation for the sentencing of 'a parched man' to six hundred strokes by those 'awful Arabs' (referring to an event in Saudi Arabia), six hundred strokes should be inflicted on an Arab in London. He nominated me for this punishment as the boss of Quartet Books and possibly 'the ugliest man he had ever met'. It was beyond comprehension that the *Spectator* should have published such offensive material, but the *Mail on Sunday* ferreted out a reason to explain 'why the genial Jeffrey is lashing out at Naim in the *Spectator*'. David Skan, the writer of the short piece, speculated that it was 'probably not unconnected with an encounter between Attallah's Quartet book firm and Bernard, who was commissioned to write a book about racing. Deadlines were missed and the book never appeared. Attallah made Bernard repay the advance.'

Then out of the woodwork there came Paul Johnson, known for his Zionist sympathies, with a very trenchant article, again in the *Spectator*, that poured scorn on the *Literary Review*. Dahl's article, said Johnson, was in his view 'the most disgraceful item to have appeared in a respectable British publication for a very long time'. He could not actually recall anything like it. Moreover, he claimed, the *Review* was 'controlled by a wealthy Palestinian who also runs Quartet Books', adding that 'the *Literary Review* has published anti-Israeli material before'. In the face of this I could not remain silent and sent a letter to the editor of the *Spectator* to challenge Johnson to substantiate his charges since he accused Dahl of a 'reckless disregard for facts'.

> Where horrendous loss of life and human misery is at stake, complaints of tendentiousness should be discounted. Johnson has no more need to apologize for the expression of his strong feelings that I have for accepting my editor's decision to publish the expression of Dahl's strong feelings in the *Literary Review*. Nor am I ashamed of my own strong feelings about the current appalling misfortunes of both the Lebanese and the Palestinians; for every comparably suffering Jew I feel no less strongly.
>
> Johnson concludes his diatribe: 'The most effective action the civilized community can take is for reputable writers to refuse to be associated with a journal that publishes such filth.' Contributors to the *Literary Review* are encouraged to write freely within the law. It is not to be assumed that the editor or publisher necessarily agrees with all the opinions of the contributors. Or necessarily disagrees with any of them.

My letter was published by the *Spectator* on 10 September. Meanwhile *Private Eye* had muscled in to comment in their 'World of Books' of 26 August that I had struck again by publishing *God Cried*, and by running a review of the book in the *Literary Review*. They claimed the staff were unhappy with the piece Dahl had produced, but were forced to run it by me, the 'Arab propagandist'. What had appalled them, they said, was the evidence of blatant anti-Semitism in the copy and how *Time Out* had published a slightly sanitized version of the review instead of doing their own. My response to *Private Eye*'s allegations appeared in their 9 September issue.

As Bookworm writes, I own through companies both Quartet Books and the *Literary Review*. Nevertheless, in no sense did I 'force' the *Literary Review* to publish the copy, nor was the staff 'appalled [at] the evidence of blatant anti-Semitism in the copy'.

The suggestion that I am anti-Semitic is as absurd as it is mistaken. If being sympathetic to the Palestinians in their plight justifies condemnation of me as a 'Palestinian propagandist' then I will live with that. But it is a mischievous distortion of the meaning of propagandist – one who disseminates 'information, allegations, etc., to assist or damage the cause of a government, movement, etc.' (Collins). I am prepared to risk such abuse as Bookworm's when I believe that the publication of a book may serve the cause of humanity. I trust the editor of the *Literary Review* to exercise her discretion in the same cause.

Running parallel to all this, a minor scuffle was set off when *The Times* 'Diary', under the heading 'Chutzpah', announced that I had entered *God Cried* for the three-thousand-pound H. H. Wingate Prize, which is awarded to an author who stimulates interest in Jewish affairs, when I knew very well there was scant prospect of the book winning. My reasoning in doing so was that it would at least give the judges the opportunity to look at the book and perhaps recognize the other point of view. The *Jewish Chronicle* came in to say that, for once, it agreed with *The Times*: it was chutzpah indeed, given the nature of the book and the intemperate language used by Dahl in his review of it.

Time Out was also dragged into the firing line for having published its abbreviated version of Dahl's piece. The magazine was flooded with letters of protest and suffered a concerted attack from the media for having dared to publish the article. Philip Kleinman, writing in the *Jewish Chronicle* on 26 August, summed up the situation by threatening that 'if *Time Out* can bash Israel, it may well be that some Jews might want to bash *Time Out*. It has a circulation of 65,000 and is heavily dependent on advertising, most of which could be placed elsewhere (*What's On, City Limits*, the *Standard*).' A few days later, in the *Jewish Chronicle* of 2 September, Kleinman picked up on a statement made by Mike Coren (himself Jewish) in the *New Statesman* to the effect that I had, as owner of the *Literary Review*, been put in a difficult position by Dahl's article, since 'not even the crudest Zionist could accuse [me] of anti-Semitism'. Yet in Kleinman's view, my remarks to Coren made it clear that it had been the proprietor not the editor of the *Literary Review* who had got Dahl to write the piece in the first place. According to *Private Eye*, he reported, the Review's staff had been appalled by its anti-Semitism but were forced to use it.

On 9 September the *Jewish Chronicle* carried a letter from me responding to Kleinman's article of the 2nd:

Sir – In Philip Kleinman's article he referred to a report that the *Literary Review* staff were appalled by the anti-Semitism in Roald Dahl's review of *God Cried*, but were forced by me to publish the article. I have already written to *Private Eye* pointing out that there is no grain of truth in this statement.

Because of the controversial nature of the article, we have published a number of hostile letters in the current issue of the *Literary Review* (September 1983). We believe a free discourse on such an important subject can only help to bring about a better understanding of the issue. May I conclude by saying that the killing of innocent people of any race, or creed, is a heinous act, and should be condemned by humanity as a whole.

The previous day, the 8th, *The Times* 'Diary' reported that Peter Hillmore of the *Observer* and their own Frank Johnson were on the point of heeding the call from Paul Johnson to boycott the *Literary Review*. Both had contributed to the current issue but neither of them was sure they wished to do so in future. Hillmore said he considered the article to be 'plain, abusive anti-Semitism which should never have been printed', while Johnson said that 'even by the standards of anti-Israel bias, this piece was above and beyond the call of duty. Gillian Greenwood, when asked for her reaction, said that other contributors to the magazine told her that nobody takes any notice of what Paul Johnson says in the *Spectator*.'

Back on 2 September, the *Evening Standard* reported how I had gone to the extraordinary length of removing from the masthead of the *Literary Review* the name of its poetry editor, Carol Rumens, in the wake of her having written a letter of protest about the Dahl piece in the magazine's letter pages. She wished to dissociate herself from it, she told the *Standard*, as she thought the review inaccurate and inflammatory. It was a bad thing, she added, when the proprietor of a magazine identifies too closely with the views expressed in it. Presumably I had removed her name because I was embarrassed that an employee of the magazine (albeit a freelance) should have criticized any of the magazine's contents. 'But at least,' she said, 'he's printed my letter.'

Again on 2 September, William Hickey of the *Daily Express* informed his readers how an almighty row had blown up in the world of literature, featuring spooky writer Roald Dahl and right-wing columnist Paul Johnson, who was calling for a boycott of the *Literary Review*. When asked to comment on this, 'Mr Attallah dismissed Johnson's call for a boycott by saying: "What do you expect from a man who changes his politics as often as I change my shirts! He has no credibility as far as I am concerned."' But then the *Express* claimed in the final paragraph that I had bowed to a swarm of protests by agreeing to publish a number of letters putting the opposite point of view. The paper agreed to publish a letter from me in reply under the heading 'Unbowed – a free forum for and against Israel':

> Sir – William Hickey highlights the fact that, following the review by Roald Dahl in the *Literary Review*, published by my company, of

the book *God Cried*, about the 1982 Lebanon crisis, columnist Paul Johnson has called for a boycott of the *Review*.

The *Literary Review* provides a forum for the free expression of opinion, and I would not expect reputable writers to refuse to be associated with the journal merely because it has published strongly expressed anti-Israel views by Roald Dahl. William Hickey is, however, wrong to say that I have 'bowed to the swarm of protest' over Dahl's anti-Zionist piece.

Letters putting the opposite point of view to Dahl's have been published in the September issue of the *Literary Review* because that is precisely in accordance with its policy.

As the row continued, Sebastian Faulks wrote in the *Sunday Telegraph* of 18 September about what he called 'a publisher under bombardment over an anti-Jewish book review'. The overall thrust of his article was, in my opinion, objectionable on many fronts. He called the review by Dahl anti-Jewish when it was no such thing. Admittedly Dahl used very strong terms in his condemnation of Israel for invading Lebanon and maltreating the Palestinians, but it was nothing more, nothing less. I also felt angry about what I felt was a misrepresentation by Faulks of the whole issue, not only where it concerned me personally but also for his evaluation of Quartet as a publishing house. The *Sunday Telegraph* agreed to publish a letter from me in reply under the heading 'A publisher's policy':

> While it is unnecessary to take issue with the sillier aspects of Sebastian Faulks's article on myself, I would question his dismissal of our publishing programme as celebrity orientated, erotic and propagandist.
>
> Quartet have some 300 titles in print. Less than 20 of these deal with the Middle East, of which 11 are concerned with the literature, folklore and anthropology of an area whose cultural influence on European civilization has been shamefully neglected. At present

we have nine photographic books on our list, and for your journalist to dismiss the talents of Helmut Newton, John Swannell, Deborah Turbeville and Angus McBean simply as 'erotic' is philistine to say the least.

To describe as 'not serious' an imprint that publishes Jessica Mitford, Lillian Hellman, Cesare Pavese, 'Multatuli', Fleur Cowles, Shusaku Endo, Robert Kee, Anaïs Nin (to name a few), and whose autumn list includes Celia Bertin's Marie Bonaparte, Ryszard Kapuscinski's The Emperor and Sue Davidson Lowe's monograph on her great-uncle, Alfred Steiglitz, rather hints that Faulks and his star-witness, Giles Gordon, might have other reasons for the sneers and innuendoes in the article. Moreover, it would seem a curious strategy for a publisher intent on 'forcing his way into the establishment' to publish Paul Robeson's political writings, Jeremy Seabrook's blistering attack on the inhumanity of unemployment, James Avery Joyce's plea for arms reduction or Ralph Miliband's socialist tract. Our list speaks for itself and we remain, whatever Faulks and Gordon may say, an independent radical publishing house. And make no mistake, there are all too few of us left.

The *Sunday Telegraph* had printed my letter, but in line with *Private Eye* practice it gave the last word to Sebastian Faulks, who said:

I wrote that Quartet has published a 'wide variety' of books but that its 'hallmarks' (i.e. those books with which it is most clearly and commonly associated) were 'pro-Palestinian books on the Middle East, collections of erotic photographs and volumes by English establishment figures'. I can still see no reason to modify that description either in respect of the 'variety' or of the 'hallmarks'.

My reaction at the time was that Faulks's riposte to my letter was ungracious if not bordering on the bloody-minded. I felt he could have been more conciliatory in the circumstances. More of a reasonable tone was sounded by Alexander Chancellor in the *Spectator* on 10 September when he suggested that the civilized community should suspend its boycott of the *Literary Review* on the grounds that we all publish rotten articles from time to time and that he 'felt a little sympathy for Miss Greenwood's employer, Naim Attallah, who happens to be of Palestinian origin'.

> Despite the fact that during the summer he was the object of vulgar abuse in the pages of this paper by Mr Jeffrey Bernard, he wrote a most gentlemanly letter to the *Spectator* in reply to Mr Johnson's attack. The letter was gentlemanly because it failed to point out that Mr Attallah is not the sole proprietor of the *Literary Review*. A chunk of it is owned by the *Spectator*'s revered proprietor, Mr Algy Cluff.

In the end, as the row continued for weeks, it became tiresome, with the same points being laboured over and over again, irrespective of which side they were fired from. I was then challenged to speak to the *Jerusalem Post*, an opportunity I willingly welcomed, for I had nothing to hide or be ashamed of. Their feature article, which covered the whole saga, included a short discourse I had with the newspaper, which prefaced our conversation by saying that neither I, nor the editor of the *Literary Review*, nor Dahl himself had the slightest regrets about the article. It went on to describe how I had been born in Haifa in 1931 but since 1949 had been living in England, where I had become a publisher. My last visit to Israel was six years before when my father died and I had never had any flair for politics.

I did not deny the fact that I was opposed to Zionism and had great sympathy with the Palestinians in their plight for statehood, but was adamant that I never used the magazine to push my own views. The editor decided what to publish, but in cases where an article might cause controversy, then consultation between editor and proprietor was the norm. I also rejected the charge that the article was anti-Semitic, despite its strong language. 'If I thought it was, I would not have published it. I'm the last one to talk about anti-Semitism. The Arabs and the Jews are both Semitic people.' In any case, I told my interlocutor, a healthy debate is far better than resorting to violence. It is an essential part of democracy that people should be free to express their own views. Gillian Greenwood was of the same opinion. She said that a contributor to the magazine should be allowed to express his view and confirmed that she had no regrets about publishing the review in question.

The scale and persistence of the Roald Dahl controversy perhaps deflected some attention from the book itself, which had been the reason for the original upsurge of indignation. When *God Cried* was published in the United States, its fate was rather different. It was virtually ignored at every level by book editors and reviewers as if it did not exist. The well-known Jewish columnist and blues historian, Nat Hentoff, wrote an article around this phenomenon that was published in *Voice* on 14 February 1984. 'Have you forgotten that summer in Beirut so soon?' he asked in his headline, referring to the 1982 massacres of Palestinians at the Sabra and Chatila camps, carried out by the Christian Phalangist militia with the connivance of the Israeli authorities during their invasion. He juxtaposed two quotes on the Lebanon adventure, the first from the Israeli prime minister, Menachem Begin, when he said, 'Never in the past was the great Jewish community in the United States so united around Israel, standing together'; the second came from the respected Israeli diplomat and politician, Abba Eban: 'Beirut for us was like Moscow for Napoleon, a place you'd wished you'd never been.'

'There is a rage in the book, and shock,' wrote Mr Hentoff, 'and much beauty in the faces of the children. I do not know of a more frightening book published last year.' It had been published by a company owned by a Palestinian Arab. 'Aha you say. This must be propaganda.' But then he asked whether, if you took up a strongly pro-Israel book, you looked to see if its publisher was Jewish. 'Yes, I guess some of you do, just as some of you will dismiss this book without looking at it because who can trust a Palestinian? That kind of dumbness cuts across ideological lines, and there's nothing to be done about it. I hope some of the rest of you will judge *God Cried* on its own.'

It was not surprising that Tony Clifton's prose should have been raw, like some of his memories. It had been 'one hell of a bloody, brutal siege of Beirut'. There was the story of an editor on the *New York Times* who cut the adjective 'indiscriminate' from the dispatch of a correspondent reporting the bombing – because he found it hard to believe. 'But ... the Israeli planes ... did not give a good goddamn what they hit. The apologists for this most shameful operation in the history of Israel – and many Israelis see it as criminal – can't have it both ways. If there was only precision bombing, why were clearly marked hospitals hit? Repeatedly.'

Hentoff conceded that Arafat and the PLO hierarchy had interspersed themselves among civilians and that it was possible that some of them took shelter in hospitals for the mentally handicapped, 'one of which was bombed five times'; but even so, how could it be worth the cost to 'kill the maimed, the halt, the blind, kids, anything that moved? What would have been worth this terrible price in Israel's first war that was not one of defence?' 'All atrocities should be written about with rage,' said Hentoff, coming to the fundamental point. 'But no one writer has space for all, and I choose Beirut because I am Jewish and feel kinship with those in Israel who do not want Jews, anywhere, to forget what happened in Lebanon in the summer of 1982. Lest it happen again under Jewish auspices, including the support of American Jews.'

REMEMBERING GEORGE HUTCHINSON

Among all the many things that happened in 1980 the saddest by far for me was the death of George Hutchinson, who departed far too young at the age of fifty-nine. He was my earliest friend in Britain; I had met him soon after landing in the country in 1949. There were many who mourned him, but for me in particular it was as the last of his kind: a gentlemanly, distinguished journalist with integrity. He had indeed belonged to that rare breed of men whose near-extinction has left the world of journalism a poorer place. The elegance of his writing, coupled with his exquisitely refined manners, made him the darling of that section of society which had an appreciation for such qualities. His readership stretched across the nation at every social level. He was the voice of moderation and invariably he had a message that was tinged with hope and optimism. For the more sophisticated, his political acumen was sharp and incisive, and he was rarely wrong in any assessment he made of an issue of national importance.

There was much I had George to thank for. In 1950, when monetary support from my family in Haifa was blocked by new regulations, the Home Office had been about to repatriate me to Israel, on the grounds that as the holder of a student visa I could no longer sustain myself financially. George's intervention, principally with the Home Office, and his rallying of MPs on my behalf secured my stay in the United Kingdom. Though we each pursued our separate paths, our friendship remained strong over subsequent years. The only blip occurred with Quartet's publication of the *Mrs Thatcher's Handbag kit*. On this one occasion George's sense of humour deserted him, and the resulting *froideur* took some time to thaw.

Eventually all was forgiven and Quartet published his biography of Harold Macmillan, *The Last Edwardian at No. 10*. It was the final work he was able to complete. At the book's launch party, a few weeks before his death, the guests included Harold Macmillan with his son Maurice. Harold stood there, leaning on his stick, and demanded, 'Lead me to the author! Lead me to the author!' There was an extraordinary number of writers and politicians among the host of friends and admirers. They thronged about him where he had positioned himself in a corner, awkwardly upright, for the illness had already taken its toll on his handsome frame. Nevertheless his face carried an expression of pleasure and satisfaction. His peers were there to pay him tribute for the last time.

The writer of the obituary in the *Sunday Telegraph* spoke of how kindly, courteous and good-natured George had been. Despite having spent his life in the often acerbic worlds of politics and journalism, he seemed to have acquired only friends and not enemies, and all the pieces that were written about him after his death mentioned the affection and esteem in which this warm and generous man had been held.

A MISSED OPPORTUNITY

In the 1980s, Quartet's New York office begun to publish more titles specifically for the US market. The office was managed by Marilyn Warnick who was more and more on the watch for likely books emanating from local contributors. Her most recent discovery was the photographer Robert Mapplethorpe, who was attracting attention not only for his outstanding talent but also because of some of the subjects he chose to photograph. He was already revered and loathed in equal measure. Everyone agreed, however, that with his unique but disturbing style he ranked among the best photographers of his generation. He pushed degeneracy to extremes and stretched the boundaries of homoerotic imagery to a level of debauchery that was wilfully shocking and unashamedly revolting.

Marilyn took me to meet Mapplethorpe in his studio cum apartment in the Bowery. With Quartet having become internationally known for publishing plush photographic books, we both had it in mind that he could be a natural addition to the list. We found him oddly dressed in leather gear, with such fetishistic sex-aids as dildos, chains and whips strewn around his living area. The walls were covered with amazing photographs of young men and women in bizarre but powerful poses. The atmosphere was disturbing and I felt slightly uncomfortable until he led us into an adjoining room to show us some of his exquisite photographs of flowers. By these I was totally enchanted, affected by their beauty and the magic they seemed to generate. There was no doubting that they were masterworks and their creator a genius. I began to warm to him and to feel a growing optimism about the chances of landing him as a Quartet author. He said that he had photographed Rebecca Fraser – who he knew worked at Quartet – when she was in New York, and offered me a signed print. Thus the meeting ended on a positive note as we agreed to think about the most suitable terms for a future collaboration.

After this first encounter I was feeling quite excited about having his name on the list of famous photographers we published. It would add to our prestige, especially in the United States. On my next trip to New York, a couple of months later, I went to see him in the Bowery again. His place was still as cluttered as before with sexual contraptions of every imaginable kind, some of them with sado-masochistic connotations. Again I felt distinctly uncomfortable and had to struggle to maintain an appearance of relaxed unconcern. Robert was as outrageously dressed as usual, all in black leather, and although he lacked a whip he seemed as threatening as if he had one. We exchanged pleasantries and then went straight to the heart of the matter. He would not mind being published by Quartet, he said, but he would have to insist on a large advance against royalties and total editorial control over what appeared in the book. The size of the advance he specified would have been difficult for Quartet to raise, but not impossible; his second demand was another matter. Total control would have been unacceptable under any conditions. My instincts told me that his choice of photographs was likely to be so reprehensible as to make any collaboration between us impossible.

When he had to leave the room to take an urgent telephone call, I wandered into another room that he used to exhibit some of his latest work. There I was brought to a standstill by a series of photographs of fist-fucking so shocking that I experienced a surge of physical nausea. The graphic images were so horribly inhuman and alienating that surely they could only appeal to psychopathic personalities. I darted back to where I had been sitting when he went to answer the phone and tried to regain my composure. When he came back I said I would consider the terms he suggested and made my exit without further ado.

I never saw Robert Mapplethorpe again, nor did Quartet ever publish any book of his. He died of the ravages of AIDS a few years later and was hailed as the most accomplished photographer of his time. His fist-fucking photographs were exhibited in New York amid a barrage of controversy. Today there are collectors worldwide of his photographs, which sell at auction for great sums of money.

A FOUR-LETTER WORD

In 1993 I went to interview an elusive and very private writer, Patricia Highsmith. The trip entailed driving through the Swiss Alps from Italy to meet her and as I never drive, I needed the help of Ros Milani-Gallieni, who was working for Garrard on special projects. Apart from her driving ability, Ros's company was a sheer delight. We flew to Milan, where we hired a car and proceeded towards Lugano, the nearest town to Patricia Highsmith's hideaway, where we spent the night before negotiating the Alps in search of her. She had given us directions to a small village, where she said she would be waiting. She was there when we arrived, looking dishevelled and rather strange. She asked Ros to stay behind and invited me into her car. We drove up a mountainous road for about twenty minutes before reaching our destination. After an interview full of drama, she drove me back to where Ros was waiting and the parting was more congenial than the reception had been.

Ros drove us down to Milan airport, handed in the car and we flew back to London. For a short trip, it had had more than its share of melodramatic moments. Ros and I often travelled together to Milan and Paris and seemed to work well together. Her grasp of languages was an added bonus, especially in Italy. I once met her parents and we spent an operatic evening at La Scala, Milan. I particularly remember the visit since we stayed at the Excelsior Hotel Gallia in the so-called Madonna Suite, named after the pop singer, who must have used it on several occasions. It happened to be the only accommodation available at the time. We had searched elsewhere without any luck, so we figured why not live it up for the night and follow in the footsteps of Madonna? Such extravagance is something I have always been partial to.

In Paris we stayed at either the Plaza Athénée or Hôtel de Crillon, or even L'Hôtel, where Oscar Wilde was said to have lived his last days and finally died. Ros's task in Paris was to coordinate the marketing and publicity of René Boivin there with its boutique within the Garrard showrooms in London. She also played a major role with her counterpart in Paris, who was in charge of René Boivin's new flagship shop at 49 avenue Montaigne together with the boutique in rue de la Paix. The new shop's inauguration party was a sumptuous affair.

In all of these activities Ros was a key figure. I met her when she was introduced to me by my wife Maria. Poised and elegant, she had perfect manners, and combined in her face the freshness of a Nordic complexion with a faint hint of the Mediterranean. She was attractive, with a mysterious air of restraint that was hard to define. My first impression was one of a young lady totally in control who would seldom allow herself to be distracted by emotional demands likely to disrupt her structured life. I was fascinated by the intriguing mix of messages she seemed to send out to the world. She was certainly someone out of the common run who had hidden depths worth exploring. Little did I know that this short encounter would lead to a working relationship destined to develop into a close and longstanding friendship that would weather the rocky patches that were to lie in its path and come through unscathed. Over time I was to discover that beneath what seemed a cool exterior Ros was a woman who was passionate about her work and passionate about people but kept her feelings in separate compartments. The phrase 'a woman for all seasons' was one that might have been used to describe her. She would write this memoir for my autobiography:

A Working Life with Naim

Ros Milani-Gallieni

Naim – a four-letter word – requires no introduction. The contacts and network flooded all around him whenever he called with a quest from his desk at Asprey plc. During my years beside him, in his role as group chief executive of Asprey, the luxury-goods consortium encompassing Mappin & Webb, Tomasz Starzewski, Asprey Bond Street, Asprey New York, René Boivin, Sangorski & Sutcliffe and the wonderfully distinguished Garrard the Crown Jewellers, my tasks took on the true meaning of multi-tasking – which I am still slave to today. In creating and running the most exclusive events for him, where aspiration turned into reality, he transmitted to me a wealth of enthusiasm and energy. This in turn opened out into an expansive vision of opportunities and developments for the benefit of the group.

My first interview at Asprey, shortly after a three-year stint with Anouska Hempel Couture – and three years before that with Mr Armani at Giorgio Armani in Milan – was a relaxed and welcoming affair. Naim offered me the opportunity to use and develop links with Europe and the five languages I had at my fingertips. It was an inspired chance. Work centred round the fourth floor at 106 Regent Street, which was the inner sanctum, buzzing with pretty girls, all of them much younger and more dynamic than I was. Security looked on approvingly as new arrivals and good-lookers asked to be shown their way to the fourth floor. As you opened a door you would invariably be met by an aroma of fresh-brewed coffee, or at mid-morning the fragrances of fresh herbs and fish dishes being grilled or steamed for Naim's punctual lunch at 12.30 p.m. Press, buyers, bankers, lawyers, writers, designers must all look back on colourful memories of those times with him, and sometimes 'one of us gals' would be invited to spice up the table, though the calibre of the guests daunted us!

The settings were carefully prepared, and it was always a greatly animated table, with lively stories shared over large goblets of Cloudy Bay white wine, and a good strong coffee to end. Then a discreet bleeper, custom-made in black croc, would summon a 'gertie' to clear us all out of the boardroom and back to our duties. Naim would then leave the room, leading his friends out and enjoying compliments about the flamboyantly colourful silk linings of his newly tailored navy-blue cashmere suit, or about an unusual stone he had set in a handsome bold signet ring – a cabochon emerald.

Among the major jewellery exhibitions I set up and oversaw was the complete rebuild of the new René Boivin store after the move from L'Opéra to avenue Montaigne with Jacques Bernard at the helm of the famous Parisian signature. The prestigious

Memories

Boivin collection was inaugurated with the grand opening of the Paris store in May 1993, celebrating over a hundred years of history and treasures – a collection I now have in a book to revive the dream from time to time. The French house of *haute joaillerie* had been brought into the Asprey group in April 1991 and boasted an exclusively designed showroom within Garrard the Crown Jewellers. Then in October 1993 there was Vienna, the venue chosen for the celebration of Garrard's 150th anniversary as Crown Jewellers to the British monarch. The British Embassy opened its doors to this spectacular one-off royal gala and exhibition, held within the rooms of the ambassador's home – quintessentially British territory in Austria. It was magnificence all round.

The pieces had been selected from the Regent Street store a month in advance with stealth-like secrecy. Antique clocks, Queen Adelaide's restored crown, silver wine coolers, each the size of a small bath, ultra-fine jewellery set with the most sought-after stones, watches and more left the West End with a code word for their destination. Long preparations had gone into emphasizing the significance of this grand opening for the exhibition, with the inauguration being marked by our most elegant and striking Princess Alexandra. She was escorted and introduced to selected guests by David Thomas, the Crown Jeweller, alongside Naim and John Asprey. A complex exhibition of this size and value was a highly intricate affair requiring many preparatory journeys to Vienna to ensure a seamless outcome for the occasion. The presentation also ran along a carefully planned series of media events, with the sexy Elizabeth Hirnigel in control, gathering all the great and good of Vienna to flock to Naim, our visionary chief executive. Elizabeth was one of that special breed of high-powered public-relations women who combine fantastic professional standards with a very impressive list of social contacts.

With Boivin the creations designed in the firm's more recent times by Jeanne Poiret, the widow of Jules René Boivin (1893–1917), are undoubtedly unique, though the life and spirit of its exquisitely created collection today lie in the dark, locked away since Boivin closed its doors. Pieces of intricacy rarely beheld – in the forms of animals, birds, flowers or fruit, each piece articulated, *tremblant*, sliding, pivoting – linger in vaults, a project that sadly never got to where it should have been: on the most beautiful girls and women of all ages, perceptive enough to understand its immense beauty.

The sadness of Boivin's current fate has its reflection in the dejection surrounding the latter days of Naim's and my projects – a friendship that at that time got locked away too when a then irreconcilable difference cut us apart. There followed a deep and complex silence, a troubled understanding of notions, of misled emotions, misguided aspirations. It all spiralled out of control and spun into free orbit. Naim was suddenly unapproachable and disappeared off to France for an entire month. How had I managed to alienate a man of such strength and emotional courage? To safeguard his well-being and allow me time to consider my work priorities, which had all along been my biggest challenge, he had set an end. I began to realize there was a gulf between us that had to be negotiated if our relationship were to survive. He wanted me to be emotionally driven in everything I did, with no defined boundaries. 'It was,' he said quite stoically, 'the quest for an intellectual climax that was missing.' Its absence was for the most part the cause of it all. I now know that this meeting of minds was to him far more potent than anything else, and certainly immeasurably more gratifying.

Memories

Fortunately, over time, we completed our journeys, our characters did grow further and stronger and more secure. The void between us became a subject we gradually started reapproaching and exploring with the confidence of reflection and thought. Through laughter and anger we came to a full circle, and are now, in these pages of Naim's third book of memoirs, within a rich tapestry of people's thoughts and feelings concerning an exceptionally driven and inspiring man and his journey through life. What I feel today about my learnings with Naim is that his style, enthusiasm, passion, spontaneity and completely sincere affection – which is still a part of our relationship – have made me understand the person he saw in me more than ten years ago through his nurturing and care; and this has also enabled me to see the person others see in me.

This person has now come into its own space with precisely the foresight he so clearly envisaged: 'When she was a girl, she was a place. Now she's a woman, she's an entire world.' A completion of the circle seems to have come about, a notion so well put by one of my dearest friends, who once wrote: 'Happiness is not about doing everything you want to do, but in wanting to do everything you do.'

Another recruit at this period was Caroline Mockett. Her mother, Ann Foxell, who was then head of the press office at Harpers & Queen, introduced her to the Namara Group. Eventually Caroline became a notable addition to the Quartet girls. In the following contribution, penned by herself in her own distinctive style, she reveals some aspects of the goings-on at Quartet that sadly had escaped my notice. I can well imagine the wicked glint in her eye as she set out to recall the somewhat nonconformist atmosphere in the Goodge Street offices at the time.

Learning the Ropes

Caroline Mockett

'*Dalleeng*! You're pretty. You'll do.' With these words – welcome and verbal contract in five words – I began my tenuous career in publishing.

My introduction to Naim Attallah had been arranged by my mother, exasperated by her daughter's consistent 'failure to launch'. By the age of twenty, I had managed to fail a secretarial course, get chucked off a cooking course and then get sacked from my first five jobs.

I returned home one evening to find mother chatting up a Middle Eastern man. This might not have been anything unusual, except that I noticed that the topic of conversation kept returning to me: my mother's laughter and energetic chat suddenly turning to sighs and sad tales of, 'I don't know what I'm going to do with her.' It took about ten gin and tonics for the charismatic visitor, Anwar Bati, finally to crumble before the twin onslaught of flirtation and sorrow. He agreed to find me a job. 'I know someone,' he said mysteriously, before swaying slightly out of the house.

Wheels turned and I was summoned to Namara House for my brief interview with Naim. Having received the seal of approval, I was whisked away to another address – Wellington Court – where I was shown into a small but pleasant office and told to sit behind a desk. Across the room was an accountant – the accountant – a breed I had never before encountered in my years of deb parties and balls. He was nonplussed by me and I was mystified and unimpressed with him. And so it was for the next three months. I had nothing to do (the accountant seemed to have guessed that I was mostly useless) except occasionally answer the phone – and then pass the call over to the accountant, make coffee (the accountant only drank a cup a day) and read the paper. As Beckett might have said in my position (hard to imagine): 'Nothing happens, nobody comes, nobody goes, it's awful!'

My dwindling will to live was given a boost by a change of duties. I was summoned to help with the launch of Bella Pollen's new collection (I thought I had joined a publishing company). I spent a few giddy days helping to hang her fashionable floral skirts and jumpers (it was the 1980s).

For these first three months of working for Naim, I caught only occasional glimpses of him. He seemed to be locked away in his ivory tower at Namara House, only to appear at parties with a retinue of pretty young women about him, all vying for his attention and favour. Seemingly shut away far from his attention, I began to give up hope of ever escaping the accountant's office and getting involved in the heart of the matter – the great endeavour of publishing. Then, just as I was beginning to work out the best way to get sacked without too many repercussions, I received a summons to Namara House.

'*Dalleeng*! I need a secretary. Come, sit there.' With that, I took up position at a desk in Naim's office. From the frozen wastes of Wellington Court, I was suddenly bathing in the continual sunshine of Namara House and the launching of the Literary Review. My initial panic about actually having to do something and so being discovered to be entirely incapable of doing anything was soon allayed: there was even less to do than there had been at Wellington Court. I sat, looked pretty, chatted to Naim and tidied my desk. A lot. Which seemed to be exactly what my job description required.

After this period of close examination, Naim arranged for me to be given a proper job in Quartet. Not for me the giddy heights of editorial; I was bundled off to sales and marketing. And here my real education began. Naim had found me a slot as post girl and general supplier for David Elliott (who called me either 'the postie' or 'the failed deb') and Penny Grant. Within the friendly chaos of the sales and marketing office, I quickly learnt the essential skills needed for success in publishing. First and foremost was the golden rule: get your work done in the morning because you never know how long lunch is going to last.

I managed to make myself useful by taking David's shaggy dog Tramp for walks and buying toasted bacon and tomato sandwiches for David and myself, a cure for a thumping hangover. And I actually did the post. The post scales I was in command of came in handy when I added to my list of job titles that of 'supplier of soft drugs to the publishing industry'. Marijuana was carefully weighed out and priced alongside letters and stamps, before being delivered – with the mail – around the office.

Occasionally I was sent out on to the front line of publishing to flog books to retailers. This operation involved the donning of an indecently short skirt, plenty of make-up and an innocent smile before targeting Harrods, Smiths and – my favourite – Mole Jazz. I would pile books into the back of my Morris Minor and splutter off to spread the word of Quartet. I soon discovered I was good at the business of flirtation – reps were putty in my hands and I rarely returned with an unsold copy.

Of course it helped that I was selling one of the most controversial lists in British publishing at the time. A mini-skirt and a car-boot load of *The Joy of Sex* was enough to get even the most jaded rep excited. Back at the office, Quartet ran an impressive after-sales service – I would take calls from keen and interested readers who wanted to discuss details of the positions pictured in *More Joy of Sex*. I happily chatted away, describing various obscene acts to male strangers. Anything to sell a book, I thought, not realizing that I had started probably the first and only free sex-chat line in the world. In the lunch break I sold books to transvestites and other colourful Soho characters. Flexibilty and an open mind was an essential part of the sales technique.

The success of *The Joy of Sex* didn't go down well with The Women's Press, whose presence within Naim's harem of publishing was probably due to a mutual misunderstanding of each other's intentions. Naim must have thought, 'How nice, more women.' The Women's Press probably thought, 'He publishes Dennis Potter – how bad can it be?' The Women's Press had a fearsome reputation; enough to put the fear of woman into David Elliott– his dog Tramp and I would be called upon as escorts when David had to venture into their territory to obtain sales figures. Little was I aware that The Women's Press was making publishing history by releasing classics such as Alice Walker's *The Color Purple*, as well as pioneering texts such as *The Lesbian Mother's Handbook*.

Looking back, I can now appreciate the innovative and risk-taking books Quartet published: Dennis Potter's *Pennies from Heaven*, Jonathan Dimbleby and Don McCullin's *The Palestinians*, Julian Barnes's *Metroland*, as well as publications by Bob Carlos Clarke and Derek Jarman. My time at Quartet was an education in many ways, a formative experience that taught me the value of originality and of thinking in brave new directions. It all helped in my later career working with artists and other creative types. For all of this, and in particular to Naim, I am thankful.

A SCOTTISH GEM

Most of my memories have described my publishing adventures but much of my working life was spent in the rarefied world of luxury retailing, especially with the House of Asprey where I was the Chief Executive Officer. And it was Asprey's, The Queen's jewellers, who were to buy the historic Edinburgh-based jeweller, silversmith and clockmaker, Hamilton & Inches, founded in 1866 and a holder of the Royal Warrant.

Acquiring a company is one thing, but finding the right person to manage it is a much harder proposition. Whenever such an appointment had to be made, I agonized over the choice, and sometimes got it wrong. People change with authority and a greater measure of responsibility; they are often overwhelmed by the enormity of the task. Although experience is a very important consideration, I have always considered it much over-valued. Energy, creativity, discipline, hard work and a sharp observant eye matter a great deal more. Along with that, the knack of enthusing people and opening their eyes to greater perspectives is equally important. Finding all these qualities in one person is seldom easy. It often involves a calculated gamble, but it is one that occasionally comes off.

This was the course I took with Julia Ogilvy, aged twenty-seven, who was running the publicity side of Garrard. She was highly disciplined, dedicated to her work and always early at her desk. We often met in the lift in the morning when everyone else was still en route to the office. Since I am a stickler for time-keeping I was naturally impressed. When her husband James moved to Fife in Scotland, Julia found it hard to keep commuting to London and asked me whether we could find her an assignment in Scotland that would make her life more practical and less exhausting travel-wise. With the acquisition of Hamilton & Inches, the opportunity arose for Julia to play an important role. Indeed, my secret ambition was loftier than people expected. I dared contemplate putting her in charge of the whole operation despite her youth.

When her appointment was announced the *Scotsman* profiled Julia with the opening statement, 'Deep within the hallowed halls of Edinburgh's finest jewellers and silversmiths insurgent forces are at work.'

> The woman prepared to ruffle such fastidiously arranged feathers is Julia Ogilvy. Three weeks ago she became the first outsider to manage the eponymous family firm ...
>
> Although she does not take over till 1 August, Mrs Ogilvy, twenty-seven, who is married to Princess Alexandra's son James, is spilling over with ideas to modernize, promote and package the firm. Marketing is Mrs Ogilvy's forte. Her post at Garrard, which she held for five years, encompassed every aspect of promoting the business. It also allowed her to indulge her love for jewellery.

Julia proved to be more than equal to the challenge. Her first priority, without any prompting from me, was to gain the confidence and respect of the staff and convince them that some of the old ways needed updating to meet the fierce competition in the marketplace. She achieved both these goals in a short time and it was plain to see that the atmosphere at Hamilton & Inches was reflecting a fresh approach and a more focused objective. The displays in the shop improved and an inspired style of management based on consultation and the full cooperation of staff was introduced. The showrooms took on a grand appearance with the hallmark of elegance stamped in every corner. A revitalized energy began to sweep through the entire premises, and Julia was like a beacon of light illuminating her domain with her ineffable charm. She became my jewel in Scotland, for I could see she was far exceeding the most optimistic expectations I had of her. Julia has made Scotland her home since then and is now very keenly involved in regional affairs devoting her time to cultural and charitable activities and is highly regarded for her dedication and love of Scotland. And here are her memories:

Rising to the Challenge

Julia Ogilvy

Naim definitely loves women. I can't believe any of his female friends would say otherwise on the whole. From the point of view of a woman, however, he does take some getting used to. I remember, from my first visit to his famous office high above Soho with its dark walls and tiger-skin rugs, the feeling of being on some kind of film set in an X-rated movie. On the other hand, the aspect that struck me immediately was his boyish enthusiasm for everything, augmented by the speed at which he spoke, his arms waving in the air. It was clear he had a short attention span and didn't suffer fools gladly. That suited me fine. Hearing good news made him happy and he always liked it if you agreed with his ideas, however outlandish they might seem. If you were lucky, he might forget about them later. It soon became obvious that life around Naim was always going to be entertaining, and often hilarious, and that when it came to women you didn't need to have any worries about being politically correct. He is an incredibly tactile and warm-hearted man and was often in need of a hug to cheer him along.

My days of working as PR manager at Garrard are a period I remember with great affection. Generally we coincided in the lift at around 7.30 a.m. It seemed to make sense to get on with the day as soon as possible if, like me, you had a husband working in the City and functioned better early on. (Even now it quite irritates me if I can't reach people in their office at 8 a.m.) Naim was obviously impressed by my timekeeping, though it never occurred to me that this might be a key reason for later promotion. I only knew it was a great chance to catch up with him and get some fast decisions. On other occasions I would be summoned to his spacious office at Regent Street (somewhat toned down in comparison with his Soho space) to discuss some new project. An even rarer piece of luck was to be invited to one of his fabulous lunches. It was always stimulating and fun to catch up on any gossip. You could rely on Naim to know what was going on. He always had gorgeous girls working for him, though it was a mistake for anyone to assume that he just liked women pretty. I certainly never met one in the entourage who wasn't brainy as well. He loved the challenge.

Among several hilarious memories I have of those times was the occasion when Naim bought one of his assistants a set of very sexy lingerie and immediately insisted she must try it on to show him. Unfortunately she forgot that the corridor from the ladies' loo to his office was monitored by security cameras. It took the security guards a long time to get over that one. I was fortunate enough to receive the occasional present, such as one of the tiny silver hearts he gave to all his visitors, but thankfully I don't think he would have dared to try me on the lingerie. He was always a little more circumspect where I was concerned, perhaps because I gave an impression of being fearsomely organized and bossy. It was still strangely flattering to be asked to sign a photo of me for his office: a rather sultry shot taken for *Harpers & Queen* by a smooth Italian photographer.

Soon after this I came to a major turning point in my life – a time in which Naim played a very significant role. My husband and I had rather rashly fallen in love with a house in Scotland and

I had begun commuting from Fife to London every week. Just as I was summoning up the courage to tell Naim I would have to leave him (he hated anyone leaving) to work in Scotland, he announced that Asprey was buying the well-known, traditional but by now near-bankrupt Edinburgh jewellers, Hamilton & Inches. His first thought was that I could work there and run the marketing side, but before long he'd decided I would make the perfect managing director. He was not at all put off by the fact that I was only twenty-seven and was restricted to a background in marketing. He had the agreement of my immediate boss, Richard Jarvis, but I knew he would have huge trouble in persuading the Asprey board, let alone me! The idea amazed me, and, overwhelmed by the prospect, I soon refused him. This was clearly not part of his plan. He introduced a diversionary tactic by saying I had to be a director and he needed me to come to the lawyer's office in St James's to countersign the acquisition papers for Hamilton & Inches. I arrived to find a room full of people and a set of papers with 'Managing Director' beside my name! Fortunately, with the support of my family, I had come round to the idea and was ready to go. The decision led to some of the best years of my working life.

Naim had known I could rise to the challenge, and he was right. I became convinced, too, that a woman was right for the role. Good 'people skills' were essential in those early days to remotivate the team, and ultimately marketing was probably the most relevant skill I could have had. Naim remained constantly in the background, encouraging me and so obviously proud of my achievements. Some years later, after Naim had left the Asprey group, I had the chance to lead a management buyout and had his full support all the way. Today I lead a different life, having left that period behind to found a charity, Project Scotland, providing full-time volunteering opportunities to young Scots, transforming their lives and those of their communities. I am proud to sit on the board of Lloyds TSB Scotland, to be a trustee of Columba 1400 and an Alpha leader. I can still look back on those earlier days and say that much of what I do now has only come about because of the faith, confidence and pride Naim had in me. I owe him a lot.

REMEMBERING THEO

A few people I have known linger in my memory. I still love them and miss them. Someone very special was the showbiz legend, Theo Cowan.

In September 1981 my links with show business were strengthened when I quietly acquired the controlling interest in one of the best established theatre PR agencies in the West End. This was Theo Cowan Ltd, which had recently changed its name to Cowan Bellew Associates. Theo was a legend who had founded his company some sixteen years earlier after working as the publicity supremo of the Rank Organization in its heyday in the film industry. During that time he enjoyed a lavish lifestyle, entertaining the stars and earning himself the reputation of a ladies' man. At one time he had a close relationship with Margaret Lockwood and it hit him very hard when they broke up. In the 1950s he helped to groom the likes of Diana Dors and Joan Collins.

Theo was responsible for launching *A Little Night Music*, *Company* and *Fiddler on the Roof*, and much more. Theo's most famous clients included David Niven, Dirk Bogarde, Michael Caine, Peter Sellers, Jenny Agutter and Jeremy Irons, as well as a host of Hollywood stars, among them the veteran actor Joseph Cotten. The firm was without doubt the absolute doyenne of British showbiz PR. Theo had worked with some of the greatest of the Hollywood greats, including Bette Davis; and Laurie's clients had included Robert Mitchum and James Stewart. In the mid-1980s, the roster still included Channel 4 Television.

On 13 September 1991, Theo died in his office at Namara House at the age of seventy-three. It happened just after lunch when, following his usual custom, he had taken a snooze for half an hour in his favourite chair opposite his long-time friend and assistant Jane Harker, with whom he shared his desk. That same morning Theo had been to see me at Regent Street to discuss various issues that were pending with regard to Namara Cowan. He was jolly, and as usual kept me au courant with what was happening in our show-business arm. We were then in a difficult period compounded by Theo's generosity in giving ample time to many of the famous stars he represented without receiving a commensurate return for his services. He wanted my reassurance that my support would continue till the dawn of better days, which we were likely to see soon. He left my office happy and reassured, and reported the gist of our conversation to Jane Harker before settling for his forty winks. When it was time for him to wake up, his staff shook him gently and he keeled over, quite dead. He had departed peacefully, having ended his journey discreetly, just as he would have wished.

Theo was a legend in his own lifetime. He was judged by his peers to be the best and, as *The Times* said, was admired by stars and scribblers alike. For more than four decades he projected or protected an élite stable of clients. In his letters to his clients, continued *The Times*, 'he would usually sign himself "Beau-nosh" – a reference to his prodigious enthusiasm for food of almost any description. "A legend in his own lunchtime," they would joke.'

The *Daily Telegraph* remarked that 'the supreme publicity agent was himself something of a mystery':

his public persona was universally loved, his private one hardly known. His life, it appeared, was his work; and the discretion which his clients valued was never applied more rigorously than to himself. Women adored him as much as he loved them, but he never married. It was known that he had nursed a special tendresse for Margaret Lockwood, and in the actress's reclusive years he was the only man who break into her isolation.

Dirk Bogarde added his personal tribute, addressing Theo's departed shade directly with his memories of the many years they had got through together with 'good movies, bad movies, and here and there a reasonably respectable one'. Theo had always been there on the journeys all over the country:

> Red carpets and station-masters in top hats. Black ties and eternal dinners with Mayors. Day after day from one city to another. You and me. Everything planned like clockwork, ready on time, never once late, not even the train ... Discipline you taught; patience, humility and tact. You did amazingly well by doing not what you were engaged to do – keeping me away from the worst excesses of the popular press. Keeping me 'out of' rather than 'in' the public eye for which I will ever be grateful. Those subtle warnings about X and Y who might look kind but couldn't be trusted with a fly-swat or a feather duster. The 'killers' of their time. How frightened we all were of them! But it was you who said: 'What they say today you'll eat your chips from tomorrow. Remember that through your tears.'

Like most of those who were well-acquainted with Theo, I can never forget him. His presence alone was a joy. At parties he knew most of the guests and his popularity was something uniquely apparent. For a number of years my wife Maria and I, accompanied by our son, went to the film festival at Cannes to be looked after by Theo, where he was king of 'The Croisette'. We attended many film premières and were treated regally by everyone we encountered for being merely in his company. Together we raided all the famous restaurants in town and the surrounding hills. It was truly a memorable experience to watch Theo as he devoured one after another of the exquisite dishes he could not resist even after being fully satisfied. I miss him often for his wise counsel, but even more for his kindness and generosity of spirit.

The memorial service for Theo was held at St Martin-in-the-Fields. It was conducted by the Reverend Albert Watson: a most moving occasion with figures from the world of entertainment there in force to pay tribute to one of the best loved publicity agents of his generation, whose popularity among the show-business fraternity was unparalleled. Readings were given at the service by Joss Ackland and Jeremy Irons, while tributes were paid by Donald Sinden, Michael Parkinson and Jenny Agutter, who also read warm appreciations from some who could not be there – Joseph Cotton, James Stewart, Lillian Gish and Barry Cryer. Ron Goodwin introduced a recording of Peter Sellers reading 'Help'; Petula Clark sang 'I'll See You Again'; and Larry Adler, accompanied by Roy Budd on piano, played the theme music from the film Genevieve. Other music was provided by a jazz band made up of Mr Budd with Ian Christie on clarinet, Richard Willcox of BBC Light Entertainment on trombone, Mike Wheeler of Rank Film Distributors on double bass, Bryan Jones on trumpet and Lon Sanger as vocalist. The organist was Mark Stringer and the whole congregation joined in singing 'On The Sunny Side Of The Street' and 'When You're Smiling'. In fact it turned out to be more of a gig than a memorial service, but that was the way Theo would have liked his life celebrated, with the merriment that was his hallmark. The ceremony was a joyous interlude for remembering a man whose legacy was laced with good memories. I left the church and went out into Trafalgar Square with feelings of mixed happiness and sadness. Theo was no more, but his unobtrusive shade would always remain with those who had had the privilege of knowing him.

MARINA WARNER

Marina Warner has had a distinguished literary and academic career since Quartet Books published the first UK paperback edition of her classic work on the myth and cult of the Virgin Mary, *Alone of all Her Sex*. She was made a CBE for services to literature in 2008; has been awarded eleven Honorary Doctorates by British universities and was asked to give the BBC Reith Lectures in 1991. Her book, *Stranger Magic: Charmed States & the Arabian Nights*, won the prestigious US 2012 National Book Critics Circle Award for Criticism. I interviewed her in 1987 for my book, *Women*. I must however admit that I was so struck by her verve and elegant use of words that I decided to revisit what I considered then to have been a memorable encounter with a charming and delightful lady whose enchantment has never left me to this day.

The Early Influences

I think, in a way, that my father and mother were such a complete contrast that I reacted across the sexes. Probably I was influenced more by my father through rebellion, though wishing to react against his prescription of what my life should be like. My father was a regular upper-middle-class man; he had been to Eton and Oxford and was a colonel in the Army. He met my mother, who had come from a very, very poor Italian family, during the war. My father was a plain-looking man, my mother a very beautiful woman. She had a complete background in Catholic service. She had been brought up happily entirely by women because her father died when she was a child, and there was a sort of sweetness in her life. She was lively and vivacious, but she is somebody who can yield, and my father had, in a way, the kind of authority of his class. He had that English mentality and he was very tyrannical. So, in a way, he influenced me more, not to conform but to fight against him. But I also didn't want to be like my mother. There were terrible rows, for instance, about her clothes. She never had any money to buy her own clothes, which seems an absolutely ludicrous detail, but I remember that I was determined I would always have my own money, that I would not be in the position of having to ask a man if I could have a coat for the winter.

My father was very ambitious for me and my sister. He didn't have any sons and always joked that, if he had sons, he would have forgotten about us. But we became his substitute sons and he had high intellectual ambitions. He became quite a famous bookseller. He was Bowes & Bowes in Cambridge, and they had a little chain of bookshops that were the serious side of Smith's in those days. It's a while ago now; he was quite old when we were born, and he's dead now. There were always books around. Any time we showed any interest in any subject, heaps of books would be brought back from the shop for us to read. So we were very fostered. My sister was good at Latin and Greek, and she got all the dictionaries and everything, immediately, which were very expensive, so there was constantly that kind of input.

My religious upbringing was quite intensely Catholic, not because my mother is a devout Catholic, which she is, but she wouldn't have imposed that on us except that she liked us to be Catholics. My father imposed it because he thought it a very good religion for a girl, which is terribly interesting. He was a Protestant – an Anglican. He brought us up as Catholics for the morality of it, sent us to convents because he thought this would make us proper young women. The Catholic religion is disciplined in a particular way for women, disciplined to self-sacrifice and sexual purity. At the same time, he wasn't an austere man. He was genial, loved company and good wine and grew roses beautifully. He had a lot of facets to his character, and not in a boring tight-arsed British way; but he was very, very dominant. And I probably caused him a lot of grief, because I was anxious to get away from that, I did want to pursue my own lines. And a lot of my attitudes were not formed by reflective consideration over books, but were immediate reactions. My politics at first were formed entirely by the flip side of his politics. He hated the trade unions, so I liked the trade unions. But then I developed a more considered view, though I still have strong visceral antagonism to certain aspects of conservatism because I didn't like them at the dinner table at home. I didn't like the *Daily Telegraph* talk which was part of the world I didn't want to enter.

He wanted me to marry a stockbroker. Even though he wanted me to have a good education, he never wanted me to be a writer. He said it was a very bad sort of income, it would never be reliable. He would have liked me to be somebody like a diplomat, and he would have liked me to do the Foreign Office, or something like it. I did languages. In that sense, he was a conventional man. He was very, very proud of me when I did become a writer. He would laugh in a sort of ironical way about the things I wrote. He was touchingly proud and his interest in me, even his antagonistic interest, was very strong and strengthening. There have been some psychological studies in which cross-identification of children apparently is a source of high motivation. Girls who identify with their fathers in some way, even as rebels, and boys who identify with their mothers can actually become more motivated, more able to express themselves, and this was true in my case, I think.

Advantages and Disadvantages

I had tremendously split fantasies. I did want to be a very girlish and perfect girl. I longed to be beautiful and spent a lot of time in front of the mirror dressing up in my mother's clothes, attempting to look like a sophisticated and beautiful woman. At the same time, all my night-time reveries before I went to sleep were of being an incredibly active and effective young man. Which really took the form, not of an intellectual thing, not of being influenced or a writer (I was about ten), but of being somehow physically free, of being able to move. I imagined adventures, and when I was in these adventures, which would be in rivers and mountains, I would be a young man. My body would not somehow be this body, which was going to be the one that meant I would marry and be confined. One of the things that possibly happened historically is that, when women are confined and attend to these private ceremonies of upbringing and meals, it actually fosters the best in human nature. We think of the feminine, in a way, as a better order, and I think it is, because it is to do with the rituals of preserving, and growth and love, and cherishing and nurturing.

I'm one of the feminists who doesn't believe that this is intrinsic to the female soul. I think it is the possibility of all humanity. When we say that Mrs Thatcher is masculine, it is more that what she is required to do has belonged traditionally to the masculine order. What we haven't sold is how you set up a society and run it, how you don't have an anarchic system in which there are no rulers, and yet avoid falling into this masculine way which is all to do with oppressions and cruelties. Different expectations of women do limit their chances, there's no doubt about it. I was lucky, I went to convent school, and I never would have had a scientific or engineering bent. So humanities, which were offered at the school, suited me, but they didn't offer the girls anything on the scientific side. I wouldn't have flourished if I had been an engineer by inclination.

Women are in an acute phase in England. The difficulty now,

of course, with massive unemployment, is that the expectations of women have been reduced even further and the birth-rate has risen terrifically among young, very young women. I don't want to give the impression that having a baby isn't a great pleasure and a great experience, but it worries me. I feel that these young women are entering into the difficult occupation of caring for a child in very reduced circumstances, and this is partly because their expectations have been cut, have been limited; they don't see their lives as offering other possibilities. That relates to some of the mythology that is becoming ever more current. One is the myth of the Royal Family, and I may be quite wrong about this, and it obviously is harmless compared to some other political systems and political ideologies, but what we see is a continual adulation of young women who arrive to greatness through chance. I think this underlines the idea that women don't take their destinies into their own hands, but, with a modicum of looks or grace and a charming way, something wonderful might happen to you. This is terribly determinist. It's not saying who I am, what I am capable of, it's floating, and it's asked of women and not of men. It is interesting that, within the Royal Family, the men are trained to do lots of things, however poorly or adequately they function at them. But the young women who enter this family and become heroines of the entire world (there is nothing in the popular press except Fergie, Diana, Caroline Monaco, Stephanie Monaco), have initially, as far as I can make out, nothing more asked of them but that they be images, something to look at.

Beauty, of course, has its place in the world, and beauty can be life-enhancing. The body is a place to start from, but it mustn't be the place where you end. Even to a woman like me, and I have every sort of advantage, there are little things that happen constantly. I get Johnnie to do things for me sometimes, because

I won't get a hearing on the telephone, they won't listen to me. The police can be very nice and they can try, but they are more likely to listen to a complaint from a man.

STING & THE DEVIL

I've always been attracted to the unusual, especially when it upsets the status quo. The BBC created another cause for me to espouse in 1978 when it made Dennis Potter's television play *Brimstone and Treacle* and then promptly got cold feet over its theme and put a ban on it, locking the tapes away unshown in the archives. It was a gruelling piece about a brain-damaged paralysed girl being raped by a con man who charms his way into her family's home and turns out to be the devil. Subsequently it had a brief West End run as a stage play, and in October 1981 I joined forces with Dennis to explore making a feature film based on his television script. The director was to be Richard Loncraine and the producer Kenith Trodd. Peter Hannan was signed as director of photography, with Milly Burns as production designer and Robin Douet as production manager.

Dennis was put in charge of his own script. Our budget was in the region of five hundred thousand pounds, with my investment, as executive producer, representing half that amount. The shooting schedule was timed to begin on 19 October, based at Shepperton Studios. Among the cast were Denholm Elliott, reprising the part of the girl's father, which he had already acted in the withdrawn television version, and Joan Plowright as the girl's mother. The part of the girl herself went to a gifted newcomer, Suzanna Hamilton. While our American backers had been attracted by the possibility of David Bowie taking the starring role of the visiting infernal stranger, in the end he was not available.

Instead the part went to Sting, the lead singer from the rock band the Police. Sting had some previous experience of working in the movies, having appeared in *Quadrophenia*, a 1979 film about the battles between the Mods and Rockers in Brighton. He now wanted the chance to do some straight acting, but the Americans insisted on a new Police album as part of the deal. Dennis was prepared to adapt the script to allow Sting a singing role, but this was an idea Loncraine promptly vetoed. He thought it would make it all seem too like a follow-up to *Pennies from Heaven*. In the end it was agreed Sting would sing a nostalgic standard to back the end credits. The number chosen was 'Spread a Little Happiness'.

When this was eventually released as a single, to Dennis's chagrin it attracted more public response than the film itself. He was quoted as saying on a Terry Wogan chat show some time afterwards, 'I think I was sent into this world to spread a little misery.' I first got to know Dennis Potter when Quartet published the novel version of *Pennies from Heaven*. He and I hit it off straight away, though he was a famously complex and cantankerous character. This was largely the result of the terrible chronic illness he suffered from most of his adult life. Known as psoriatic arthropothy, it affected his skin and his joints. He had to endure constant physical pain and was incapacitated in many ways, which gave him a focus for his anger. Despite these handicaps, he was a man of the most remarkable achievements whose delving into the seedy depths of human motivation riveted his audience. He had a feeling for the drama and its need to defy convention which gave his work a rare quality seldom equalled by any of his contemporaries. He had an obsessive nature that in some ways was not dissimilar to my own. Artistically he was driven and inflexible.

He loved a quarrel and his relationships with close associates were always tempestuous. This was especially so with Kenith Trodd, who had worked with Potter over many years on his television projects. Theirs was a relationship that oscillated between love and hate and caused consternation within their circle. Dennis's perception of women was strange as well as intriguing. He was attracted to the dissolute type of woman whose sexual vibes stir man's most basic instincts. He certainly preferred the image of woman as sinful to the idea of her as pure. The seething underbelly of nightlife with all its sexual connotations was a theme he was drawn to explore time and time again. The association between disgust and guilt was very real for him.

Somehow he felt at home in an environment where prostitutes lurked or had a dominant presence. But his was a unique talent and his output was prodigious, given the health constraints under which he worked. Of my own involvement I said in an interview with *Screen International* in early 1982 that 'investing in films is a logical progression to my publishing activities'; that 'I've always been interested in the media and I've always wanted to take risks. I do not see the point in investing in things that you know are going to work. For me the gamble of doing something you believe in is vitally important.'

Dennis told the *Daily Mirror* that in his ambition for the play to be turned into a film he was prepared to work for nothing to see the project through. The subject matter of *Brimstone and Treacle* was guaranteed to attract controversy. In the mixed reception given the movie by the critics after its London première in September 1982, discussion undoubtedly centred more on its theme than its artistic merit. There was a general consensus that Sting's performance was a triumph, and most commentators agreed he was not its only revelation and *Brimstone and Treacle* was definitely a film to watch out for. It was remarked that it represented 'a most impressive move into film production for the publishing impresario Naim Attallah'.

The party following the première was a lavish affair at a mansion in Regent's Park. Billy Connolly and Pamela Stephenson were there, deep in conversation with Captain Sensible (wearing a skirt), while Lyndsey De Paul giggled with her new man, designer Carl Dawson. Sting arrived alone but was soon surrounded by a cluster of beautiful women, including Selina Scott and the singer Marsha Hunt. Everyone at the gathering heaped praise on Sting for his acting ability. 'He was so good, he made me sick,' joked Bob Geldof. Sting was in his element as he gasped, 'It's all so amazing.' His sudden transition from rock star to film star left him quite bemused.

Even the great photographer Helmut Newton, who took the publicity photos for the film and had seen plenty of sights in his time, was dazzled by the event. Only one dissenting voice was raised: that of Virginia Gallico, the mother of Ludmilla Nova, my friend who had been lead dancer in *Arabian Fantasy* at the Royal Albert Hall. Virginia, who was also lady-in-waiting to Princess Grace of Monaco, was outraged and appalled by Dennis's fable. She let me know her views in no uncertain terms but I chose not to engage in any heated exchange with her in case it damaged my relationship with her daughter. Years later, when I bumped into Virginia and Ludmilla by chance in Budapest, the incident was apparently forgotten and all was well.

When Quartet gave Dennis Potter a commission to write a novel treatment for *Brimstone and Treacle*, he passed the task over to his daughter Sarah, whom he was encouraging to do some writing. His utter devotion to Sarah suggested she was the closest to him of all the women in his life.

ARABELLA POLLEN

In January 1982, Arabella Pollen, daughter of Sotheby's then vice-chairman, Peregrine Pollen, became part of the Namara Group. Arabella's project was to launch a fashion company under her own name, with my financial backing and the full resources of Namara at her disposal. Though Arabella possessed no formal qualifications in dressmaking or design, I could see she had ability and drive. She combined beauty with energy and her elegance and poise were enhanced by her piercing blue eyes. She was, moreover, being helped in her adventure by one of the rising stars at *Vogue* magazine, Sophie Hicks – today a well-known architect. I was very taken with Arabella, and although fashion was not an area on which I had set my sights, I was carried away by her aura. It was overwhelmingly seductive. She was every man's dream: youthful, zestful and self-assured. There was also that indefinable quality about her that made a man wish to protect her and gave him the impression that she needed him when it was in fact not the case; nevertheless the sensation was gratifying.

She took over my old office at Wellington Court and the process of promoting Arabella started in earnest. I was determined to make her a household name. The strategy was to establish Arabella as *the* fashion designer for the young – the new generation of hopefuls who formed the nucleus of a trendy society with their boundless ambition and natural *savoir-faire*. Arabella's beau, Patrick Benson, was referred to by *Tatler* as her chief button-sewer, whereas he was in fact a multi-talented artist whose many sketches provided her with inspiration. Sandra Marr, Viscountess Weir's daughter, was listed in the team as head mannequin, and the indefatigable Sophie Hicks was chief adviser. In due course, a young lady with a lisp, Kathryn Ireland, was appointed special publicity person cum personal assistant.

Katherine was a great operator and a real go-getter. At one point, however, I felt that her influence on Arabella sometimes veered from the positive to the reckless, diverting Arabella towards more recreational pursuits. No doubt I was being over-protective, worried that, because of her youth, she might be led seriously off course. Following through from those early days, Katherine has since moved on to become the hottest property in Hollywood, running her own interior-design company that caters mainly for the stars.

Arabella's rise to prominence happened in no time at all. Among her clients she was soon counting Princess Diana, a fashion icon of her day, and a large majority of the Sloane Rangers who graced the London social scene in that *époque*.

When I asked her to contribute her memories of that period for inclusion in my volume of autobiography, *Fulfilment & Betrayal*, she supplied the following which well captures our special time together:

Growing a Business

Arabella Pollen

When Naim called me out of the blue one day to ask whether I would write something for his memoir, my initial reaction was panic. I have almost zero recall of my twelve-year stint in the fashion business, maybe because it was a long time ago, or maybe it's the onset of premature Alzheimer's. Either way, only the barest threads of memory remain: the up-all-nights and the seven days a week, the brilliance and dedication of my studio workforce. OK, so there was that two-year commute to Paris – Fashion Aid, of course, and the craziness of the Studio 54 shows – but almost all the rest of it, the people, the parties, the excitement, tears, triumphs and disappointments, have merged into one great kaleidoscopic blur stored somewhere deep inside my head. Not Naim, though. Naim Attallah is not a person you forget.

We met in 1980. I was nineteen and a year out of school. I had spent the first six months of that year working odd jobs in advertising and the latter part of it holed up in a crumbling mill in France with a Super 8 movie camera, earnestly attempting to write, shoot and direct a satire on the business. This high-falutin project left me profoundly broke and I was eventually forced to return to London, engage with the real world and look around for a way to make ends meet. Having crashed through my

A-levels with a spectacular mix of bad behaviour and complacency, the only asset I had of any real value was a cupboard full of textiles which I'd collected over the years and – for reasons that still escape me – I decided to make clothes out of them. This resulted in a small collection, mostly constructed from stiff and itchy Hebridean tweeds, which somehow caught the attention of an editor at Vogue magazine, and before very much time had passed I found myself sitting in the air-conditioned offices of Namara in Poland Street, clutching a portfolio between my knees. 'If he likes you,' the *Vogue* editor had said, 'he'll be back.'

Quite what I was expecting in a publisher who might be interested in starting a fashion business with me, I can't say. Certainly Naim Attallah was not it. First of all, he was extraordinary looking: tall, broad, enormous hands, odd-shaped ears. He was a Palestinian 'Mr Potato Head', but with a charming face and rather beautiful eyes that folded into multiple creases when he smiled. There was his voice: versatile in its range, capable of soaring and dipping through several octaves whenever he became excited. There was his manner: utterly disarming, every gesture expansive. On top of all there, there were his clothes: flamboyant, foreign, yet, conversely, impeccably English. Something bright flashed as he seized my hand. A piece of jewellery, a silk tie? I don't know. There was just so much detail to take in. All I remember is that he gripped my arm, launched forth with great enthusiasm on a variety of seemingly unconnected topics, flipped through my portfolio, and the deal was done.

Later that day, I walked slowly out of the Notting Hill tube station and blinked disbelievingly into the afternoon light. I had a job. More than a job, I was about to have my own business. I assumed he was mad, certifiably insane. But what I came to understand was that Naim didn't believe in business plans or spreadsheets. He believed in people, and once he put his faith in you, it was absolute.

Some of us are dreamers, some are thinkers. Naim is a doer, a nurturer of talent and ideas. Together we put down roots and grew a business. God knows, neither of us knew what we were doing, but we muddled through. It was a lot of fun. We had more than our share of success and I loved how proud that made him.

Random things stick in my mind from those days, like Naim's zeal for cats, not the kittycat variety but animal skins, oil paintings and two enormous white and gold china tigers – maybe kept at Namara, maybe perched on a white rug at his house in Mayfair. I remember the window of our Knightsbridge offices shattering when the Hyde Park bomb exploded. I recently found a gold egg on a chain he gave me from Asprey, which I wore for a while, then temporarily mislaid. I remember the other girls downstairs, bluestocking and studious, working for some mysterious outfit called The Women's Press.

Naim and I would have lunch together. These were three-course affairs, cooked by someone pretty with a cordon-bleu diploma and served with great style. We talked about everything – his myriad of ventures – film, theatre, art. We talked about Palestine, women, publishing, food, love. He was endearing, passionate, funny, enthusiastic, and just a little bit mad. There wasn't a soul who knew him who didn't imitate his delighted shriek of a greeting when you walked into a room. We all took to answering phones 'in the style of Naim'. I think he probably knew. I suspect he kind of liked it. He was happiest being the sun around which lots of interesting people revolved.

From time to time we argued. Then he was infuriating, bombastic, stubborn, arrogant – but so, of course, was I. I was always in a hurry. I wanted Pollen Inc. to be bigger and better. I wanted success and recognition. I wanted greater financing, higher turnover, more staff. He was slower; and a lot wiser. When the time came for us to head off in different directions, I'm pretty sure I was the one who behaved badly, a touch furtively, unsure quite how to approach the matter, while Naim behaved, as usual, like a gentleman. Twenty years later I still count on Naim's loyalty and friendship. When I wrote my first book, a truly dire spoof on the fashion business, it was Naim who, with great generosity of spirit, was the first to review it. We still have lunch from time to time. The cordon-bleu days might have gone, but the panache remains. Naim's enthusiasm and passion for life have never faltered. I am always more pleased than I can say to see him – and I wear my gold Asprey's egg a lot.

THE BLUE ROLLS-ROYCE

I once went with John Asprey for a quick bite to eat at Brown's Hotel in Albermarle Street and, for no other reason except that it was such a sunny spring day, we decided to walk to Berkeley Square and look at the array of Rolls-Royce cars in Jack Barclay's showrooms. There a long-base royal-blue Rolls-Royce attracted my attention and we went inside to give it a closer inspection. Jack Barclay's son, who knew John from their schooldays, came up to greet him warmly and showed us round. I could not take my eyes off the blue Rolls-Royce. I asked for details and found out it was a second-hand car that had only one owner on the logbook. The mileage was low and the asking price was seventeen thousand pounds.

I became overwhelmed with excitement, and although I did not possess anything approaching the funds for the purchase, immediately said I would like to buy it. John Asprey looked at me with a stunned expression. He knew perfectly well that I could not afford the car, and, what was even more crazy, I was on the verge of purchasing a vehicle which I could not even drive. John kept reminding me of these salient points, but I was adamant.

Naturally, I said, I would also have to hire a chauffeur – which was something else I did not have the means to do in my present circumstances. Everything happened at bewildering speed. In a moment of madness, I had irresponsibly purchased a Rolls-Royce to fulfil a dream that had been with me ever since the early years of my marriage. Basically I could not afford to pay for the car, let alone maintain it, but just the same I told Jack Barclay I would take delivery in three weeks' time as I was having to go on an urgent trip abroad. This was quite untrue but the only ploy I could think of to give myself time to sort things out.

I asked John Asprey meanwhile to leave his visiting card with Barclay's as a token of validation for the purchase. John complied, to indicate solidarity with me and not let the side down, but as soon as we were outside the showrooms his reaction was more of disconcerted wonderment than of admonishment. Even so, as soon as he got back to his office, he could not resist mischievously phoning my wife Maria to forewarn her how her husband had, in a moment of wild exuberance, bought himself a Rolls-Royce – emphasizing the make of car to get the maximum rise out of her. It worked. Maria was livid, though the word is too mild to describe her actual response. She would never set foot inside such a car, she swore to John Asprey in her fury. I would either have to return it or ride in it alone.

John then phoned me to report Maria's displeasure and alert me to the row awaiting me at home. I braced myself to face the music. But while Maria was truly upset, she came to accept the fact that it was too late to do anything about it without an embarrassing loss of face. She also realized that if she pursued the matter too fiercely she could undermine my morale and shake my confidence. That was the last thing she wanted to do. In times of crisis it was typical of Maria to close ranks with me so that we could present a united front. Whatever chastising was done was carried out behind closed doors. She never allowed her anger to spill beyond the confines of her own home.

There was actually very little time in hand for me to arrange for the financing of the car. I spoke to Lord James Crichton-Stuart, who was on the board of Coutts, and the board agreed to advance me the purchase money. Lord James, whom I knew rather well, was always sympathetic to me and had helped me in the past. The question of a driver was also soon resolved. A chauffeur who had formerly been in the service of Princess Margaret came forward to apply for the job after he heard about the vacancy on the grapevine. The scene was therefore set for me to be driven about in grand style, giving the impression of wealth without actually having any. The paradox was that owning the Rolls-Royce probably did indirectly bestow on me many of the things I was seeking to achieve. It was still an era when ostentation played a major part in the making of a business magnate, though the principle does not necessarily hold true today.

REBECCA FRASER

Rebecca Fraser, now a distinguished biographer and historian, left Quartet in 1986 having been with Quartet for many years in a variety of roles, culminating in her running of Robin Clark, a literary paperback reprint list which Quartet incorporated. Here, in her own words, she recalls her time spent in the bosom of the Namara Group:

For Naim: A Tribute

Rebecca Fraser

Almost a quarter of a century ago, in the autumn of 1982, I arrived at the publishers called Quartet Books, to work in the art department. I was very interested in book production and illustration as I had just illustrated two books myself, and had also done so as a child for Sidgwick & Jackson.

Having a mother who was a writer brought additional interest to working in publishing. I liked the whole pernickety process of bookmaking which I had seen going on in our house from my earliest youth – the book-jacket proofs, the colour plates, the prelims, the acknowledgements, the footnotes, the index. Just how complex the whole process was had recently been brought home in New York where I had been a researcher for the investigative journalist Edward Jay Epstein on two complex books, one about diamonds and the other about Armand Hammer.

But Quartet was a publisher with a difference or 'a tweeest!' as my new employer liked to say, drawing the word out as he always did into a sort of shriek of highly contagious excitement. Like everything to do with Quartet, starting with my immediate hiring over a delicious lunch, the whole experience would be faintly surreal, but wonderful. Mr Naim Attallah, the boss, was absolute emperor and lived in a magnificent and flamboyant fashion. Every day his uniformed chauffeur was to be seen whizzing about London in a large Rolls-Royce, mainly taking Naim to power breakfasts, or occasionally rushing proofs to a libel lawyer far away in the Temple if Naim or an editor had got the wind up about a book. I found that by and large Naim aimed to be in the newspapers a great deal, whether on his own account or with his publishing, which was daring and challenged the status quo – as all good publishers do. Naim had the mind of a Bletchley Park computer, strangely allied to the exuberant temperament and creative passion of a conductor or a great opera star. Having been a banker, he insisted that he personally rechecked all the costings which are the integral part of the publishing process. He never stood still.

As in *Alice in Wonderland*, what I thought was a publishing house was always becoming something else as well: a chocolate shop, parfumerie, jewellers and so on. For like a true empire it expanded all the time with the sort of relentless energy of my new employer. And oh the extravaganzas that flowed from Naim's fertile and enthusiastic mind – the plays, like *The Beastly Beatitudes of Balthazar B* and *Trafford Tanzi* starring Toyah Wilcox, then at the height of her fame, the magazines, many of which have become literary institutions – the *Literary Review*, the *Oldie*, the *Wire* – and the Academy Bookclub. The whole operation was backed by the legendary PR company Namara, also housed in the empire's engine room, Namara House in Poland Street. At the top of this narrow house sat the imposing, enormously tall figure of the charming Naim behind his vast custom-made desk, while in and out rushed captains of industry, famous figures like Fleur Cowles, editors, reporters and photographers. They were all desperate to be published by Naim and wined and dined and promoted by him. For Naim loved people and they usually returned his affection. Naim was kind-hearted, generous and trusting in the extreme.

I soon realized that my real passion was editing, and after a period learning the black arts of publicity, I moved to edit Robin Clark books. This was a very nice little paperback imprint that had begun as a humorous classics list but which I was keen to make a showcase for exquisite first novels and literary nonfiction. We discovered some terrific writers even off what was known as the 'slush pile' – novels sent in without an agent, something unimaginable today with uberagents presiding as chick lit goes for six-figure sums. The great thing about Naim was that he was prepared to take the risk on first novels which other, bigger houses would not. We began to specialize in literary trade paperbacks like the Bloomsbury Frances Partridge's *Memories*, Allan Massie, Peter Vansittart and Auberon Waugh's five novels. We published Peter Handke, Julian Barnes's first novel and Heathcote Williams's classic *The Speakers*. Christine Sutherland's marvellous *Princess of Siberia*, which continues to sell twenty years later, was a huge hit, as were *Marie Walewska* and *Monica: Heroine of the Danish Resistance*.

No. 27 Goodge Street, a tiny little walk-up opposite a stationer's just off Tottenham Court Road, was the nerve centre of the editorial department. It contained within it many fierce spirits battling for dominion. They were also battling with Naim's taste, as most of them were women and most of them had an inbuilt resistance to Naim's default position *vis-à-vis* publishing. Despite his passionate interest in current affairs, what made Naim really happy was a photography or art book – 'Very erotic, beloved!' he would call out happily – and the saucier the better. There was usually a great deal of annoyance and rolling of eyes about the photography books at 27 Goodge Street, to which Naim paid very little attention. He continued to commission them imperturbably and they rolled inexorably off the presses. At the same time Naim was also truly contributing to feminist power by bankrolling the ground-breaking feminist publishers The Women's Press, which published seminal works by Elaine Showalter and Kate Millett, while Quartet itself published the 1980s classic, Anne Dickson's *A Woman in Your Own Right*.

Some of the Namara empire's contradictions were embodied in the figure of the sales director, David Elliott. David was rather like Naim in character. He was extremely kind and very mischievous. Although he was also the sales manager of The Women's Press, he took huge pleasure in annoying every member of their staff. He rushed about in his combat jacket and his desert boots, thinking of remarks to enrage 'the Sisters', as he called them, his black eyes snapping with pleasure, his bushy hair bristling with aggro for the sake of it. His close ally was the Scots accountant, Olive, who had very black eyebrows and white hair. Every week, as she distributed the pay slips made out in her tiny precise writing, Olive sniffed in a way that suggested that Naim was quite mad to pay anyone except herself. She was guarded by her huge Dobermann pinscher which she had bought as a tiny sweet puppy. But David also enjoyed baiting the bluestocking editors at Quartet. Just when everyone had had enough and would rush round to kill him, he and his terrible dog Tramp, the worse-tempered mongrel I have ever known, would make you scream with laughter.

Despite his naughtiness, David was extremely well-read, had been in books for years and had all kinds of brilliant ideas. He forced me to seek an audience with Dame Nora Smallwood to get her permission to do a V. S. Pritchett omnibus. That was quite terrifying – she was then the doyen of English publishers – as was meeting the great man V. S. Pritchett himself in Gloucester Terrace. *The Pritchett Omnibus* was a smash hit for Robin Clark, which under Jeremy Beale began to expand. Since then the imprint has published a great many jewels of English writing that should always remain in print: Thackeray's *The Book of Snobs*, Herbert Read's *The Green Child* and W. W. Jacobs's terrifying 'The Monkey's Paw', with a selection of his humorous stories. Of course, we could never compete with the bigger trade paperbacks starting up at the time, but we published many literary books which in today's climate might remain unpublished.

At night as the dusk fell and the office workers started leaving Goodge Street, it was a perfect life for a twenty-four-year-old. One could either work late in the cosy little offices looking out on Fitzrovia and roam through the amazing Quartet backlist, or increasingly one could go to Naim's parties! By the time I left in 1986, having begun to write a biography of Charlotte Brontë, Naim was one of the most fêted men in London. He had begun a successful literary career of his own with several wonderful books published. His warmth, charm and sheer niceness persuaded many icons of our age to 'fess up all to him.

I met some of my greatest friends at Quartet, where the atmosphere was serious, hardworking and enormous fun. We all wanted to get on and Naim had a wonderful ability to give responsibility to the young. The thought of children and marriage left me cold. The word was what mattered. I then went on to work for a Maxwell paper and *Tatler* magazine as features editor, but the seminal period in my life was working for Naim. Gentle, kind and thoughtful, he was a great creative force and true Maecenas. There should be more like him.

RANA

In 1985 an event took place that was stranger than fiction. It began as a whimsical exercise in curiosity. Word had reached my ears of a beautiful Syrian girl called Rana Kabbani, said to be full of cultural graces and exceptional talents. She was married, twice, to the Palestinian poet, Mahmoud Darwish, and when the marriage failed the second time she left Paris, where she was living, and returned to Damascus, the city of her birth. There, I was told, she was contemplating her future. The details were sketchy, but the more I heard about her the more intrigued I became. I grew intent on finding out as much as I could before making any overtures. In time the pieces of the jigsaw came together to reveal more: she was a Cambridge graduate who had broken many hearts during her sojourn at the university; an Eastern beauty who was endowed with outstanding intellectual gifts; a woman whose abilities could take her in any direction she chose.

I became determined to bring her into the Quartet fold. My obsessive nature gave me no rest until I had managed to track her down. As we spoke on the telephone I found myself babbling about a job at Quartet to someone who was a complete stranger. She must have thought me a dangerous lunatic, ringing from London for a reason beyond her comprehension.

That conversation was the first of many. In the end I persuaded her to pack her bags and head for the airport and a new life. The strangest thing about the whole business was that neither of us had laid eyes on the other, yet both were willing to be hostages to fate. For me it was an inspired gamble, though I cannot guess what went through Rana's mind. That is why she has penned her side of the story especially for this book and given me permission to reproduce it along with a letter she wrote a week after joining Quartet. My own recollection is as vivid and vibrant today as it was when she came into my office for the first time, bringing with her a bright light that somehow illuminated the premises.

Naim's Harem

Rana Kabbani

I came to London in 1985 in answer to a job offer from Naim Attallah. I had lived in many of the world's great cities – Damascus, New York, Djakarta, Washington, Beirut, Paris, Tunis, Cambridge – and was native to the very oldest of them, Damascus. But London would prove to be the most significant for me. It was the place I came to consider my home, where I would throw myself into work and political causes; where I would marry and have children; where I would make my most important, sustaining and wonderful friendships. And all because of Naim, that improbable *deus ex machina*.

I had lived in England before, spending three years at Jesus College, Cambridge. From there I came away with a PhD, my first published book and something of a broken heart. My plan was to return to my country of origin and look for a university teaching post, which was what I did in 1985. Syria in the meantime had become a very sinister place. Two years earlier an armed uprising by the Muslim Brotherhood had been put down by the regime in the most violent and ruthless manner, resulting in a massacre in the city of Hama, where thousands of civilians were slaughtered. The regime then extended its crackdown to crush all dissent and, besides, every shade of Islamist, targeted leftists, communists, Nasserites, students, poets, teachers and actors – activists and intellectuals of every kind. These found themselves in horrifying dungeons from which there was often no way out alive. In this way they were silenced from speaking out against the macabre methods of the state. Thus did many of my generation perish and join the unaccounted for, the 'disappeared', who to this day in Syria number some 14,000 missing.

To survive in the country, get a job, remain free, remain alive, one had to show total allegiance to Big Brother. The army was on the street; the vicious security services ruled everywhere, helping themselves to whatever and whomever they wanted. You crossed them at your peril. I had applied to the English faculty at Damascus University to teach the nineteenth-century literature that had always been my passion. I was well qualified for the job, but it was soon made clear to me that I would only get it if I became a Baath party member. But I was not a joiner and one-party rule sickened me.

My family had been deeply implicated in the making of Syria's history. On both sides its members had respectively served the Ottoman Empire, fought the Ottoman Empire, fought French colonial rule and been imprisoned; had penned the Syrian constitution, had thrown themselves into establishing democratic elections after independence; had been elected to ministries and premierships; had been outstanding citizens and patriots; had used their personal fortunes and patrician positions to serve their country in every conceivable field. It may therefore have been in my genes to look askance at the angry country boys who had come to power on the back of tanks, replacing a budding, democratic Syria with fascism and thuggery. Urbane, middle-class professionals had already left the country, realizing that Baathist Syria saw them as class enemies and would never treat them with justice. Yet still I lingered a little longer. I did not want to be cut off from my language and family, or to become dispossessed – the invariable fate of exiles.

Then a man I had never heard of, let alone met, began to ring me persistently from London, insisting he had a job for me. Since he sounded like a demented cartoon character, calling me

'Dahling' in an extraordinary accent and an over-excited manner, I became intrigued. I promised I'd consider his offer, but this wasn't good enough. Naim Attallah wouldn't leave it there, but rang me every day, four times a day, demanding to know when I would arrive. He cajoled, scolded, joked, pleaded, ordered. Finally I cracked and thought it best to get on a plane to London. It is only now, as I write this twenty years later, that I realize Naim Attallah probably saved my life.

Quartet Books, where I arrived to work, was in a broken-down area off the Tottenham Court Road, miles away from the gentrified bit of Kensington where I was staying. The buildings were Dickensian in their ramshackle mess; everyone working there looked like a character from a novel – lush, mad, exotic and highly strung, with a hilarious sense of humour. Naim operated, like the Wizard of Oz, from somewhere else and was still no more than a voice to me as I climbed the stairs to find my office. I was in luck. The spirit of the place, a man possessed of the most beautiful eyes I had ever seen, Stephen Pickles, took a shine to me. With my very high heels and very long hair, my scarlet nail polish and lipstick, I was everything his rigorous, homosexual rules wanted a woman to be – overtly feminine and utterly unapproachable.

Pickles at once voted me the perfect arm candy to take to swish London parties. We settled into a comfortable routine: books and gossip by day; more books and gossip on our evening prowls. It would have been hard to find two more contented cats. In Pickles I had discovered a sensitive, ferociously well read, elegant and sardonic navigator and translator. London was a mysterious place where everyone spoke in code. Thanks to Pickles I was given the key to break the code, and very soon break it I did.

On my first morning, right on cue, having checked me out

first, Pickles walked me through a few streets and across Oxford Street to meet Naim. We went into the most amazing office, full of colours I had never seen used before on walls and floors in such extravagant profusion. Entering Naim's inner sanctum was a mind-altering experience: all shocking pinks and animal skins and precious, eroticized objects. Naim himself was larger than life: very tall, elegant in a startling and unforgettably vivid way, with an amazing lining to his jacket and a brilliant tie. His features were all wrong if you took their components separately, but joined together they made a unique and loveable face that was forever working itself up into spasms of high excitement, like a child's. Pickles slipped easily into being the gruff, nonchalant, understating foil to his boss's florid dramas, and I could see within a few seconds that everything was going to be fine. I had landed in a sort of recherché zoo, and being a wild animal myself – part panther, part peacock – I began to feel immensely happy.

'Is your office comfortable, my dahling?' Naim enquired as he hugged me again and again, as though recognizing a soul-mate.

'No,' I said as petulantly as I could manage. 'My office is awful, because there's no bed in it, and I need a bed so I can have a siesta in the afternoon, as I always do at home.'

Naim froze in horror – not, as it turned out, in a reaction to my utterly preposterous demand but because he felt he had been found wanting.

'We must get you a bed at once!' he announced, turning pale. 'Pickles, who should we call? Harrods?'

Next morning I had a bed, which soon became the social focus of the building, just as in a student bedsit. Pickles would sometimes sit on it as he ploughed through a typescript he was working on. Then rumour began to circulate that this was no mere bed, but a harem divan covered in silks that Naim had had made for the new Sultana Valideh, who could wrap him round her little finger and made her terrifying demands in Arabic. Quartet was a rumour mill and the pecking order among Naim's harem of women employees was as ferocious as it must have been at Topkapi. The bed story duly reached the ears of the two Great Beauties who shared an office downstairs: Nigella Lawson and Rebecca Fraser, who had shared power quite amicably prior to my arrival. Rebecca, who possessed a fierce intelligence, extraordinary beauty and the skills of a virtuoso fencing master, decided she must see for herself what was going on. She came up to introduce herself, saying we must have lunch in a few days. On her way out of the office she smiled and said in her most imperious tone, pointing at the bed, 'Oh! How sweet!' Thus I was put in my place for ever as her second in command.

In this respect, too, Naim had come to my rescue, saving me from existential loneliness in the England that gradually became my home through a precious introduction to the formidable Rebecca Fraser. She was to become my dearest friend, and her family was to adopt me as yet another wild and wayward 'gel'. Her clan – generous, rowdy, erudite, affectionate, supportive and inhumanly clever – was all you could wish for. Rebecca's mother, Lady Antonia Fraser, and Rebecca's sister Flora also became my adored friends. Her daughter, Atalanta Fitzgerald, born years after our Quartet era, is my goddaughter, of whom I am more than usually proud.

Naim had an uncanny ability to talent-spot. Many of those he employed, or whose careers he supported or encouraged, became high-flyers in their fields. A list of their names would come close to constituting a British cultural who's who. Despite an *embarrasse de richesse*, my favourite of Naim's 'discoveries' is the use made in Jonathan Dimbleby's book *The Palestinians* of photographs by Don McCullin, showing haunting images of people in refugee camps. Don was then known only as a photo-journalist within press circles, but he has since come to rank, quite rightly, as one of the world's most moving, profound and serious artists. Naim could see this quality from the start. But then Naim was always in advance of everyone else, blazing ahead in a flurry of ideas and enthusiasms. It always makes me secretly pleased that a maverick Palestinian, and a self-made one at that, should have had such a profound effect on English society, giving such a tremendous leg-up to so many of its gifted sons and daughters from such a range of social backgrounds.

Whenever he entertained he was wildly extravagant and generous. His parties – whether they were seated affairs for a few in his office, with delicious food served by stunning employees, or cocktail gatherings for hundreds of the famous, where champagne flowed and canapés never stopped circulating – were forerunners in the 1980s of what would become 'lifestyle' events in the 1990s. No one in England, certainly no publisher, had thought before to entertain as he did. He was the king of parties. Everyone who was anyone wanted to be included. Other people's book launches were shrivelled, mean, puritanical affairs by comparison, with undrinkable plonk.

The person I came to worship most at Quartet was Olive, Naim's amazing accountant. She was a great woman, 'worth a guinea a minute', as Jeremy Beale, my fellow editor, liked to describe her. Olive was matter-of-fact and funny at the same time. She came out with the best throwaway one-liners I have ever heard, delivered in her inimitable Aberdonian accent. She was scary and made you want to behave; and behave I always did, when she was around at least. I was dumbfounded when, on the eve of my marriage, she called me up to her office and gave me the most beautiful porcelain candlesticks and bonbonnière, ornately worked with delicate grey and gold roses. These, she told me, had been given as a present at her own marriage, half a century before. To this day they remain my most treasured possessions. Working at Quartet was a dream. I was doing what I liked – reading and editing books. I was partying with friends and discovering a great city, all on Naim's time and pay. No boss could have been more magnanimous or asked for so little in return. He allowed me to be myself – lazy, free, crazy and ungovernable. He understood me instinctively and never tried to change me.

The letter Rana wrote me soon after arriving in London was as follows:

> Dear Naim – A strange Sunday afternoon this as I read *The Shah of Shahs*. This Polish man [the distinguished journalist Ryszard Kapuscinski] knows more about our displaced history than all the specialists; for in the end, it is his own wound which he is describing, his own country's wrench between fragrant church and the sorrowing democrat's dream. Certain lines stay in my mind like Mozart's phrases: ousted politicians entering history, blinded children singing their pointless tragedies – all of our untidiness is here, all our panic and passion.
>
> I go for a walk in the park on this first Sunday of my new existence. I'm settling in with the frenzy of a bird after rain. A woman on a nearby bench is exiled in a particular sorrow. She must be Iranian, her eyebrows and hair come straight out of Hafiz. She sits on this green bench in remote Holland Park – how very far from Tabriz! A park full of exiles stunned by the sudden sun.
>
> I'm happy, and bursting with language. I think our commerce will be rich beyond calculation. Leave me some scope to wander and some freedom to dash off to Beijing when the

mood hits me and I will always meander back to the genteelly shabby premises of drab Goodge Street. Whatever I make of myself in the heady and luxuriant years to come will be of your making too. I am so excited by possibilities, by the wandering restless fanatical mind's voyages. And I am utterly contented in the choice I've made to come under your wing.

Yours, Rana

CELEBRITY PUBLISHING

1987 established a new Quartet departure and gained an exposure for the imprint in a field that was entirely outside its normal range. We began to publish various celebrity books, and one in particular sticks in my memory. It concerned an actress and was entitled: *Charlotte Rampling with Compliments*. It was a collation of snapshots, fashion shots and movie stills of the star over a period of twenty years. The *Standard* commented:

The divine Charlotte Rampling has been turning strong men to porridge ever since her début in 1965 as a water-skiing nymph in Richard Lester's *The Knack*. Now one of her most devoted fans, Mr Naim Attallah, the Arabian connoisseur of the fair sex, is bringing out a book ...

Another admirer, Dirk Bogarde, who starred with her in *The Night Porter*, contributed an introductory portrait of the actress: 'She was as free, simple and skittish as a foal, hair tumbling in a golden fall about her ... the grace of a panther ... the almost incredible perfection of her bone structure.' The Japanese film director Nagisa Oshima, who had recently directed her in *Max My Love*, in which she co-starred with an ape, contributed four pages of painstakingly drawn Japanese ideograms in celebration of his leading lady. Both contributions gushed shamelessly and showed the amount of love and admiration people in show business felt for her.

Memories

I was particularly glad to be publishing this book. In 1973, when Charlotte Rampling starred in *The Night Porter* with Dirk Bogarde, she began to inhabit the dreams of a whole generation of men. I, for one, had never recovered from the sight of her straddling Dirk Bogarde, and the image remained in my mind like an old sepia photograph. In the film she played a young girl who blossomed into a sophisticated woman, and her performance was so haunting as to move one critic to compare her with Garbo. Two years later, in the 1975 remake of *Farewell My Lovely*, her seductiveness was supreme yet perfectly contained.

When I met her in the 1980s, I found the real Rampling even more compelling than the screen version. She struck me as both exotic and English – a near contradiction in terms – and she underplayed her sex-symbol status with a rare intelligence, despite the allure of her emerald-green eyes, her velvety voice and the perfection of her bone structure.

Underneath the poise, however, Charlotte Rampling seemed haunted by demons. As the daughter of an army colonel, she had had an unsettled – and sometimes unhappy – childhood. She had felt rejected by her mother in favour of her older sister, who later died tragically at the age of only twenty-three. Charlotte reacted by exceeding the traditional boundaries of women's lives. During the 1960s, when everyone else was on CND marches or off to India doing ashrams, she went to live with gypsies in Afghanistan (a dangerous and violent experience) and later to a Tibetan monastery in Scotland. By the time she was twenty-two, she was in Hollywood and had earned herself the title of 'Europe's kinky sex-film queen' by living in a *ménage à trois* with Brian Southcombe and a male model. Later she told me that she had loved both men but, to spare her parents' feelings, thought it best to marry one of them.

In 1976, she met Jean-Michel Jarre at the Cannes Film Festival after what she described as a *coup de foudre*, and the following year they married; unfortunately they are now divorced. Jarre was a highly successful composer and musician with an international following.

Looked at from the outside, they seemed like a dream couple, combining art, beauty, glamour and intelligence in enviable proportions. It could have been an ideal partnership, but it was never likely that Charlotte Rampling would subscribe to the Jane Austen view of marriage as a woman's principal act of self-definition. Rampling was always far too unconventional ever to be defined by marriage. 'Jean-Michel and I are very *marginale*, as we say in French,' she told me. 'We do things which are off the beaten track.'

Just as she had always chosen cinematic roles that explored the darker side of human nature, so she was given to delving deep into her own soul. More than once she had suffered depression and come close to nervous breakdown.

Evidently it was improbable that marriage would ever bring her stability in the conventional sense; rather, it was always likely to be a continuation of the restlessness from which she could never find a refuge. *Plus ça change, plus c'est la même chose.* She was truly a woman to break boundaries.

Charlotte Rampling with Compliments was virtually a biography, but it told its story visually. It illustrated the early modelling career of the beautiful girl in the London of the swinging sixties as well as documenting the international film career that followed for her soon after. Fashion photographers, including the world-famous Helmut Newton, David Bailey and Cecil Beaton, captured her compelling, enigmatic moods, which were often mysteriously melancholic and invariably conveyed an erotic aura of unique intensity. The volume was also beautifully produced and it did well commercially. It created a good rapport with Charlotte, which led to her becoming yet another candidate for my projected book of interviews with women.

A MORE INNOCENT TIME?

The recent brouhaha about the sexual antics on various TV programmes reminded me of a time, not that long ago, when a suggestion that wives sucked their husbands' toes was ridiculed as if we had faced the end of civilization.

In 1987 Quartet published a book whose reception provoked a response that was never intended (though that ancient adage about no publicity is ever that bad does apply in the publishing trade). The hilarity arose partly because of its subject and partly because of the identity of its author, who happened to be married to David Stevens, then the press baron of Express Newspapers who had been created a life peer as Lord Stevens of Ludgate. Melissa Sadoff, as she called herself, possessed an inherited family title from central Europe and was, formally speaking, Melissa, Countess Andrassy. The book she had written was *Woman as Chameleon: or How To Be the Ideal Woman*. It was the very antithesis of feminist doctrine, aiming to teach women ways to keep their marriage exciting by pampering their man and acceding to his every wish and whim. Melissa was flamboyant in her views and Lord Stevens gave the impression of taking his wife's attentions in his stride. She described the treatment she gave him in rather embarrassing detail, which opened up an opportunity for the critics to have a field-day in leg-pulling. 'Grovel' of *Private Eye* immediately dubbed Melissa 'Countess Undressy' and claimed to have suggested the book after hearing her speak about her husband's 'Ugandan preferences'. He was able to quote her verbatim for his own purposes.

> 'There is nothing,' she says, 'that can be called perverse between husband and wife so long as it relates to the husband's need and the wife's willingness to do it.' I have advised her to put it all on paper with a view to publication in book form. I tell her that my

friend the seedy Lebanese parfumier Mr AttullahDisgusting could well be interested, as he is currently obsessed by all aspects of the Ugandan situation.

Two weeks later 'Grovel' followed through with the latest development:

> As I suggested, the Countess Undressy ... is to write a book of Ugandan hints, which will shortly be published by the swarthy Lebanese sex-fiend Naim Attullah-Disgusting. The 'Countess' will not mince words when she describes how she sees the duties of a wife. 'Always kiss your husband's body, starting from his toes,' she writes. 'After kissing his toes and sucking them, proceed to kiss every inch of his legs ... 'She should then perform the oral act. Many women feel an aversion towards this form of sex ... Women who feel this way need to be asked what they would prefer – to have their husband go to a prostitute for such a service?' (What's the oral act? © Norman Fowler '87) (That's enough filth. Ed.)

The launch for *Woman as Chameleon* was held on 10 February, with 'Londoner's Diary' of the *Evening Standard* citing the toe-kissing routine before asking 'a pale, nervous and uncomfortable' David Stevens, 'Well, does she always?' He had to confess that he hadn't yet read the book, and didn't intend to do so till he'd sifted through the reviews. 'Otherwise I might be embarrassed.'

The nearest the party came to being risqué was when Jubby Ingrams's (the daughter of Richard Ingrams, and who worked at Quartet) shoe was removed from her foot by an admirer with a view to kissing her from the toes upwards. Ms Sadoff rushed over to intervene. 'No,' she cried with a Transylvanian lilt. 'It must be the other way round.'

Henry Porter in the *Sunday Times* 'Notebook' judged David Stevens to be 'rather more reticent about his home life' than was his wife.

I would estimate that this book ... is going to cause considerable embarrassment to Mr Stevens ... None the less, he has taken steps to purchase the serial rights if only to keep it out of the hands of the Daily Mail group, which naturally was keen to enhance his discomfort by publishing extracts like this: 'Become your husband's own prostitute ... if your husband is in his study, workroom or garage in the wintertime put on a sexy slip, wrap yourself in a coat, slip on suspenders, black stockings and surprise him wherever he may be.'

Unfortunately the fun and games of the press diverted attention from the rest of the book, which threw many a light on relationships, friendships, motherhood and divorce, with sound philosophical reflections. Melissa was of Hungarian origin, a talented concert pianist and an accomplished hostess. She was perhaps a shade over the top in her enthusiasm, but being an eternal optimist her heart was in the right place. In retrospect, I believe she deserved more praise for the book than she ever received. Throughout the merciless lampooning from *Private Eye* and the barrage of snide sarcasm aimed by the rest of the press against the book, which inevitably earned the displeasure of the feminist lobby, she remained in control and outwardly unaffected by it all.

Her husband, despite the newspapers' determination to embarrass him, was extremely supportive. He did not seem to be in any way phased by the teasing of friends over the rumpus caused by some of the book's intimate passages. Sadly, only two years later, Melissa died when she got up in the middle of the night to eat a peach and choked on the stone. I was in Los Angeles at the time and was woken to hear the dreadful news. It left me feeling very emotional. I had grown to like Melissa immensely. Her colourful personality and boundless zest for life were her enduring strengths and ensured she could not be easily forgotten.

A MAN FOR ALL SEASONS

Quartet first published Colin Spencer nearly 40 years ago when *Victims of Love* completed his brilliant sequence of novels – *The Generation Quartet* – which has been shamefully forgotten by the literary establishment. I remain convinced their quality, insight and compassion will come to be seen by future generations as one of the great literary achievements of the mid twentieth century.

The recent revival of Colin's play, *Spitting Image*, at Islington's King Head theatre, (originally staged in 1968, and the first play to be openly about a homosexual relationship put on in Britain) gives me the opportunity to highlight our publishing in 2013, Colin's wonderful volume of autobiography, *Backing Into Light, My Father's Son*.

Just read the first two paragraphs:

> A few weeks before I was born, sometime that June in 1933 in the small back kitchen of 12, Redford Avenue, Thornton Heath, my father was intent on murdering me. Drunk and amidst a tirade of vituperation, waving a kitchen knife he was threatening to stab my mother in the womb. 'Doing you and the kid in,' is what he would have shouted, spitting and weeping ... though he would have referred at that as 'blubbing'... 'and then myself.'
>
> My foetal self, almost ready to be born, would have expected immediate annihilation, as the mother did that bore me. I believe in that moment I became terror struck, a terror of him that continued throughout my life. I must have curled up more tightly, unwilling to venture into this violently angry world outside. This, in fact, has always been my reaction; timidity, caution, shyness, expecting the worst, yet I think these fears are also balanced by the opposites, many of these latter qualities, I suspect, I inherited from my father. So his heritage has been a strange and complex one, a heritage that I have had to fight as much as accept.

Colin Spencer remains one of our very best writers and it's an outrage he is not better appreciated. Buying this volume of autobiography is a fitting counterpoint to the establishment's brutal indifference. This gem of a book is also a stunning account of art school life in 1950s Brighton and London's literary bohemia during the 'swinging sixties'.

TAMARA

Sheer impulsiveness accounted for my meeting with Tamara von Schenk at a cocktail party. I must have sensed I would be on the same wavelength as Tamara, a striking blonde of German stock, for I homed in to speak to her without waiting for an introduction. Why overlook such an opportunity, I reasoned, when I was fortunate enough to be caught in her magnetic field? I found myself talking to an elfin-like creature who was elegant without being sensational, sultry without being threatening, and who possessed an aristocratic look that was apparent even if you knew nothing of her background. Tamara was every inch an aristocrat, with the sort of complexion and comportment men dream about. She cast a light, unobtrusive shadow for one with such a rich, distinctive aura. I felt comfortable in her presence. It was nothing like a first-time encounter but felt as if our paths had crossed many times before. Each responded to the other with the sort of ease that usually develops after many years of acquaintance. I firmly believe in the concept of our destiny preordaining every step we take and that it is pointless to fight it, but I am equally convinced that we can help it along in our chosen direction. This may sound like a paradox, but the undeniable truth of it emerges as the years pass. Tamara's life took on a new dimension after our first meeting. I offered her a job at Quartet. She was not trained for it, but proved equal to the challenge. She accompanied me to Cologne for a chocolate fair to act as my translator, and later performed a similar role at the Frankfurt Book Fair. In the piece that follows, Tamara gives her recollections of her time with Quartet and the friendship that developed between us.

Dealing with Variety

Tamara von Schenk

It wasn't too difficult to establish who the infamous Naim was the evening I met him in 1993. One man alone managed to dominate a large group of charmed women. His body language, enthusiastic and energetic, coupled with colour flashes from his vibrant suit lining, matching tie and large ring adorning his left hand, singled him out as some exotic species among the rest of the grey and drab business-suited men. I decided to take a closer look and forty minutes later walked away, slightly stunned, as I had just been hired, having had no experience, as publicity manager for Quartet. I tried to dismiss his reputation as a serial womanizer and the fact that I was a slightly overweight blonde in heels and put the whole thing down to utter madness. It was only later that I understood that this was part of an extremely generous, if somewhat obsessive, and spontaneous nature which made up the complex persona of Naim Attallah.

The glamorous reputation of the Attallah posse of well-bred, rich, partying girls had worn off by the time I joined Quartet in May 1994. From day one my friendships with Georgia de Chamberet, Pickles and especially Susie Craigie Halkett were sealed. I felt lucky to be working with three such strong individuals in one of the last remaining independent publishing houses that still adhered to the original ideas of publishing. The variety of material that came through our doors ranged from the avant-garde to more traditional material covering the latest in photography, gay literature and a mixture of undiscovered gems from Europe. Naim's roots were important to him, and this was strongly reflected in the extensive Middle Eastern list, which was quite a novelty at the time.

A week-long trip to Cuba to compile an anthology of young Cuban writers was an unforgettable privilege. The days were spent collecting a wide breadth of material from a stream of struggling and often highly talented writers, desperate to smuggle out what they had written to bypass the harsh restrictions of the Castro regime. Those we met came from all walks of life and our journey was a tremendously humbling and thought-provoking experience and definitely a sharp contrast to the madness and predictability of the Frankfurt Book Fair, which came a few months later.

Of the many books that passed through my hands, the one I worked on in my last few months at Quartet was the most memorable. It involved a close association with the author herself, Elizabeth Wurtzel, whose work and private life fused together with her hugely successful book, *Prozac Nation*, which besides being my last was also my most challenging project. I went beyond the call of duty as publicity manager when I invited Elizabeth, depressed, paranoid, self-obsessed and
highly complicated, into my home, where she stayed far longer than expected. I chaperoned her day and night during her publicity tour – an interesting experience to say the least. This title was the first personal account of a life of depression eased by the wonder drug Prozac, and as such both marked a turning-point in Quartet's history and an end to my time there.

To this day I have the valued friendship of Naim, a fiercely loyal man who in return expects no less from those close to him.

Being the colourful character he is, he has so often been misunderstood and surrounded by rumours. Those who know him well are aware of his extreme vulnerability. In difficult times, he has maintained his dignity and the high standards he sets for himself. I can truly say that I am happy to have met such a man.

HARRY WINSTON

Being often in Geneva, John Asprey and I had the good fortune to meet the legendary Harry Winston, who was undoubtedly the most successful diamond dealer in the world. He maintained a large office in Switzerland to cater for wealthy clients who came to see him in search of important stones, unique for their size and colour. He had set up his own business, the Premier Diamond Company, on Fifth Avenue in New York in 1920 when he was only twenty-eight, and went on to become the most prolific gem salesman of his generation. He revolutionized the way precious stones were set, shifting the emphasis on to the stones themselves and away from the ornate settings popular in the earlier twentieth century. Many of the most famous diamonds in history passed through his hands, including the Hope Diamond, which he donated to the Smithsonian Institution as a gift to the American people. On Oscar nights in Hollywood many of the sparkling diamonds worn by the stars had been loaned to them by Harry Winston. In 1958 his firm created the Nur Il Ain tiara for Queen Farah to wear at her wedding to the Shah of Iran. Among Harry's royal clients were members of the House of Saud in Saudi Arabia.

The history of what became known as the Taylor-Burton Diamond turned into one of the most extraordinary episodes of Harry's career. The original stone, of over 240 carats, had been found in 1966 and Harry bought it at once. He and his master cutter then studied it for six months before attempting the cleaving, which was successfully carried out live in front of television cameras. The largest piece eventually yielded a classic pear-shaped gem of 69.42 carats, which was sold to Harriet Annenberg Ames, the sister of Walter Annenberg, an American diplomat. In 1969 it reappeared in the auction room after Mrs Ames tired of having to keep it always hidden in a bank vault. The actor Richard Burton was well known for his habit of buying diamonds for his wife Elizabeth Taylor, and the Burtons certainly took an interest. The bidding started at two hundred thousand dollars and swiftly rose to a record price of over a million dollars; at which point Burton's representative dropped out and the stone went to the chairman of the Cartier parent company in New York. Richard Burton then became even more determined to acquire it and opened negotiations with the owner's agent, saying, 'I don't care how much it costs – go and buy it.' He got his way, for an undisclosed sum, but only on condition Cartier could first exhibit it in New York and Chicago and it would be named the Taylor-Burton Diamond.

The *New York Times* took a mordant view of this spectacular flaunting of wealth and commented: 'The peasants have been lining up outside Cartier's this week to gawk at a diamond as big as the Ritz that cost well over a million dollars. It is destined to hang around the neck of Mrs Richard Burton. As someone said, "It would have been nice to wear in the tumbrel on the way to the guillotine."' Miss Taylor wore it for the first time in public in Monaco at Princess Grace's fortieth-birthday party. After her divorce from Richard Burton, she resold it in 1979 for five million dollars, putting part of the proceeds towards building a hospital in Botswana. Harry, who died at the end of 1978, did not, alas, live to see this final act in the drama.

Harry had made it his speciality to purchase from governments and diamond corporations the largest uncut diamonds he could locate and then take the inherent risk of having them cut and polished. Whenever John and I visited him we heard stories of the millions of pounds' worth of diamonds he had sold and of how he achieved this against odds that his competitors (who were few) would have considered unbeatable. He was a rotund, jovial little man with boundless enthusiasm and unquenchable optimism, which had enabled him to do what most people would find impossible. He gave us an insight into the trade, emphasizing above all the importance of perseverance when early signs are discouraging. He taught us a great deal and we looked upon him as our guru in the world of precious stones.

In 1972 Harry Winston had acquired the Star of Sierra Leone, which came from the largest raw diamond ever to be excavated from the Diminco mine in Sierra Leone. Originally it had weighed 968.80 carats and at that point was the third biggest raw diamond ever found. The largest single stone as Harry bought it was 143 carats, emerald cut, brilliant, yet ever so slightly flawed. It was then the largest diamond of his career to date. In what was a tricky operation, he cleaved away the imperfections, thus greatly reducing the size of the stone. Many in the trade called him mad even to consider it. However, the triumphant outcome was a 33-carat D-flawless stone alongside sixteen smaller stones, thirteen of which were flawless. Collectively they far surpassed the value of the original rough stone.

John and I had the privilege not only of seeing the Star of Sierra Leone but also of being responsible for the sale of some of the smaller gems to clients in the Middle East. Harry encouraged us to have faith in our ability to sell important stones by going about it the way he would himself. 'If you have that measure of self-confidence,' he said, 'you'll travel the path of success.' He would insist we take a whole tray of diamonds worth millions on a sales trip. He would not have it otherwise, however much we protested that we could not possibly take the responsibility. 'Listen,' he said, 'it's not your responsibility, it's mine. I'm insured. If anything goes wrong, it's my responsibility.'

To convince us further he would recall the time when he sold over twenty million dollars' worth of gems to a single client, an absolute monarch who was on a visit to Geneva. The monarch's personal secretary phoned Harry in New York telling him to come to Geneva and bring some diamonds with him. Harry called on all the dealers he knew in New York and collected from them on a consignment basis every available quality diamond. He ended by scooping the market in good stones, and when he told his fellow dealers why, they laughed and thought he'd gone crazy. In Geneva he went to see his client with the stones in a black bag and was granted a single audience. The monarch asked him to turn the bag upside down and tip out its contents in the middle of the room. As soon as the glistening treasure lay on the carpet ten or so women appeared from adjoining rooms and fell on it. Within five minutes they had cleared the whole pile. 'Send me the bill,' said the client. The lesson Harry learnt then was that nothing is ever impossible. It gave him great satisfaction to return to New York and tell his colleagues how he had sold the lot.

Faced with tales of such audacity, John and I could no longer refuse to do his bidding. We would take the tray of diamonds worth millions without even signing a receipt and venture forth in the footsteps of the master. To say we ever matched his level of success would be untrue, but we managed to make our mark and he was never disappointed.

Our close association with Harry Winston, the grand master of his trade, continued until his death. The last time we saw him was on a flight to New York in Concorde in the autumn of 1978. He was seated not far from us, and throughout the flight we observed in amazement as he ordered from the stewardess vodka after vodka and never betrayed the faintest sign of inebriation. He was a most extraordinary man. He had a very expressive type of Semitic face and when he spoke about his diamonds his features seemed to become strangely illuminated. His love for and affinity with his stones instilled in us a lasting appreciation of the perfection and beauty that only nature can produce.

The Namara Follies

Princess Katarina of Yugoslavia

I came to work for Naim during the heyday of his entrepreneurial activities that were in many ways the talk of the town. Assembled around him was coterie of the most desirable young ladies, all of them noted for their profiles, intelligence and social graces. The atmosphere throughout the group was mesmeric. The papers seemed to pounce constantly to catch the tidbits and cover every nuance of all that happened. They unabashedly reported in full what amounted to high-octane gossip, as any girl who worked in the group became newsworthy and was likely to find herself turning up in the diary columns of leading newspapers. I was no exception, especially when I found myself as one of the six Namara girls dressed in rubber dresses for the launch party of Naim's perfume Avant l'Amour and Après l'Amour. Black rubber stood for Avant, white rubber for Après. I was chosen to represent Après. Heaven know why.

We first had to be photographed in the basement at Namara House, which was transformed into a studio for the occasion. We had chiffon arranged round our bare shoulders and were professionally made up, with our hair done in readiness – my hair being quite long and curly, like a subject in a Pre-Raphaelite painting. As I faced the camera, I had to gaze up the ceiling as if at someone I was in love with. This was in order to make my neck profile seem quite elongated with the shape to echo to erotic curves of the scent bottle designs. When the prints arrived back for Naim to check, we were perturbed at how transparent the chiffon looked in the photographs. At the launch part it intrigued the press to find me there attired in a rubber costume as well as appearing on a six-foot poster.

This was one of many incidents that kept us au fait with the latest follies that were always a feature of the place. All in all, working for Naim was a madly unpredictable but enlivening experience. His energy and lack of inhibition were object lessons in how to work and play, and all those who had the chance to share in his merry-go-round of remarkable adventures have been touched by them ever after.

A CHILDHOOD FANTASY

As a boy, I spent most of my time shut away from the world by well-meaning parents who fretted constantly about my frail state of health. Adopting a strange form of escapism, I had fantasized about being a general directing my troops on the field of battle and being saluted according to my rank.

Three decades later in Abu Dhabi, following my founding of the Al-Manara Trading Company, I found myself at the helm of a small outfit consisting of former officers from the British army and one ex-Royal Navy officer. All were employed by Al-Manara and its subsidiaries and I was their chief. The naval man was Mike Mackinley, and the others included Mike Brennan, a former army man who was in charge of Falcon Enterprises. This was a sister company of Al-Manara, which was engaged in entrepreneurial activities to do mainly with contracting.

The irony of it would have eluded any observer of the scene, but for me they became the little army of my dreams. My forces were engaged not in conflict but in battling on the highly competitive field of commerce. Their brief, as pioneers in a region that was rapidly meeting the challenges of a modern economy, was all-embracing. They were accustomed to inhospitable conditions in rough terrain and had the discipline to adapt to whatever they came up against. The problem-solving skills they had learnt in their forces careers were carried across a completely different set of circumstances. Best of all, the local inhabitants took to them and they seemed able to blend with any sort of background.

Whenever I flew in on one of my monthly visits to Abu Dhabi, my little platoon would be there to meet me, drawn up at the airport. They would greet me in the manner taught by their training, evoking their previous military roles translated into civilian courtesies. It was for me as if an innocent dream, born out of sheer frustration, had turned itself into a fragment of substantiality, allaying any resentment I might still be harbouring about my lost childhood.

It's lovely to evoke childhood memories later on in adulthood, especially if converted into reality.

MORE ROOTS

My domestic life was well established in Royal Crescent, Holland Park, where I lived with my wife, Maria, in the modest flat we had moved into soon after our marriage three years before. I had taken up the position with a French bank, even though it was not one I had particularly sought. It had taken several years of dreams and experiments and wild adventure for me to reach that point. In the eyes of my manager I was fortunate, in such an insecure world, to enjoy the security of what was potentially a job for life – a concept still very much alive in Western business society. The manager made it clear that his employment with the bank represented an investment and they expected to see it repaid in the years to come. I was also well aware that, having taken a wife, I had also taken on other responsibilities that could not be pushed aside.

The days of sowing my wild oats were over – or at least put on hold, for in the depths of our inner being all men would like to believe the option never goes away, marital commitments notwithstanding.

Where their spark for the joy of living remains unabated, then the paradoxical dream of freedom is one men take with them to their graves. They seldom allow it to surface for fear of being accused of inconstancy.

The background tone to the Holland Park house was set by the landlord, John Kirby, and his ups and downs with his live-in girlfriend, Nita. John was one of those who had lived by his wits in the London of the war years and who never lost the habit of cutting a quick deal whenever he saw the chance. The atmosphere between him and Nita was volatile, alternating between the tempestuous and the tranquil. She had been jealous and moody from the beginning and John took delight in winding her up mercilessly. Their consumption of booze was partly to blame for their more raucous outbursts. On such occasions it was prudent to steer clear of any contact; otherwise there was a risk of getting caught up in the general discord. Even so, the drama made fascinating, almost compulsive, viewing, and though the tension was extreme, it was often relieved by outbursts of hilarity.

Maria and I kept a low profile whenever the war of attrition between John and Nita flared up. We would wait until the confrontation between the lovers, having culminated in an explosion of lust which left them in too exhausted a state to indulge in further bouts of rage, was over and an approximation of normality was restored. It was an in-house soap opera in which the main actors lived in full view of their audience, sparing neither shame nor verbal abuse.

John's motivation was clear as he needled Nita to get a rise out of her. She played her part to the hilt as she gave vent to her jealousy of other women with a devastating ferocity that spurred John into further provocative outpourings. Then it would be back to the calm after the storm and a stillness would prevail until the first rumble of new hostilities set off the whole cycle again. John shared with Maria a genius for trade and barter and they pitted their wits against each other in the buying and selling of the desirable trinkets and small ornamental objects that could be found on the traders' stalls in Portobello Road.

Their bargaining and sparring over prices and modes of payment went on constantly from the time when Maria and I first moved to Royal Crescent. Each party seemed to derive pleasure and satisfaction from outwitting the other for sheer devilment. There were no hard-and-fast rules. Like rivals in a game of chess, they each saw their objective as being to come out on top at the expense of their opponent. It was a relationship based on commercial principles, expediency being the common denominator. Yet it was also apparent that a genuine mutual affection existed behind the façade of trading activities. It brought into the turmoil of John's life an emotional directness that made a welcome contrast with the highly strung relationship he had with Nita.

Maria meanwhile kept on with the job she had with ABC Cinemas, at their head office in Golden Square, Soho. The privilege of two complimentary tickets a week to see any current movie playing at an ABC cinema was a perk we greatly appreciated. We never failed to make use of it. So far as we were concerned, other forms of entertainment lay beyond the bounds of affordability, and we had to be content with films rather than theatre or opera. In any case, we were aware that our education was lacking in those areas. We hoped one day to catch up on what we had missed during the early years of our struggles for survival. For the moment we had no means to exist except through our own hard work, no one to fall back on in an emergency except ourselves.

Life in the past had often been too desolate for comfort. Maria was a victim of the Second World War, when she endured terrible hardships separated from her Polish mother, who spent a large part of the war in a concentration camp. She never experienced the joys of childhood. Instead she saw only death and devastation on a horrifying scale and feared for her life as the Allies bombed Germany, where she had been placed in the care of a middle-aged couple while her mother was incarcerated. Yet although she had missed out on her youth, she remained focused and never let the experience blight her future. She had survived the harshness of the elements and the inhumanity of man.

Memories

I considered it a privilege and a sign of good fortune to have her as my wife, my living companion and soulmate. My life would be meaningless without her. I could not countenance an alternative. As for myself, there were no damaging effects of the Second World War I could point to, but against a different background I had had my share of hardships. The upheavals and civil conflicts in Palestine that resulted in the creation of the state of Israel had cut me off from my roots. Thrown into a void, bereft of an identity, I had been forced to fend for myself at an age when I was both unprepared and ill equipped. Sent to England to continue my studies, and struggling to find my feet in a strange country, I had known fear and periods of deep anguish. Loneliness and privation played havoc with my mind and forced me into sheer desperation. The bleakness of my situation made me an easy target for depression, but somehow I managed to overcome each and every crisis and tap into a resilience that I had no idea I possessed. Maria and I were both therefore hardened by the events of our early lives and equally determined to build ourselves a viable future. The odds may have been stacked against us, but we felt this would only make the achievement greater, the rewards of success more satisfying.

The cross-section of people I was getting to know through my work at the bank became steadily more diverse. One day a young Lebanese woman turned up at the counter to change some money. London being new to her, she also wanted some information. Her whole manner was of someone with a vibrant personality. No one could have let her pass by in the street unnoticed. When she spoke, the lyrical edge to her voice had a resonance that drew immediate attention. Her attractive looks exercised the same effect. Her skin, with its rich and even Mediterranean tan, glowed with the fervour of youth. Her glance had depth and fieriness to it. She involved her body in every animated gesture and statement as if she were all the time hinting at hidden emotions.

There was no doubting that she possessed an exceptional self-assurance and presence. I felt no surprise when she said she was in

London to study acting and that her greatest ambition was to enrol at the Royal Academy of Dramatic Art, otherwise known as RADA. She had the air of a born actress, eager to emerge from obscurity and display her talent to the world. First, however, she was going to have to face the hurdle of gaining acceptance and any success with that was going to hinge on her audition. At once I felt a pang of doubt about her chances. Competition for admission to RADA was fierce. There was always an abundance of youthful acting talent trying to make its way in London. The girl herself had no such reservations. Her enthusiasm and determination simply swept aside the possibility of failure. 'Doubt' was not a word that found a place in her vocabulary.

The audition would go well, she predicted. There would be nothing to hinder her in embarking on the course she wanted. And, indeed, everything went as she expected. In no time she was one of RADA's star students. Her name was Nidal al-Ashkar.

Nidal's father was a prominent member of the PPS, a political party based in Lebanon which had as its main policy the creation of a 'Greater Syria'. This was to be achieved by working for the unification of Lebanon, Syria, Jordan and Iraq. With politics in her blood, Nidal felt as strongly about them as she did about becoming an actress. Later a major crisis was to affect her life when her father was arrested and imprisoned for his part in an attempted coup to seize power in Lebanon. Her father had always been her hero. She and her eldest sister, Amal, had often acted as his bodyguards, standing at his side with submachine-guns during his public appearances. After he was released from prison, he confided to me that he had never felt safer than when his girls were guarding him. The two girls were better than four men in his opinion.

My chance encounter with Nidal in the bank led to a friendship that would span many decades. While she was still in London, she became an integral part of the flourishing community that came and went but had as its centre Maria and mine's flat at Royal Crescent. The flat continued to be a tiny enclave for both rich and poor. Here they could come together to relax and find solace and comfort. Hardly an evening passed without some visitor, friend or well-wisher negotiating the stairs to the third floor. Whatever went on in the outside world, the flat continued to be a meeting place: an open house where warmth and informality made up for the lack of amenities in post-war Britain at a time when things considered basic essentials today were still seen as luxuries.

Nidal became one of those who saw the flat as a haven whenever a crisis she could not cope with loomed large in her life. If she fell ill, I would go to where she lived and carry her back to Royal Crescent to ensure she would be properly looked after and make a quick recovery. She shared the big bed, huddling on top of it on the cold winter days and watching television with me and Maria. Once, after giving a strenuous performance at RADA, she arrived too exhausted even to take a bath. Maria said she would scrub her clean, and the bathroom being then free, she took her upstairs to run a bath. In a fit of mischief, Maria came back to the kitchen and asked me how much I would pay her if she let me peep at Nidal naked through the large keyhole. It was only a tease to provoke me into having a rush of blood to the head. When the bathroom session was over, and Nidal had emerged looking clean and refreshed, I told her about my wife's offer but omitted to say that of course I had not taken her up on it. Nidal at once assumed the role of outraged womanhood. She began to grill me mercilessly, demanding to know exactly what I had seen. 'You bastard,' she stormed, 'I shall never forgive you for this.' The running joke went on long afterwards, and always she pretended to turn deaf ears to my denials.

Secretly she had been flattered by the innocent fantasy that I would willingly pay money to my wife for the chance of seeing her naked. Nidal graduated from RADA with flying colours. She then worked in London and Europe for a while with the legendary Joan Littlewood, the inspirational spirit behind Theatre Workshop, which made such a mark on the British theatre scene in the 1950s and 1960s. After that she returned to Lebanon to set about establishing a career in her homeland, founding her own ensemble in Beirut and working initially along Theatre Workshop lines. Later she transferred her talents to Amman in Jordan, which was where I last saw her live on stage; but when the violent upheavals of the civil war in Lebanon were finally over, she returned to Beirut to start on a new performing-arts project.

This was the Masrah al-Madina ('the City Centre'). It became a vital component in the regeneration of the wrecked capital. Nidal saw how important it was to maintain a base for the arts in the rebuilding of Beirut, avoiding the danger of the city being transformed 'into one big restaurant, without any culture'. For ten years she battled to obtain finance, beating against a wall of political indifference. The closure of al-Madina through lack of funds was forced in 2003, but the original determination that I saw in Nidal when I first met her was quite undimmed.

In 2005 al-Madina reopened on the site of the old Saroulla Cinema in the Hamra district, once the city's bohemian café quarter. The triumph was somewhat muted by the brutal car-bomb assassination earlier in the year of the former prime minister, Rafik al-Harari, who had been one of Nidal's leading supporters in the venture. Nevertheless she was able to proclaim it as an assertion of human integrity and the civil society for which her war-weary country had struggled through years of invasion and strife.

Nidal, having worked with a legendary heroine of the Western theatre in Miss Littlewood, herself became a legendary heroine of theatre in Lebanon. She directed and acted in many theatrical productions as well as in Arab television and films. I saw her at last on screen when in 1998 she was given a role alongside Catherine Deneuve in a stylish French thriller directed by a fellow actress, Nicole Garcia, called *Place Vendôme*.

When Maria and I made our first visit to Beirut we had got to know Lydia, the mother of Salwa Hannoush, secretary to a great Lebanese banker. She had helped to make our stay in Lebanon fruitful and enjoyable and shown us a lot of hospitality. Her baked cakes were a speciality and we had sampled them often when we were regularly invited to tea. She also made sure that we met a few of their friends within the family circle, including those of Salwa and also of her son Raja, who worked at the British Embassy in Beirut. Lydia was a frequent visitor to London and a great admirer of the British way of life, so it was natural that Maria and I became her first port of call whenever she was in town on a visit. She loved our company and our little flat in Royal Crescent. In fact she began to spend most of her time in England with us and became a family fixture by adoption. Lydia's sense of humour was boundless, with the result that she sparked me off into ribbing her incessantly just to see the reactions my teasing induced.

She was a great sport, however, and took it all in her stride. The Cold War was then at its height and for Lydia, who had been brought up in a God-fearing Protestant family, the Communists were everything that ought to be opposed. She did not object to their concept of equality, but only to the fact that they were heathens by definition. They lived solely within the narrow bounds of the material world, she used to say, and had no aspirations to lift their souls towards the glory of God and eternal life.

Out of a pure sense of mischief I began to call her 'comrade'. Whenever her name was mentioned or I had to address her for any reason, I always referred to her as 'Comrade Lydia'. The sobriquet in due course became permanent and even stopped being a tease. Lydia was apparently able to embrace the title without the least embarrassment and become attuned to it. I even called her 'Comrade Lydia' when I telephoned Salwa in Beirut and asked after her mother. At first Salwa giggled at the idea of her mother being one of the comrades, but then she began to take it as a matter of course.

The sound of 'comrade' evoked a deep warmth of affection in everyone who knew her mother. At the time when Comrade Lydia was a regular visitor to Royal Crescent, there was a friend of mine from bygone days called Claudine who was literally camping out in the cramped flat. Claudine, the daughter of a fashion designer and herself a painter, was attractive in a bohemian sort of way. Her body mysteriously gave off a broad hint of a strong sexual appetite and she had a weakness for men with big bottoms: she always claimed it was the size of their bottoms that turned her on. She was waiting to go and live in Rome and in the meantime she slept on a mattress on the kitchen floor.

The kitchen was the largest room in the flat and was therefore multifunctional. It was also the dining area, and the sink, because of the shared bathroom, often provided an alternative facility for a hurried wash in the morning before setting off for work. I was usually the first to be up and about and would go to shave in the kitchen. Claudine would be still asleep – half naked, or even naked in the warmer weather. Maria would be the next to rise, leaving the big bed in the bedroom empty.

I then gathered up Claudine, and carried her, half asleep in a total haze, to dump her in the newly vacated warm bed, where she could stay undisturbed till late in the morning. It became a necessary ritual so that the kitchen could be returned to its proper use – the mattress folded and placed in a corner where it no longer intruded into the restricted space.

Comrade Lydia, who made an arrangement with John Kirby the landlord to stay in a basement room in the house for a while, witnessed these goings-on without turning a hair. The weird spectacle of a naked female being carted out of the kitchen in a state of somnolence was hardly conventional in any domestic setting, yet the operation was only performed as an expedient chore and was devoid of physical connotations. Comrade Lydia became so attuned to this new environment that nothing shocked her any more. She knew she was seeing all the frailties of the human condition mixed up with the kindness and solidarity that binds people together wherever survival is the common goal.

Many were the tales that Comrade Lydia took with her to Lebanon every time she departed. The stories found their way back to London in no time at all after she had recounted them in Beirut, knowing they would set off ripples of laughter or a torrent of scandalous gossip. She never did this out of malice, but only to demonstrate how eventful and full of surprises her own life had become, showing herself to be a raver at heart and completely adaptable when circumstances demanded. She told Salwa how kind I was to this Claudine – how I would cook for her, comfort her when she was down and even wash her knickers. The last service was emphasized as an act of particular significance. I would always think of Comrade Lydia as a true comrade in arms in a battle where desire for dramatic effect was indeed the mother of invention.

WHY I PUBLISH WHAT I PUBLISH

One of my initial objectives in becoming a publisher was to publish books of Middle Eastern interest, covering not only the Palestinian conflict and the suffering of the Palestinian people – which we did comprehensively – but also to promote Arab culture that had been so long ignored in the West. Historically the Arabs of ancient times contributed to the fields of science, medicine, mathematics and the arts. The eclipse of their contribution was largely due to the colonizing powers, which for centuries suppressed knowledge of their cultural evolution and almost destroyed the resulting heritage. Tribal strife was another key factor, impeding progress and diverting attention to more mundane pursuits which stifled learning and higher ideals. There remained, however, a rich crop of emerging writers whose work deserved recognition in the West, and especially in the English-speaking world.

I was determined to do my part in having the output translated into English to stand alongside Quartet's international list, which was made up of sometimes obscure or newly discovered talent together with established writers. Although, from the commercial perspective, it was unrealistic to expect good financial returns in the short term, the inclusion of books emanating from or relating to the Middle East enabled Quartet to extend its frontiers to a readership in areas hitherto unknown to it. Leaving politics on one side, our Arab contribution in fiction was substantial. While Zelfa Hourani took charge of the Arab fiction list and developed it to great effect, I remained in direct control of what we published under the headings of non-fiction and politics.

A title of particular importance was Najib Alamuddin's *The Flying Sheikh*, published in 1987, which chronicled the whole story of the founding and establishment of Middle East Airlines, of which he was chairman and president for twenty-five years. Sheikh Najib, who came from an eminent Druze family in Lebanon and became known as 'The Flying Sheikh', had a more detailed understanding than most of the complexities of Lebanese politics. He steered the airline through the stormy passages of Arab–Israeli conflict and sectarian strife in Lebanon, and ultimately ensured its survival in the face of formidable intrigues that had both internal and international origins. In 1993, Quartet went on to publish *Turmoil: The Druzes, Lebanon and the Arab–Israeli Conflict*, in which, with a vivid sense of history, Sheikh Najib traced the origins of the Druzes, of their relationships with other Islamic and Christian groups and of their position in Lebanon's modern times of strife. He had many insights on the influence of the oil wars and the disastrous effects of the international arms trade in the region as a whole.

Dina Abdel Hamid told a more personal story in *Duet for Freedom*, published in 1988, with an introduction by John Le Carré. As a member of the Hashemite dynasty, Princess Dina had been briefly married to King Hussein of Jordan, but her book gave an epic account of events following the capture of her second husband, Salah Ta'amari, a spokesman for the PLO, during the 1982 Israeli invasion of Lebanon. By an extraordinary chance, her attempts to contact Salah and free him from the hidden labyrinth of the notorious prison camp of Ansar, opened up the chance of negotiating with the Israelis for the release of thousands of Palestinians and Lebanese in exchange for six captured Israeli soldiers. *Duet for Freedom* was a true love story with many wider implications.

Princess Dina is honorary godmother to our son Ramsay – honorary because of our religious differences, she being of Islamic descent while we belong to the Greek Catholic church.

In 1993 Quartet published Pamela Cooper's lively and readable memoir, *A Cloud of Forgetting*. Pamela's first husband was Patrick Hore-Ruthven, the son of the first Earl of Gowrie, who died on a commando mission in the Western Desert during the Second World War. She was the mother of Grey Gowrie and the Islamic scholar Malise Ruthven and had a long-standing connection with the Middle East from the time when she worked with Freya Stark in Cairo on her Brotherhood of Freedom project, designed to promote ideas of democracy among influential Arabs. With her second husband, Major Derek Cooper, she became active in the post-war years in humanitarian relief work. They were instrumental in founding the charity Medical Aid for Palestinians (MAP) and in 1976 dramatically got themselves expelled from Israel for their outspoken expressions of indignation at the treatment they saw being meted out to Palestinians in the country. For six weeks in 1982 they were trapped in Beirut during the Israeli siege and bombardment in the events leading up to the massacres of Palestinians in Sabra and Chatila. Derek's side of the story of their adventurous life together was told in a biography by John Baynes, *For Love or Justice: The Life of a Quixotic Soldier*, which Quartet also published three years later.

It was a sign of the mark being made by Quartet that in 1994 Peter Lewis made us the focus of an article in a double issue of a prestigious literary journal, *Panurge*, entitled 'Quartet & Arab Women'. He selected four Quartet titles: Djura's *The Veil of Silence*, Aïcha Lemsine's *The Chrysalis*, Sabiha Khemir's *Waiting in the Future for the Past to Come* and Hanan al-Shaykh's *Women of Sand and Myrrh*; but first he assessed the situation in British publishing for translations intended for the domestic market. The situation in general, he concluded, was dire, John Calder's departure in despair for Paris having said much about the 'closed, reactionary intellectual climate in Britain'. Calder and Marion Boyars had previously made great efforts, together and under their separate imprints, to introduce into Britain new writing from abroad, but now silver linings were hard to find. Quartet Books, on the other hand, had 'been pursuing what may be called the Calder–Boyars enterprise with considerable imagination'.

> In 1993, for example, Quartet published fiction and non-fiction titles translated from a number of European languages, including Romanian and Swedish as well as French, Spanish and Russian. In spite of having high reputations in their own countries, most of these authors are unknown in Britain, although the list does include Julien Green, translations of whose fiction first appeared decades ago.
> Even more unusual and enterprising, however, has been Quartet's commitment to what it calls the 'Middle East', but which includes most of the Arab world.

The evidence indicated that writing in such countries as Morocco and Algeria was 'flourishing as never before'. The French 'colonial connection and its francophone legacy' meant there was a significantly better situation in France for the publishing of this new literature, but recognition in Britain was still 'barely perceptible'. The common thread in the four books he had under consideration was that their authors' primary purpose was to 'explore and give voice to the experience of women in their cultures', though none of them could be said to be writing feminist polemics. The lack of educational opportunities would have made such attempts at writing impossible for even the preceding generation. Djura, in telling the story of the violence against herself encountered within her own family in *The Veil of Silence* (translated by Dorothy S. Blair), was speaking for all those women 'who keep silent out of fear, who seek a decent life while they are forbidden even to exist'. Yet she still tried to hold on to those positive elements in her heritage that she could identify with, her song troupe, Djurdjura, having the aim of singing 'out loud what their mothers would only murmur under their breath'.

In *The Chrysalis*, Aïcha Lemsine gave a historic sweep to these cultural changes in Algerian society over two generations, where a young woman who has broken free to become a doctor is sucked back into and almost destroyed by the old ways, the situation only being redeemed by her stepmother's defiance of convention and show of womanly solidarity. Sabiha Khemir's *Waiting in the Future for the Past to Come* was unusual in that it was written in English in the first place. It reached out for a more mythic, storytelling way of giving an account of the changes in women's experiences and expectations in post-independence Tunisia. The collision between tradition and modernity was there, but with 'a sense of new life emerging from the old without a radical severing of connections with the past'.

Hanan al-Shaykh's *Women of Sand and Myrrh* was a follow-up to her first translated novel, *The Story of Zahra*, that Quartet published with success in 1986. *Women of Sand and Myrrh* (translated by Catherine Cobham) interwove the stories of four women living in an unnamed Arab country in the Arabian Gulf. Two of them belong to the country itself, the other two are Lebanese and American respectively. Al-Shaykh, said Lewis, 'is primarily a psychological novelist, exploring the inner lives of her main characters as they try to define themselves through their relationships with women and men ... in a social context that inhibits their potential for development and fulfilment'.

In Lewis's view, only one of the four books he had listed would have been available in Britain had there not been a publisher in London committed to issuing 'a substantial number of books in translation'. On the continent most countries – including a large one like Germany with no shortage of writers of its own – had an abundant supply of books translated from English.

The reverse is not true. To its credit, Quartet has been doing a great deal to rectify this state of affairs, and its advocacy of writers from the Arab world is particularly to be applauded. Very little normally reaches us from these countries, and this is most regrettable when literary activity there is flourishing as never before. Perhaps the next time an Arab writer is awarded the Nobel Prize for Literature, Brits will not look totally mystified and resort to snideries about positive discrimination being exercised in favour of unheard-of second-raters from the Third World.

The following summaries of other selected fiction that we published in this area will help to give the reader a flavour of what was certainly expanding into a major list worthy of close attention. *My Grandmother's Cactus: Stories by Egyptian Women* (translated and introduced by Marilyn Booth) was an anthology of stories by the latest generation of women writers in Egypt. Like some of the others already mentioned, they often featured experiments with new narrative patterns that drew on legend and myth. *Beneath a Sky of Porphyry* (translated by Dorothy S. Blair) was a second novel from Aïcha Lemsine, this one being set at the time of Algeria's war of liberation from the French, telling of the effects of the conflict on the lives of a group of villagers. In much the same vein was *Fantasia: An Algerian Cavalcade* by Assia Djebar (translated by Dorothy S. Blair), which set the life of a young girl against the same background of conflict, based in part on eyewitness accounts of ruthless acts of barbarism by the French colonial forces. *Return to Jerusalem* by Hassan Jamal Husseini, a leading Palestinian diplomat and businessman, was a novel (written in English) that told the story of a Palestinian journalist arrested in Kafkaesque circumstances in Jerusalem by the Israeli security forces and absorbed into Israel's prison system to suffer the authorities' interrogation techniques alternating between brutality and cajolery.

The genre of historical novel was also represented, including an international bestseller, *Leo the African* by Amin Maalouf (translated by

Peter Sluglett), based on the colourful life of the sixteenth-century geographer and traveller Leo Africanus, author of the renowned *Description of Africa*, written in Italy after he had been captured by a Sicilian pirate. *Elissa* by a Tunisian author, Fawzi Mellah (translated by Howard Curtis), was set between the eighth century BC and the present, and concerns a scholar who purports to be translating a letter from a collection of Punic tablets that tells of Elissa's fabulous voyage after fleeing Tyre, which leads to her becoming Queen of Carthage (aka Dido); though he loses track of what he has translated and what he has invented.

Another novel set in Alexandria by Edwar al-Kharrat, *City of Saffron* (translated by Frances Liardet), centred on the growing up of a boy who slowly gains an awareness of the nature of the lives of the adult men and women around him. *Behind Closed Doors: Tales of Tunisian Women* by Monia Hejaiej described the importance of oral storytelling in the lives of three women of Tunis, their views competing and contradictory, in preserving a conservative, moralistic attitude to set against the rebellious and subversive. From Libya there came a distinguished trilogy, *Gardens of the Night* by Ahmed Faqih (translated by Russell Harris, Amin al-'Ayouti and Suraya 'Allam), published in one volume. It began with *I Shall Present You with Another City*, where the narrator is in Edinburgh as a student, writing a thesis on sex and violence in the *Arabian Nights*; the second title in the sequence, *These Are the Borders of My Kingdom*, found him back in Libya in a loveless marriage, suffering a breakdown which brings on trances that make him think he is a prince in the *Arabian Nights*, falling in love with a beautiful princess; and the third was *A Tunnel Lit by One Woman*, in which a female colleague seems to embody the princess of his visions, though the reality gradually evolves towards disillusion.

The theme of North African migrant workers in France was the subject of *Solitaire* by a Moroccan author living in France, Tahar Ben Jelloun. Ben Jelloun had a powerful imagination, as *Solitaire* (translated by Gareth Stanton and Nick Hindley) showed. His twenty-six-year-old central character is condemned by emigration and exile to be trapped in both internal and outward isolation – his own thoughts and the hatred and racism on the streets. Another novel by Ben Jelloun, *The Sand Child*, was the story of a family where the father can produce only daughters, and when the eighth arrives vows that she must be brought up as a boy; with the result that her/his future is marked by the deceptions and hypocrisies that dissect Arab society. The sequel to this, *The Sacred Night* (translated by Alan Sheridan), took up the story of the boy becoming a woman after the father's death, struggling to be reborn in a corrupt, enslaving society through suffering and mutilation. *The Sacred Night* was winner of the 1987 Prix Goncourt.

THE WAY THINGS WERE

The weather must have been very cold at the end of November 1989. The girls at Goodge Street began complaining to the *Evening Standard* that they were freezing because of Quartet's lack of central heating. The paper was quick to make a story out of it, though it got the location wrong, saying that 'Antarctica' was at Poland Street rather than Goodge Street. The trio who led the protest against their Spartan work conditions were Anna Pasternak, Jubby Ingrams and Nina Train. They went so far as to claim they had resorted to thermal underwear in their efforts to keep warm. The *Standard* went on to embroider the piece:

> But Attallah, who once spent six months as a steeplejack in the south of England, is deaf to their heart-rending entreaties. 'My girls will stay slim and beautiful operating in the cold,' he told me wisely. 'And carting books up and down stairs will certainly add to their fitness.'

That was one of the most endearing aspects of the place, the way it was viewed by many as a nest of left-wing idealists and blue-blooded socialites who loved the frisson of perversity.

Quartet was many different things to many different people. It was a paradox that challenged conventional analysis and the unpredictability of its publishing programme won it a high share of public attention.

A NIGHTCLUB BOUNCER ON THE RECEIVING END

After the Elizabeth Garret Anderson hospital, a job was offered to me as a bouncer by a nightclub proprietor, a former Oxford graduate who had been through a stretch in prison for a drug offense involving cannabis. He and I had formed a kind of friendship and as a consequence was asked to act as his personal bodyguard as well as a bouncer in his nightclub. My duties would not begin until after 2am; the first part of the night was taken up with the club's function as a jazz club.

The club premises were situated on the second floor of a dilapidated building down an alley off Charing Cross Road, directly opposite the famous Foyle's bookshop. It was the sort of joint you would be more likely to come across in the Bowery district of New York, though it was perhaps less seedy and certainly not in such a dangerous neighbourhood.

The jazz played was mostly in the New Orleans revival style; the so-called 'Trad fad' was taking off in Britain among many young, up-and-coming popular musicians. Skiffle – the poor man's music using washboards was already an influence and would soon turn into a profitable craze for the music business.

I was a jazz novice in so far as it was kind of music completely new to me. I responded to it instantly and found myself caught up by its insistent, powerful swinging rhythms and the improvised melodic lines of trumpet, saxophone, clarinet or piano soaring above the bass. I was thrilled to the more elegiac numbers based on the twelve-bar blues; the fall of the melody seemed to contain all the sorrow of an enslaved race over 200 years of suffering. There was sadness on the one hand, but on the other an unquenchable resilience and capacity for human joy. It was music I could relate to. The club's patrons were mostly committed jazz enthusiasts who I appreciated and revelled in the intensely charged atmosphere.

During its brief life, the club became well known for the quality and brilliance of its players – some already famous and on the way to international stardom.

With gigs from such established figures as Chris Barber and Ken Colyer, it attracted a class of musicians keen to find a testing ground in which to improve their skills and try out their music in front of a live audience.

Many of the Soho landmarks were well known to them. Some they visited for pleasure; others out of sheer necessity. In particular there was Chiquito's, a coffee house in Hanway Street, off Tottenham Court Road.

With its bohemian, easy going policy, its unpretentious and friendly atmosphere, it virtually fulfilled the role of a dating agency without intending to be one.

I became particularly well known there as I used to hold court at one of its tables in the afternoon and early evenings before going to work, usually in the company of women. It became a second home. Another favourite was the pub adjoining the dominion theatre on the corner of Tottenham Court Road and New Oxford Street, where one could sample a variety of Barley wines, very strong brews in small bottles.

My duties as a bouncer had its bad moments as well as its perks. That in the job I was sustained various minor injuries was only to be expected. There was one incident, however, which could have had serious consequences.

A burley Scotsman, who had been drinking heavily, became

obstreperous and threatened to cause major disruption in the club. As I went to eject him, I found myself on the receiving end of a well-crafted blow, delivered with deadly precision, that sent me tumbling down two flights of stairs. I was quite badly hurt and shocked and had to be taken to the Charing Cross hospital, then still at its old address in the Charing Cross district to be given casualty treatment. My back was injured and I had bruises on both legs. From this I drew a useful lesson; never underestimate an opponent, not even one who appears totally uncoordinated and off guard with inebriation. I had dropped my guard when I tried to throw out the Scotsman and I paid a heavy price for one moment of inattention.

At a later stage in my life, after I was married, I needed to attend the Charing Cross hospital as a patient for a minor swelling of the thumb. To my utter surprise, the hospital register recorded the number of times I had attended for treatment in my former rackety existence as a Jazz club bouncer. Although I was embarrassed when the nurse mentioned how well known my name was for my regular visits during that period, I also felt a kind of nostalgia for those days that I could hardly conceal. I remembered how most nights, after the band had packed up and gone and the club had been closed, the proprietor would lead the way to Archer Street on the Southern edge of Soho, the reason for going there was to pick up what was usually a small packet of cannabis to see us through the small hours. An old barber shop in the same street was where, during the day, we would go to shop for our French letters (as condoms were called in those days).

From Archer Street, I and the proprietor would go into the Soho jungle to track down some weird party or other, news of which had been picked up on the grapevine.

Soho, at the time, had a sort of lured sleaziness that has completely gone from it today. It formed the underbelly of a sin conscious Britain, where all that was forbidden could be obtained at a price. The area was popular with poets and artists, who were drawn to the raffish pubs and drinking clubs, and with East End gangsters like the Cray Brothers, who made it their stamping ground when they were 'up west,' as well as with all sorts of other characters from the fringes of society.

The parties to which I accompanied the nightclub proprietor usually went on until dawn. At these libertarian gatherings I met many numbers of the Bohemian demi-monde, musicians and budding actors and not to mention lots of females in search of a little craziness and out for a good time. It was a milieu of louche behaviour which was commonplace. To me, the scenes of abandon that resulted had an irresistible appeal and the attraction got me into some odd situations. Some of which are hard to relate!

Suffice to say that, as usual, I soon moved to seek more fertile ground and abandon old ones for prosperity's sake.

HOLLYWOOD AND ME

There is a nineteenth-century saying: 'What the fool does in the end the wise man does at the beginning.' I was never sure in which category I belonged. There were times when I was an odd mixture of the two. Sometimes I faltered at the start and redeemed myself at the end; on other occasions the reverse was true. But I always learnt the lesson, even if I forgot it soon after. That, in brief, was the essence of my life – a long hazardous journey, punctuated by great moments of triumph and short periods of disenchantment.

My business career in banking and commerce followed a somewhat unconventional pattern, and 1975, a year of major diversification, proved true to form. Opportunities opened up and my agenda began to brim with new enterprises. Show business was one of them. I had become director of Paradine Co-Productions Ltd, a company formed with David Frost to produce a new film adaptation of the story of Cinderella.

The script, based on the French version of the folk tale written by Charles Perrault in the late seventeenth century, was to be a collaboration between Bryan Forbes and the song-writer brothers Richard and Robert Sherman.

Bryan was an experienced actor, scriptwriter and director who had worked on many successful films, among those he directed being *Whistle Down the Wind* and *The L-Shaped Room*. The brothers Sherman, whose previous credits included such hits as *Mary Poppins* and *Chitty Chitty Bang Bang*, were to write the score, which would include twelve original songs. Bryan would direct. It was an ambitious project requiring a budget of two million pounds which was secured from an overseas source.

In May we announced the film was going into production. Richard Chamberlain, famous for his role as Dr Kildare in the television series, was to play the charming prince, with a relatively unknown young actress, Gemma Craven, as his Cinderella. Others in the cast included Margaret Lockwood and Kenneth More, Michael Horden and Dame Edith Evans.

An unusual amount of press coverage followed the announcement, focusing on my involvement. The journalist George Hutchinson, who had been a friend since my early days in England, featured me in his weekly column in *The Times* as 'the one who intends to save the British film industry from eclipse ... for which', he added, 'we would have cause to thank him'. Others took a more political approach, the show-business journal *Variety* heading its report 'Palestinian Financier Invades Showbiz with Shangri-La Coin', while the *Jewish Chronicle* asserted that there were 'No Strings to Arab Film Money'. The film's profile received a further boost when the Queen Mother, accompanied by Princess Margaret, visited the set at Pinewood Studios to watch Bryan Forbes directing his illustrious cast.

Since several scenes for the film were shot on location in Austria, I went with my wife Maria and son Ramsay, then aged eleven, to stay five days with the crew. It was a novel and exciting experience that left us with some vivid memories. Richard Chamberlain pranced around, looking rather effete in his costume and keeping to himself most of the time, whereas the rest of the cast were more sociable and warm. Kenneth More in particular displayed an affable humour and entertained us with some amusing stories. He had an immediate rapport with Ramsay, taking him under his wing throughout our stay to explain all the intricacies of film-making.

Kenneth closely resembled in real life the characters he had portrayed on screen in films like *A Night to Remember*, *Genevieve* and *Northwest Frontier*. He was a British actor of the old tradition, possessing a special quality of poise and charm all but extinct today. In his memoirs, *Kenneth More or Less*, he recollected the scene we shot in Southwark Cathedral by special dispensation of the bishop, Dr Mervyn Stockwood, when the aged Dame Edith Evans, who had only one line in the scene, 'That girl ought to go', kept nodding off. Every time Kenneth nudged her awake she immediately delivered her line, 'That girl ought to go', with impeccable professionalism.

All the signs for the film, given the title of *The Slipper and the Rose*, looked promising. Only a few days before the performance, on 24th March 1976, *The Slipper and the Rose* received its première at the Odeon, Leicester Square, having been selected as the Royal Command Performance film for the year. As I stood waiting to be presented to the royal patrons, the Queen Mother and Princess Margaret, the press-camera lights flashing all around, I felt I had entered a new world.

What a journey I had travelled since the early days of my marriage, when we lived in a small flat in Holland Park that did not even have its own bathroom. There, in sheer frustration, with my life still going nowhere, I once wrote a fan letter to my hero of the time, Marlon Brando – hoping to find a way into the film industry. Of course, I received no reply. But here I was now in this select line-up, among stars and show-business celebrities. The Sherman brothers, being American, were every bit as elated as I was to be waiting to meet the Queen Mother and Princess Margaret. The Queen Mother took everything in her stride.

One of the brothers had a girlfriend in tow – a stunning blonde, dressed to kill and exhibiting a most impressive cleavage. The Queen Mother didn't bat an eyelid.

Afterwards, along with David Frost, Bryan Forbes and Stuart Lyons, we partied till well beyond midnight and sent out for the morning papers to read the press notices and comments. Critics hailed *The Slipper and the Rose* as a shining example of what the British film industry was capable of achieving if given the chance.

WARMING THE COCKLES

In January 1984, David Elliott had flown to Montreal from London to host a sales conference for our North American reps. It was the first time he had undertaken such a trip, brought about by Quartet's expansion in the region. David was there to brief the sales force on those forthcoming publications that were likely to be of interest in their territory. Marilyn Warnick and I flew up from New York to join him – her involvement was vitally important since the whole American operation came under her jurisdiction. My purpose in being there was to become more familiar with what was going on and then to wrap up the conference with a short address to give the occasion an air of *gravitas*.

Beyond its successful outcome, nothing unusual happened except for the weather. It was bitterly cold, with temperatures the lowest I had ever encountered. I had a single worse experience a decade or so later when I visited China in mid-February and hired a car to drive me out from Beijing to see the Great Wall of China. I took the precaution of putting on many layers of warm clothing complemented by a fur coat and hat, and a pair of thick gloves, but my ears and eyes were difficult to shield from the cuttingly icy wind that swept in from Mongolia and seemed to penetrate into every fibre of my body. The resulting pain was excruciating as my face was pelted with particles of ice which stung any bit of flesh they managed to land on. I never felt so helpless and desperate as I did when negotiating the Great Wall, hardly daring to open my eyes for fear of some crippling injury to my eyesight.

The Montreal winter, bad as it was, was not in the same league as its Chinese counterpart, though it was still my first taste of extreme weather conditions. Marilyn, David and I wore heavy overcoats as we set out on our last day to brave the elements by taking a walk in the city centre, looking for places of interest, especially the leading bookshops. Our ears and hands were already painfully numb when we chanced on a cinema showing 3D projections for adults only. Marilyn held back, perhaps embarrassed at first, but then decided anything would be better than freezing to death! We bought three tickets at the box office and were given special coloured glasses for viewing the film. It had to be admitted that the spectacle was technically sensational, though the content was nothing more than a pornographic display of sexual acrobatics. The images hit you from every side until you felt you were yourself a participant in the ongoing orgy. For the first ten minutes the senses were stunned, but the novelty began to wear thin when the action became so confused it was impossible to distinguish who was copulating with whom. When we left the cinema the crisp cold outside air had become less of a problem. The hour spent watching people engaging in libidinous activities had given our blood circulations a boost to fend off the cold. We spent the evening quietly before flying back to New York the next day.

A NIGHT TO REMEMBER

On 28 February 1984 Quartet celebrated the publication of Derek Jarman's autobiography *Dancing Ledge* by throwing an outrageous party at the Diorama in Regent's Park. All a guest needed to do to gain entry was buy a copy of the paperback edition of the book for a cut price of five pounds. A large proportion of London's gay community converged on the venue in a state of high anticipation and were admitted so long as they were clutching a copy. The numbers who gained access rose dramatically till they reached a figure later estimated at twelve hundred. The crush became so intense that there were fears for public safety and damage to the very fabric of the building. It was far from being an exclusively gay affair. The crowd was made up of a heterogeneous mix of literati, aristocrats, Sloane Rangers, showbiz personalities and punks. Collectively they represented the most colourful of London's hedonistic high-camp society, as well as its most illustrious. All the beautiful people stood side by side with the ugly, the profane and the bizarre, and were letting their hair down without the least regard for propriety or convention.

The all-night event turned into an orgy of excess resembling a saturnalia. Into the midst of this phantasmagoric confusion and merriment there erupted a surprise cabaret organized by Derek Jarman, the star of which was Elisabeth Welch, the sultry-voiced singer who, at seventy-six years old, was a veteran of numerous musicals and for many a living icon. Escorting Miss Welch was a troupe of fire-eaters who set off total panic among the crowd. The observer who best summed it all up was Auberon Waugh in a piece in *Private Eye*, written in his uncannily insightful style and accompanied by a cartoon by Willie Rushton (the original of which still hangs in my office today):

> Latest entertainment idea to hit the London scene is a group of hideous naked women and one man called the New Naturalists. I saw them at a party given by Naim Attallah the Lebanese [sic] philanthropist, but now they are everywhere. They come on stage completely naked except for combat boots, their bodies painted in green and blue. Also painted blue is what could be described as the man's generative organ, but might more accurately be called his willie. They start peeing all over the stage and everybody shrieks

with laughter. Those who stayed on at the Quartet party – for a sensitive autobiography called *Dancing Ledge* by 1960s raver Derek Jarman – had the enjoyable experience of seeing it all cleared up by Miss Bridget Heathcoat-Amory, one of the most enduringly beautiful of Naim's string of delicious debs. I wonder if the Church of England should consider a Thanksgiving Celebration Service of Relief along these lines.

The party was widely covered by the press, with pictures of the Marquess of Worcester with Lady Cosima Fry, Aileen Plunkett with her granddaughter Marcia Leveson-Gower, and Viscount Althorp, now Lord Spencer, brandishing cash in hand to acquire his passport to entry.

Dancing Ledge was Derek Jarman's first major work of autobiography. He was already established as Britain's most controversial independent filmmaker and the book gave a kaleidoscopic account of his life and art up till then, from sexual awakening in post-war rural England to the libidinous excesses of the 1960s and subsequently. He told his story with openness and flair, describing the workings of the imagination that lay behind the making of the films *Sebastiane*, *Jubilee* and *The Tempest* and the frustrations he was suffering over his as yet unrealized project, *Caravaggio*. This was to be made in 1986 with Nigel Terry, Sean Bean and Tilda Swinton, the same year in which he discovered he was HIV positive. *Dancing Ledge* was republished by Quartet in 1991 in response to public demand. Working in the shadow of his diagnosis, Derek Jarman managed to fulfil himself as a unique creative spirit, with an extraordinarily productive output in various fields, in the few years he had left. He was a prophet of punk who linked homoerotic imagery and thought with increasingly profound themes of time and death. More films were produced and he painted and wrote poetry. He died from the effects of AIDS on 19 February 1994 at his Prospect Cottage on the shingle banks at Dungeness in Kent, where he created an extraordinary garden in his closing years. It mixed indigenous maritime plants with stones from the beach and sculptural *objets trouvés* washed in by the sea, and it makes a strangely haunting and touching memorial.

REMEMBERING BEASTLY BEATITUDES

The actor Patrick Ryecart had acquired stage rights from J. P. Donleavy for his novel *The Beastly Beatitudes of Balthazar B*, and was looking for a backer. Patrick's links with my family went back some two decades to the time when he lived in Haifa as a young boy, his father having been the Anglican vicar who looked after the British community. Whenever his parents had to travel to visit their flock in the Holy Land, his mother would leave him at my parents' house, where my little sister had the task of minding him. Being already in England by then, I only heard about him at that stage, but we did finally meet and become friends a year before his marriage to the Duke of Norfolk's daughter Marsha.

Given the childhood connection, I felt a certain obligation to back Patrick's project as a sign of solidarity; though I also had high hopes that this time round we could be on to a winner. The plot told the story of Balthazar, 'the world's last shy, elegant young man', who as a zoology student at Trinity College, Dublin, meets up with an old school friend, Beefy, who is studying for holy orders but not averse to amorous adventures. When their student careers come to an unholy end, the pair decamp to London, Balthazar to search for true love and Beefy to find a rich wife. I sought the advice of another friend, Howard Panter, and we agreed to collaborate on the play's production.

Patrick was to play the part of Balthazar opposite the Shakespearian actor Simon Callow as Beefy, so we began with the advantage of a strong cast. I also found myself hitting it off well with J. P. Donleavy, despite his reputation for being a tough negotiator who could adopt an inflexible attitude once he got a bee in his bonnet. He was good company and we became friends as a result. The promotional campaign began a few weeks before the play opened at the Duke of York's Theatre, spearheaded by Theo Cowan as a newly joined member of the Namara Group.

I took overall control of the publicity machine and pulled out all the stops. Laura Sandys, the sultry youngest daughter of Lord Sandys, who was barely seventeen when she came to work for me, joined forces with a gamine young lady, not much older, called Serena Franklin. Together they went around the West End in a yellow jeep, wearing T-shirts that bore the logo, 'I Love Balthazar B'. They were an instant hit with the media and were chased everywhere by every member of the paparazzi brigade in town. As far as exposure was concerned, we won hands down, and the play opened with excellent reviews.

Unfortunately it was a dark period for West End theatres in general. We hoped to keep it going by word of mouth, for there was no doubting the play was a crowd-pleaser once we managed to get them inside the theatre. For the next six months I did not miss a single night's performance, counting the audience in like sheep. I stood in the lobby watching people as they arrived, always hoping for a last-minute surge before the curtain went up. I became a fixture, almost part of the furniture.

As the performance began, both Patrick Ryecart and Simon Callow would instinctively look at the box where I sat to assure themselves I was there. Sometimes I was rewarded with a wink from the stage – their gesture of appreciation. With steely determination we gradually managed to improve ticket sales, but Simon Callow had a previous commitment that he could not postpone. His run in the play had to end and a replacement needed to be found very quickly. It was no easy task. We racked our brains for inspiration, when suddenly a mad idea came into my mind. I was very friendly with Billy Connolly and Pamela Stephenson, who were regulars at my parties. What about Billy Connolly taking over Simon's role as Beefy? He had a tremendous following and his popularity would surely ensure a box-office bonanza.

But he was not then known as the actor he showed himself to be later, and his act as a comedian was based on his brilliant ad-libbing.

Taking on a stage role was a different proposition altogether, requiring discipline in memorizing and sticking to the script. Could he do it, would he do it? And if he would, what were the chances of his being able to prepare himself in such a brief period of time? I invited him to lunch at Namara House, where my excellent cook, Charlotte Millward, an adept in the art of gastronomy, was the envy of the town. For Charlotte food was the spur to creativity, and her inspired invention and improvisation knew no bounds. She could offer avant-garde cuisine to equal that of any famous chef in the metropolis.

Disconcertingly, Pamela Stephenson had by then performed a miracle on Billy and he was a reformed character. Not only had she stopped his drinking, she had also turned him into a vegetarian. Charlotte, undaunted, arranged a sumptuous meal made exclusively of vegetables, and was greatly flattered when Billy sought her out in her kitchen, asking for some recipes. The lunch went well, and although Billy was astounded by my proposition, he did not turn it down flat. Having seen the play and liked it, he was very keen but doubted his ability to rise to such a serious challenge. He promised I would have his answer within a few days. Instead of just waiting for it, however, I telephoned Pamela, asking her to urge him to say yes. Her reaction gave me a heartening boost, for she felt sure that this could be for Billy a good career move.

He went into rehearsal almost immediately, though there was one remaining hitch. Because of a previous commitment he could do it for only a few weeks. This being better than nothing, we readily agreed. The casting of Billy as Beefy turned out to be inspired. He took the part in his stride and if ever he forgot his lines fell back on his variety-act technique of improvisation. There was one seduction scene where he had to rip a girl's knickers clean off, a manoeuvre which dear Simon Callow could only approach with fastidious distaste. Billy, by contrast, tackled the task in a state of heightened heterosexual excitement and performed it with such relish that sometimes he used his teeth as well as his hands. The crowd howled with approval and loved every minute of his antics, not all of which were strictly in the script. They caught the bawdy spirit of the piece, however, and with his manic exuberance Billy never failed to bring comic genius to each performance.

The play took on a new lease of life and the queues outside the theatre went round the block, with people hoping either to get tickets or catch a glimpse of their hero. If only Billy had been able to stay on for a few more weeks, then the new capacity audiences would have turned the play into a smash hit in every sense. As it was, it ended up with a good run and earned me the respect of theatre folk for my tenacity and resolve in not being easily dismayed by the capricious nature of theatre. There were other bonuses. During those few months when I stood every evening in the lobby of the Duke of York's Theatre I encountered a host of people. They would come up to me to talk, and introduce me to whomever they were with.

Two meetings in particular were significant. The first was with Sophie Hicks, today a successful architect but then an up-and-coming girl about town who worked at Condé Nast on Vogue; the other was Nigella Lawson, a student at Oxford who was up in London to see the play. Sophie in turn introduced me to Arabella Pollen, an ambitious and rather delectable young beauty of eighteen who, with my backing, would become Princess Diana's favourite fashion designer. Nigella, with her persuasive charm and expressive good looks, secured from me a written undertaking to employ her at Quartet after her graduation from Oxford in a year's time.

AN EXCLUSIVE BUNCH

November 1981 had seen the publication of *By Invitation Only*, a softcover book in which Richard Young's lens and Christopher Wilson's pen recorded the famous, the glamorous, the ambitious, the tasteless and the shallow as they socially revered, engineered and mountaineered their way amid the party set of the day. In its pages could be found the chic and cheerful of café society hard at their occupation. The tools of their trade were a champagne glass and a black bow tie; their place of work could be anywhere within the gilded environs of Mayfair. Their only task was to have fun; their only ambition was to come by as many different pasteboard passports to pleasure as possible – each one engraved 'By invitation only'. Peter Langan, the infamous owner of Langan's Restaurant in Stratton Street, wrote in his foreword to the book, which he had scribbled on the back of David Hockney's menu:

> God alone knows why I should introduce you to this book. The people in it veer between the awesome and the awful. Wilson and Young who wrote it and took the pictures are the only two people who can grease their way through a door without opening it. Café society will suffer as a result of its publication. They'll all buy it, and they'll all condemn it. They'll also want to take a quick peek at the index to see whether they're in it. I don't want discarded copies cluttering up my restaurant after they've finished reading it for the 297th time, so I beg you to take it home with you, put it out on your coffee table, and remind yourselves not to be so silly as to want to take part in the high life. They're a lovely lot but sometimes they give you the skids, you know.

The cover of the book featured a dazed looking Lord Montagu clutching a glass with both hands and a cigar between his fingers. The inside cover flap stated that

> such is the paradox of café society that many of its components who appear in these pages would, on the whole, prefer to be absent. Many others who have been excluded would prefer to be included in. It must be made clear that some of the more arcane

practices described herein apply to the latter grouping and not the former.

The illustration on the back cover showed Peter Langan in a total state of inebriation face down on the floor of his own restaurant. Appropriately enough it was at the restaurant that the book launch was held. On the night, a party for two hundred and fifty people turned into a bash for five hundred of London's most diligent freeloaders, or so reported the *Daily Mail*, which then went on to say:

> Naim Attallah's penchant for bacchanalia was put sorely to the test. He played host to the cream of Nescafé society which featured in the tome. But the cast was studded with faces who did not possess the necessary encrusted invitation card. At one point the crush was so great the PR man Peter Stiles felt it necessary to elbow his way out of a corner where he was trapped by columnist John Rendall and his PR wife Liz Brewer. Alex Macmillan the publishing mogul and grandson of Harold Macmillan and Prince Charles's personal valet Stephen Barry made sure they were adjacent to the food, whereas Gary Glitter and Bryan Ferry stuck to the wine on offer.

The book sold extremely well. It was predictably considered scandalous by some, entertainingly outrageous by others, and people outside café society did not give a jot about it either way. I came in for some personal admonishment from certain close friends who thought I should have imposed a more selective policy on who actually got into the book; there were faces whose presence in its pages could cause great embarrassment and even grief to others. They failed to understand how for me, as a publisher, any form of censorship would have gone against the grain.

WHAT'S THE PARTY FOR?

In 1983, I threw a party at the Arts Club in Dover Street to launch a Quartet book on the Bee Gees, the vocal trio of the three Gibb brothers who were around in the early days of pop and became one of the world's most successful music groups. It was written and created by David English and produced in gorgeous colour with illustrations and lettering by Alex Brychta. The theme was how funny it is, the way people often resemble animals. 'Think of Barry, Robin and Maurice Gibb ... Barry as a Lion, Robin the Red Setter and Maurice as an Eager Beaver. Now come with me, says the author, and experience the legend of the Bee Gees.' It was basically a children's book, dedicated to children everywhere and to the fourth Gibb brother. Its style of telling was unique and reflected all the hopes, frustrations – even heartache – as well as the joy and happiness life has in store for us.

Certainly the launch party was a joyous event. The three brothers were there, wrote David Thomas in the Standard, 'standing in one corner of the room pretending it was still 1978. Meanwhile the London lit. crit. set, never known for passionate disco fever, milled around asking one another whether they knew what a Bee Gee looked like, pointing at strangers and enquiring, "Do you think that's Barry?"' Then, Thomas went on to say, 'as if to underline the changes that have come over the pop scene since the days that the Bee Gees ruled the airwaves, there were some newer stars in attendance. Like Marilyn (né Peter Robinson), a good friend of Boy George's who used to model frocks for Vivienne Westwood and who is now, in the best music-biz style, about to sign a six-figure deal with a major company.' Finally Thomas went on to query the purpose of throwing a party when the guests had little to contribute to the selling of books. When he put the question to Juliette Foy, Quartet's press officer, she replied that, 'Primarily we are promoting our publishing house as much as the book.' I thought that was a good response since we could never justify the cost of a party if we were to equate it with the number of books we sell as a result.

My own thoughts are that parties are also useful for meeting people who might have a book in them, and that if, as a publisher, you do not circulate widely, then opportunities will pass you by. The Bee Gee soirée in particular was heavily attended by show-business personalities, including the likes of Billy Connolly, Christopher Reeve, Sting, Bob Geldof and Jeremy Irons. The presence of celebrities will invariably ensure a good deal of press coverage, which in today's world gives a vital boost to any business.

DIRTY WEEKEND

Quartet has never run away from a fight with the Establishment and over the years, gained a reputation for taking on books whose subject matter were often too radical or mischievous for the Establishment publishers. One such book was published in 1984 when we were about to celebrate a forthcoming Quartet publication, *The Dirty Weekend Book*.

One of the participants in the book, Catherine Ledger, decided to jump ship at the last moment after suddenly finding she had principles. Her fellow contributors, Alexandra Shulman, Charlotte Du Cann, Gillian Greenwood, Emma Duncan and Kathy O'Shaughnessy – a dynamic bunch of aspiring, intelligent young women – were naturally disappointed by this change of heart and the sort of publicity it provoked. Miss Ledger, who worked for Virgin Books, gave her reasons, claiming it was too upper class for her liking. The intention, she said, had been to make it self-mocking and funny, but it turned out to be socially divisive, sexist, old fashioned and full of joyless cliches. She asked for her name to be taken off the cover and title-page.

The scheme of the book was to list sixty hotels that would be congenial for an amorous weekend break, mostly in Britain but a few abroad for the more adventurous. Unfortunately the press attention that followed in the wake of Miss Ledger's withdrawal endowed the book with an unwelcome hint of turpitude, calculated to stir up spasms of moral outrage. The newspaper headlines varied from 'The Dirt Flies' to 'Fur Flying', with them all, even such a responsible paper as *The Times*, reporting the same story from different angles. The claim was put forward that certain 'respectable' hotels listed in the book's pages were threatening injunctions to stop its publication unless all references to them were excised. The *Daily Mirror*, despite its sensational headline, 'Lovers Get the Good Sex Guide', was more sympathetic, quoting Mrs Pamela Neil, of the Highbullen Hotel at Chittlehamholt in Devon, who said commonsensically, 'Thirty years ago we would never have accepted an unmarried couple. But nowadays who cares?'

Another headline, this time in the *Standard*, declared 'No sex, please, we are Scottish'. The hypocrisy in the reaction was becoming too ludicrous for words. Mr Ron Lamb, proprietor of the Balcary Bay Hotel at Auchencairn, had his complaint put on record. He objected to his establishment being included, he said, despite the glowing report it was given. He was extremely annoyed that it had been mentioned without his permission and all reference to his hotel should be removed. Furthermore, unless the publishers acknowledged his letter of protest, the matter would be placed in the hands of his solicitors. 'An injunction is a possibility,' he threatened, 'but the least said the soonest mended. I don't want to give the publishers cheap publicity,' he concluded.

As always, I was relishing the fight. 'What kind of a reply did he [Mr Lamb] expect?' I retorted. 'People don't go to hotels for meditation or prayers; as far as I know there are no restrictions on making love in a hotel. If you were to write in your memoirs that on your honeymoon you made love in the Dorchester, is the hotel entitled to sue you?' It was a storm in a teacup. All the hotels that threatened legal action were ignored and melted away without a murmur.

Private Eye remained true to its principle of never missing out on having the last word if it could possibly avoid it. Under 'Books of the Month' at the end of June it included this little squib:

The Dirty Publisher's Guide
(Compiled by five young Sloanes who work for Naim Utterlahdisgustin) Utterlahdisgustin comes out tops in this raunchy survey of the world's dirtiest publishers.
(*That's enough books. Ed.*)

A BOY IN ENGLAND

Even as a child of eleven, I was captivated by the written word; prose, poetry, even the art of calligraphy – all held an endless fascination for me. Because of my frail health, I rarely engaged in sport; or, to be more precise, I was never allowed to do so. The time that I had on my hands as a result was mostly spent on reading and writing, or on analysing political events in the manner of a grown-up. I was unduly sophisticated for my years and preferred the conversation of adults (which added substantially to my store of knowledge) to the company of children my own age. I already saw my future as lying elsewhere from my family environment in Haifa. I did not know where that would be, but the world I built around myself out of my vivid imagination was that of a dreamer. This world had no conventional boundaries and little regard for the established rules that had so far governed, perhaps orchestrated, my life.

I was a revolutionary at heart, in spite of possessing a pronounced sensitivity – a trait not generally associated with those who seek to enforce radical change or ferment rebellion. I loved to read the works of those philosophers with whom I felt I had common ground. I could not hope to grasp everything I read, but the challenge of trying to unlock the complexities of their arguments exercised my intellect, nourishing the mind in the way that food nourished the body. I was constantly scribbling things down; no matter where I happened to be I was quick to observe anything bizarre or out of the ordinary so I could record it for future reference. I had a love of learning that grew with me into my adult years and remained with me through all that happened in my life.

My habit of writing to try to give voice to my imagination became a refuge for me when I first arrived in England. Alone in my room, I battled with how I could stretch the possibilities of the English language in my creative writing. I wrote a piece I called 'Between Night and Morning', using a – no doubt outmoded – parable style for a prose poem. It began in tones of melancholy:

> Hush my heart, the sky does not hear you.
> Hush, the ether is burdened with lamentations,
>   and wailings will not carry your songs and chants.
> Hush, the phantoms of the night do not care for
>   the whispers of your secrets, and the processions
>   of darkness do not stop before your dreams.

As the poem proceeded, I imagined my thoughts in the form of a boat:

> Hush my heart and hear me speaking.
> My thought was yesterday a ship on the undulating
>   waves of the sea and voyaging with the air from
>   shore to shore.
> The ship of my thought was empty save for seven
>   glasses full of various colours resembling the
>   colours of the rainbow in bloom.
> And there came a time when I grew weary of
>   wandering on the surface of the sea and said,
>   'I shall return with the empty ship of my soul
>   to the port of my native country.'

> I painted the corners of my ship with yellow colours
>> for the sunset, green for the heart of spring, blue
>> for the linen of the sky, red for fraternal love, and
>> sketched on its sail and rudder strange pictures
>> which attracted the eyes and brightened the view.

When the ship arrives, the people come out to welcome it with drums and trumpets, but all they see is the painted exterior. The ship inside is empty. It sails away again and gathers treasures from the seas of the world, the people only regard it with derision. All they can see is the outward appearance of things.

In 1948, I was sent to England to further my education, safely away from the burgeoning conflict in Palestine. I was apprenticed to a large industrial concern in Stafford where my spare time was very limited. I did as much overtime as I could in the English Electric factory to earn extra money. The living conditions in the homes where I stayed were hardly conducive to creative effort and the whole atmosphere was rather stifling. It was a depressing time for me. I considered that my social roots had been put down in London and I was not happy with having to live anywhere else. I knew I must somehow counteract the dangers of sinking into a clinical depression. One prescription I arrived at was to embark on writing letters to all my friends to give me solace. Any time I had over from that activity I allocated to composing short pieces of prose on the imaginary encounters of opposites. I was coming more and more to see the world in terms of contrasts: the beautiful as opposed to the ugly, evil in conflict with goodness, light breaking through the darkness and life walking hand in hand with death. Each extreme had its own role and special significance, but the extremes were at the same time interdependent. No extreme could exist without its opposite: the train of thought was an absorbing one.

A piece I wrote in Stafford was called 'Conflict between Opposites'. In my imagination I saw a gigantic, grotesque figure raise itself up on the summit of a mountain in the moonlight to address the moon with special pleading.

> O Queen of the Heavens ... I have travelled many weary miles for this audience, I have climbed precipitous and hostile rocks. I have braved heat and cold, that the winds may carry my voice to your gracious ear, bearing the burden of my one small request.
> As your light reveals, I am indeed ugly. Through long ages have I suffered because my appearance causes men to shudder. It is such that I cannot bear to see my own reflection mirrored in a pool of still water.
> Therefore, O Queen, I pray you, make me good to look upon. Make me handsome and fair of face.

The Moon replies:

> O Son of the Unfaithful, you come with a wish that has been denied because of your evil heart. You have transformed beauty into ugliness, you have wrecked loveliness, you have destroyed fairness of form and face. It is not a change of face and figure that you need, but a change of soul. You cannot borrow beauty as I borrow it from the Sun.

The Figure presses on with his request:

> O Queen of the Heavens, I am the most obedient of all your slaves. You can give me beauty as you give all things on earth beauty. You give your

> pale, soft light to mills and alleyways, to crude and clumsy things. And lo, your magic touch makes them as lovely as lilies.
>
> Give me, I beseech you, beauty also. I am most wise. My wit is subtle, and none can match me in persuasiveness. Sages and philosophers stammer or fall silent when met by my matchless arguments. None is so clever as to delude me, none so cunning as to outwit me.

The Moon acknowledges that all that he says is true but asks to what purpose he has put his great gifts:

> You have used them to snare the innocent, to destroy the wise, to bring derision upon the ignorant. You have employed flattery to trip the weak and vain, and you have used terror to bring down the strong.

She does not accept that he can learn humility, or that beauty of face could give him humility. When the Figure promises that he will charm poets, painters and architects if freed from his ugliness, and build vast and stately cities, she does not doubt it, but has no wish to see such cities:

> They are merely gigantic traps in which millions of men are caught. It is in cities that your darkest deeds have been done. It is in cities that all the seeds you plant ripen. Lying, cheating, killing are three of these things … You seem to forget that I have looked down upon all cities that man has ever raised. I saw Sodom, Babylon, Nineveh and

Memories

> Tyre. I saw Thebes, Athens, Pompei and Rome. Some of those cities were jewels, shining with so many splendours that they dazzled the eyes of men. Yet the people in them were corrupt, cruel, lascivious and full of guile.

Finally the Figure concedes:

> It seems, O Queen, that I am to remain ugly.

And the Moon replies that she cannot give him beauty:

> That must come from within yourself ... Only when your thoughts are pure, when your heart is full of good intentions, when your soul is inspired by truth and goodness and beauty, only then can you have external beauty. Therefore begone, for I cannot bear to look upon you longer.

The figure vanishes, and there follows a universal silence, broken only by the long and wistful sighs of the wind.

I was intrigued by the power complementary opposites exert over our lives. This happens regardless of the far-reaching impact they also have on our intellectual evolution with the onset of maturity. I began to see that there was also a parasitic dimension as these factors fed on the mind. This, too, was largely overlooked, because superficiality remained the easiest way to define the indefinable. Few dared to delve deeply into the origin of those causes that they saw as the reasons behind their very existence, for each had an advantage in denying alternative versions of the truth.

Beauty inspired music, poetry – artistic creativity in all its sublime forms. Evil brought conflict, desecrated noble values, ravished innocence and fuelled temptation at its most base. The irony was that evil in the end gave birth to goodness, for extremity could bring in its wake extraordinary reversals. As in nature, the storms of conflict blew themselves out and gave way to repose and tranquillity. Light nurtured and boosted growth in nature, while darkness induced rest. Each element was equally necessary to maintain the ecological balance.

Death, as the conclusion of life, hovered inexorably, reminding mortals of the transitory nature of terrestrial existence. Yet death could be a welcome relief, even a friend, when all else had failed. Certain fanatics even celebrated death as the ultimate sacrifice, which they believed would unlock the doors of heaven. The civilized and the barbaric alike had a special relationship with death. Religious devotees saw it as the final moment of redemption before eternal life. Yet in the end all these mysteries of polarity were too complex to unravel. I would pour my thoughts out on paper, in the hope that elements might emerge to illuminate more clearly the uncertainties that I had racing through my mind.

While in Stafford I also tried my hand at writing short stories. These featured the same boldness of ideas, but were in search of the shape and style they needed to put them across. One, called 'The Dance Hall Girl', described the scene in the sort of city dance hall that was still the focus for the social life of young people in the 1950s. It picked up on the changes in dance convention that were then in the air:

> On the one side, the orthodox dancers swayed with the music, following the conventional, less exhausting steps. On the other were dancers who indulged any and every step, many of them ugly, clumsy improvisations which were merely confusing and bereft of all rhythm. A couple in the far corner of the hall were performing an extremely strenuous dance, their own version of a

barbarian love sequence. The subtle gestures and the supple movements of their bodies at times revealed sex in its most acute form, thrilling the young people who knotted about them.

In contrast with this, there was a genuine performer, a solitary black man from Africa:

He was doing it all after the manner of his own people, with agility, grace and a remarkable sense of artistic inspiration. It was a skilful display of an art which the new world has borrowed, without acknowledgement, from the old. In it there was nothing new, for the passion typified was as old as man and equally enduring. The black man, though exhausted, kept on dancing, whipped on by the music, oblivious of the outside world, defying the prejudice and unkindness in the hearts of men.

Close by, meanwhile, a crowd of bebop boys was jiving in the modern American manner, but they lacked that depth of feeling which makes dancing an unconscious art. They were not absorbed by the music. Instead they were its slaves, spending their energies in a futile effort to match their movements to its rhythm.

The scene then became phantasmagorical, leading up to the narrator finding himself dancing with a Salome-like figure:

Here was the spirit of youth in all its boundless aspects; in its indomitable search for erotic adventure, the escapades, the follies, the whims, the intoxication of the nerves ... the dancers, with pale, sick faces, strained features, half-doped eyes, whirled, swung and clenched to the frenetic music of the band ... I was overcome with a compelling desire to take part in this eruption of gaiety and found myself jiving with the devil's own image of temptation ... Her lips burned with the fire of cupidity and in her eyes was a light never seen on earth.

The couple danced themselves to a standstill. As he leant over her collapsed figure, she opened her eyes and he saw the promise of a night of love such as few had ever known.

While this story was, in its immature way, about the combination of the sacred and profane in ecstasy, another, called 'The Last Noble Breath', attempted to deal with the whole problem of love and loss. Here the narrator faced the imminent death of his partner after a life of complete understanding and sharing – the perfect union that everyone longs for but few attain. 'I am the one who should be dying,' he protests. 'That would be easier.'

'Yes, it is hard to live at times,' she said, 'harder than it is to die. But life is more than a bond of affection which unites two people. It is much more than the love of a man for a woman. Life is achievement, the answer to a challenge, the realization of hopes ambitions. Your purpose is not yet complete ... Only when you have created the beauty and uttered the truth will you be ready to re-join me ... The universe is grounded on beauty and based on truth.'

'Is it?' he asked, and only by a great effort did he restrain himself from crying out. 'What beauty is there in you dying, what goodness? ...'

'A rose is very beautiful, my darling, but it lingers a very short time. A few dancing days in the sun while it flashes splendour from golden brightness, and then it withers and begins to perish. So much beauty for such a short time. But that is not surprising, really. The creator has such an immense store of beauty... and you know, too, that all his worlds are wonderful ... Look at the sky. It has more worlds than men can ever number, all bright and all lending brightness to each other. They fade, but others take their place, and the world and all infinity is charged with a beauty that is renewed and increased.'

'But such a large universe,' he said, 'such a large universe in which to be alone.'

'You will never be alone,' she said, so softly that he could barely hear her ... 'Be proud and happy for me ... And I shall be waiting for you.'

Those prose writings from Stafford were perhaps not so much stories as imagined situations reflecting my inner preoccupations as I came to terms with the world about me. After I returned to London, my time in Acton at Mrs Rudzka's house was not only a period when my wildest physical impulses were gratified. It was also a productive period in a different sense. Although on the one hand I had constructed a hedonistic environment about myself, on the other I went on trying to express my inner thoughts in a morbid sort of writing that had a poetic edge to it. My dream since childhood had been to write, for in writing it is possible to give free rein to one's most intimate feelings without constraint; writing is a solitary, painful task but it may dare to show its faceless side without fear of a more tangible confrontation. My literary creativity was perhaps at its zenith during those days when I felt most forlorn and isolated. At those times I was acutely aware of being almost an orphan. I thought of how my family had been brutally separated by the events that led to the formation of the state of Israel. One way or another, they had all ended up living in what was a foreign land, for the Palestine I knew and loved had ceased to exist except as an idea in the heart. Although the family ties remained as strong as ever, I was having to fend for myself in a situation where it would have been unthinkable to ask for any assistance, especially on the financial front. Dreams help to maintain morale, but they can be very dangerous if they lull us into a false sense of reality. The rich can implement their dreams almost at will, but those less fortunate have to tread a rocky road. For them dreams can only be made to come to true through toil and sweat and a steely resolve.

One piece in the sequence of my writings in Acton, 'A Pause among the Graves', was typical in its gothic, over-the-top, possibly hashish-induced imagery:

> I thrust at the gate of the dead and walked in the lair
> of ghosts with lurid face and broken heart. I
> entered the placid cemetery where the bitter
> secrets of many poor souls flapped as leaves in the
> wind. The phantoms of life, like the nocturnal
> beasts, quit their dens in the darkness of night.
> They terrified men of feeble heart and abducted
> their will to a hell of dumbness. These creatures
> are the slaves of humanity – the slaves of their
> passion and enjoyments. I stepped along the
> clumsy,sinuous paths and stumbled on the skulls,
> and bones of the wretched people who had died
> under a veil of pain, love and patriotism …
> I sat in the place of rendezvous where I could mourn
> my beloved and kiss the earth she dwelt in.
> I sat and heard the floating whispers of the soft
> breeze swaying with the flowers mutant with
> reverence and awe …
> There I bent over the grave of my spirit and watered
> the lilies, the symbol of her soul, with a flood of
> tears – tears of the fragrant blood of the victims of
> love.

There was much else in the same vein: a morose sort of writing, but the words were signposts on the road to maturity, however obscure the goal remained. In Acton, while I sat for many hours reading and writing, I also pondered philosophically. Were we predestined to follow a given path? Or could we truly be masters of our own destinies irrespective of time and place? I asked the questions repeatedly. Was a person cast into the wilderness ever likely to achieve the same measure of success as someone born into a thriving society that offered opportunities every step of the way? What would have become of me if I had remained in Nazareth? Could I have lived happily near to nature and survived the vicissitudes of every day life as my grandmother and great-aunt had done in the past? Times had changed, I argued. Their sort of spartan existence – pitted against the elements, winning nature's benefits only through constant struggle – was no longer regarded with the same degree of respect and admiration.

At least my tendency to dwell on these things sharpened my awareness and made my mind more analytical. All the time I was adding depth to my perceptions of beauty and ugliness, which to me represented the poles of good and evil. Their contrasting differences were another dimension that I needed to dissect if I was ever to understand the true meaning of life.

The morbidity in my writing sprang from the noticeable change in my lifestyle that came with my move to Acton. I was perceiving things through the perception of jazz music intermingled with the occult. It was a weird period in my life when I was lost between distorted imagery and the real world. The one thing I knew was that nothing was for ever. The world's conventional forces must eventually compel me to turn back towards conformity. How this would happen I could not foresee.

SOME FINAL MEMORIES

Anna Therese Lowe worked at Quartet. She was a bright young thing, rather slim and pretty, with a gift for words. When my wife Maria opened her shop Aphrodisia in Shepherd Market, Anna penned a description of the shop and the philosophy behind its exclusive merchandise that was lyrical in its composition and showed a flair for sensitive and romantic writing. I was very fond of her and rather spoiling. I took her to stay in our house in the Dordogne and she blended with the countryside like a budding flower undulating in a gentle breeze. A year later she had a serious riding accident when she fell from her horse head first. Luckily she recovered, but only after a long period of rest and recuperation.

A loss more painful to record was that of Jubby Ingrams. Her death at such an early age from a heroin overdose had a shattering effect, not only on her family but on all those who knew her. She and I were great buddies and I saw her grow from a bubbly girl into womanhood without ever losing the impish zest of youth or the determination to live life to its fullest degree. Always entertaining, she was the soul of any party and had a magical aura that captivated everyone who had the good fortune to know her. Her funeral service was as sombre as it was touching, with everyone close to tears as the various tributes came from people of widely diverse backgrounds. Jubby was loved by all and for them her death was a tragedy of incalculable proportions. The mere mention of her name still brings a lump to the throat.

Another sad break with the past was the death of Tony Lambton at the age of eighty-four in his home at Villa Citenale near Siena. In the mid-1980s I and my wife had stayed there and been given a guest bedroom that he claimed was haunted. It was typical of Tony to try to unnerve his guests while playing the perfect host. The ghosts must have been hibernating when we were there as they never made their presence felt. Any discomfort we experienced was of a less ethereal kind, for the old-fashioned bed had a sinking mattress that made sleep virtually impossible. During the night we were forced to lift it off its base and deposit it on the floor to give it a flat, stable surface on which we tried to get a night's repose. Tony's response was to be rather amused when he realized his guests had spent the night on the floor in preference to making the most of an imposing bed that had no doubt been witness to many an indiscretion, perhaps even of an ecclesiastical nature.

The villa had been the family home of Fabio Chigi, who became Pope Alexander VII in 1655 and rebuilt the house for his nephew, Cardinal Flavio Chigi.

Tony's life could have been described as having much the same flavour as that of a dissolute monarch of a bygone age, but in his case his wicked sense of humour redeemed his less orthodox indulgences. There was also a counterbalance in his notorious frugality. Once, when there were several people expected for lunch at Villa Citenale, he suggested we should have as a starter a tomato salad. He then led the way into the gardens where there was a vegetable patch he tended, of which he was very proud. Dozens of tomatoes were flourishing in the Italian sun, but I had only picked a few before he commanded, 'Don't pick any more.' I tried to say there wouldn't be enough for everyone, but he was adamant: 'I can't stand wasting food!' Another time I took my wife and Lambton's live-in companion Claire Ward into Florence for a sumptuous meal. When we got back, Tony was furious at what he called our wasteful pursuit of gluttony. He had his eccentricities, but was a great friend and, to some, a much feared enemy. His departure made our world a duller place.

The world suffered a tragic and irreparable loss with the death of Auberon Waugh. His memory is for me as sharp today as it ever was. His uniqueness as a person, one who combined wit with a sardonic sense of humour and whose eloquence drew on the music of words, stood supreme and unassailable. The years we worked together were the happiest I can remember. Soho is, as a result of his death, no longer a place where I hanker to be. The void his departure created is too painful to bear, especially for those members of the Academy Club who, as I did, saw him in his element on almost a daily basis. It is only England that can produce the likes of Bron to enrich future generations.

While going through some research, I came across a vignette by Sam Leith, today the literary editor of the *Spectator*, describing how Bron took him on as the unpaid 'slave' in the *Literary Review* office. Sam had written to a number of newspapers and magazines, looking for openings as a gap-year student. The only reply he received was from Bron, who told him, 'We would love to have you here as long as you are available. Unfortunately we have no money of any description. Would you be prepared to work as a slave for no wages?' Bron, Sam remembered, may have been sharp in print but was an exceptionally nice person. Having arranged to lodge rent-free with relatives in London, he then spent 'eight extremely happy months slaving at the *LR*:

> This involved reading proofs, helping with commissioning, running errands (one important duty was to scamper to Fortnum's to buy fruitcake when the Academy Club ran out), playing bridge in the office on Wednesday afternoons and, when he decided to treat the staff, going out for lunch with Bron.
>
> I returned from one such lunch with my eighteen-year-old brain soused with claret and port and my eyes visibly rotating. The then deputy editor, Lola Bubbosh, directed me to a sofa to sleep it off. Bron himself slept off lunch in his own chair, his snoring rising in crescendo until it became unbearably loud – at which point he'd wake with a start and look round crossly to see who had disturbed him. My eventual leaving present to him was a pillow, stencilled with the magazine's logo.
>
> Bron's genius was to charm big-name writers into contributing for peanuts; but he had to pay Julian Barnes in wine from his own cellar. There was visible pain on his face as he'd lift the telephone with the words: 'All right, Barnes. We're talking some serious claret.'

This to my mind is vintage Bron. Surprises have always awaited me. Once, whilst boarding a No. 38 bus at Green Park, I was to get a friendly wave from the woman driver. It was Mary Hemming, the ex-joint managing director of The Women's Press. What a transformation: from a rabid feminist to a paragon of public service! 'Tout passe, tout casse, tout lasse,' as the French say.

ENVOI

Quartet Books have been in the vanguard of British independent publishing since its formation nearly half a century ago, in 1972, when four directors of Granada Publishing left that conglomerate to establish a radical list, concentrating on new fiction, political debate and social issues. After a successful launch – its bestseller, *The Joy of Sex*, was one of the most successful books ever published – the fledging company hit cash-flow problems and was rescued when I bought it in 1976.

The range of titles produced by Quartet in its first four years of publishing was quite remarkable. It quickly established its radical credentials, issuing work by politicians such as Aneurin Bevan, David Owen, Neil Kinnock and Ian Gilmour. It was the first to publish the first book written by the now world-renowned civil rights lawyer, Geoffrey Robertson, *People Against the Press*. The paperback-fiction reprint list came to include such works of literary distinction as Shusaku Endo's *Silence*, George Mackay Brown's *Magnus*, B. S. Johnson's *House Mother Normal* and *Christy Malry's Own Double-Entry*, Brian Moore's *The Luck of Ginger Coffey*, Mordechai Richler's *A Choice of Enemies*, Alexander Trocchi's *Cain's Book* and Jack Kerouac's *Satori in Paris*, *Vanity of Duluz* and *Pic*. Among non-fiction reprints were the poet P. J. Kavanagh's *The Perfect Stranger*, Lillian Hellman's biographical volumes, *An Unfinished Woman* and *Pentimento*, Robert Kee's unmatched history of Irish nationalism, *The Green Flag*, Richard Holmes's major biography, *Shelley: The Pursuit*.

One of Quartet's major achievements was the development of the Encounters paperback series of twentieth-century European classics – publishing, among others, Aharon Appelfeld, Giorgio Bassani, Hermann

Broch, E. M. Cioran, Stig Dagerman, Heimito von Doderer, Julien Green, Pierre Klossowski, Ismaïl Kadaré, Miroslav Krlezˇa, Arnosˇt Lustig, Osip Mandelstam, Pier Paolo Pasolini, Fernando Pessoa, Fyodor Sologub, Abram Tertz, Boris Vian – over 100 titles, bringing great intellectual kudos to the company. It also championed the publication of translations of works by important authors largely unknown to the English reading public – notably Thomas Bernhard, Per Olov Enquist, Tahar Ben Jelloun, Annie Ernaux, Ernst Jünger, Eduardo Galeano, Hervé Guibert, Juan Goytisolo, Witold Gombrowicz, Antonio Muñoz Molina, Manuel Vazquez Montalban, Yves Navarre, Juan Carlos Onetti, Giorgio and Nicola Pressburger, Pascal Quignard – which attracted the attention and the praise of leading British and American critics of the day. ng public – notably Thomas Bernhard, Per Olov Enquist, Tahar Ben Jelloun, Annie Ernaux, Ernst Jünger, Eduardo Galeano, Hervé Guibert, Juan Goytisolo, Witold Gombrowicz, Antonio Muñoz Molina, Manuel Vazquez Montalban, Yves Navarre, Juan Carlos Onetti, Giorgio and Nicola Pressburger, Pascal Quignard – which attracted the attention and the praise of leading British and American critics of the day.

This wide-ranging and distinguished literary taste is still reflected in Quartet's current publishing programme with an emphasis on original manuscripts, many by first-time published writers. Recent successes have been Nikesh Shulka's novel of first generation immigrants, *Coconut United*; Alba Arikha's memoir of a growing up with a famous painter father haunted by the impact of the second world war, *Major/Minor*; Brian Sewell's two volumes of autobiography, *Outsider I & 2*, and a selection of his art criticism on modern British painters, *Naked Emperors*; Desmond de Silva QC's riotous legal memoir of his dramatic judicial career, *Madam, Where Are Your Mangoes?* and much more. A full description of Quartet's publishing list, both current titles and continuing back-list can be seen on its website – www. Quartetbooks.co.uk.

Though Quartet's reputation has stayed at the forefront of independent British publishing houses, recent developments in British society and the wider world – the worldwide economic crisis of 2008, Brexit, the impact of the new technologies, the ever increasing amalgamation of media companies into huge multinational megaliths, etc. – have all impinged on the profits and turnover of much smaller publishers, however prestigious.

But as the song goes ... I'm still here!